Contract Law in Japan

Contract Law in Japan

Hiroo Sono
Luke Nottage
Andrew Pardieck
Kenji Saigusa

This book was originally published as a monograph in the International Encyclopaedia of Laws/Contracts.

Founding Editor: Roger Blanpain
General Editor: Frank Hendrickx
Volume Editor: Jacques Herbots

Wolters Kluwer

Published by:
Kluwer Law International B.V.
PO Box 316
2400 AH Alphen aan den Rijn
The Netherlands
E-mail: international-sales@wolterskluwer.com
Website: lrus.wolterskluwer.com

Sold and distributed in North, Central and South America by:
Wolters Kluwer Legal & Regulatory U.S.
7201 McKinney Circle
Frederick, MD 21704
United States of America
Email: customer.service@wolterskluwer.com

Sold and distributed in all other countries by:
Air Business Subscriptions
Rockwood House
Haywards Heath
West Sussex
RH16 3DH
United Kingdom
Email: international-customerservice@wolterskluwer.com

ISBN 978-94-035-0741-5

e-Book: ISBN 978-94-035-0742-2
web-PDF: ISBN 978-94-035-0743-9

The Authors

Hiroo Sono (LLB/LLM *Hokkaido*, LLM *Michigan*) is Professor of Law at Hokkaido University, Japan. His main fields of research interest are in contract law and international commercial law. He is one of the founding members of the CISG Advisory Council (CISG-AC) since 2001 and the Global Private Law Forum (GPLF) of Japan since 2014. From 2006 to 2008, he served as Counsellor, Civil Affairs Bureau, Ministry of Justice where he was responsible for Japan's accession to the CISG. Since 2008 he serves as the Japanese delegate to UNCITRAL Working Group VI (Security Interests) and since 2015 he is a correspondent to UNIDROIT.

His recent publications in English include 'Introductory Note (Uniform Law Treaties; Their Reception, Implementation, Success And Failure)' and 'Going Forward with Uniform Private Law Treaties: A Study in Japan's Behavioral Pattern', 60 *Japanese Yearbook of International Law* (2018); 'Articles 85–88' in *UN Convention on Contracts for the International Sale of Goods (CISG): A Commentary* 1129 (S. Kröll, L. Mistelis & P.P. Viscasillas eds., C.H. Beck, 2nd ed. 2018); 'Integrating Consumer Law into the Civil Code: A Japanese Attempt at Re-Codification in Codifying Contract Law' in *Codifying Contract Law: International and Consumer Law Aspects*, 107 (M. Keyes & T. Wilson eds., Ashgate 2014); 'Private Enforcement of Consumer Law: A Sketch of the Japanese Landscape', 16 *Hokkaido Journal of New Global Law and Policy* 63 (2012); 'The Diversity of *Favor Contractus*: The Impact of the CISG on Japan's Civil Code and its Reform' in *Towards Uniformity*, 165 (I. Schwenzer & L. Spagnolo eds., Eleven International Publishing 2011); 'Japan's Accession to and Implementation of the United Nations Convention on Contracts for the International Sale of Goods (CISG)', 53 *Japanese Yearbook of International Law* 410 (2010).

The Authors

Luke Nottage (BCA/LLB/PhD *VUW*, LLM *Kyoto*) specialises in contract law, consumer product safety law, foreign investment regulation and international arbitration. He is Professor of Comparative and Transnational Business Law at Sydney Law School, founding Co-Director of the Australian Network for Japanese Law (ANJeL) and Associate Director of the Centre for Asian and Pacific Law at the University of Sydney (CAPLUS).

Luke's publications include *Product Safety and Liability Law in Japan* (Routledge 2004), *International Arbitration in Australia* (eds., Federation Press 2010), *Foreign Investment and Dispute Resolution in Asia* (eds., Routledge 2011), *Consumer Law and Policy in Australia and New Zealand* (eds., Federation Press 2013), *International Investment Treaties and Arbitration Across Asia* (eds., Brill 2018), ten other books, and many chapters and refereed articles.

He has or had executive roles in the Australia–Japan Society (NSW), the Law Council of Australia's International Law Section, the Australian Centre for International Commercial Arbitration, and the Asia-Pacific Forum for International Arbitration. Luke is also a Rules committee member of ACICA and listed on the Panel of Arbitrators for the AIAC (formerly KLRCA), BAC, JCAA, KCAB, NZIAC, SCIA and TAI. Luke has consulted for law firms worldwide, the EC, the OECD, the UNDP, ASEAN and the Japanese government, and has made numerous public Submissions to the Australian government on arbitration and consumer law reform. He qualified as a lawyer in New Zealand in 1994 and in New South Wales in 2001.

Andrew Pardieck (AB *Harvard*, JD *Indiana*, SJD. *Hokkaido*) formerly served as General Counsel for Temple University, Japan Campus. He is currently Associate Professor of Law at the Southern Illinois University School of Law, USA, where he teaches civil litigation and comparative law courses.

He researches and writes on varied topics, including 'America Seizobutsu Sekinin Sosho no Genjo to "Kanri Sareru Seigi" [Products Liability Litigation in the United States and "Managed Justice"]', in *Festschrift in Honor of Professors Nobuhisa Segawa & Katsumi Yoshida, Vol. II* (M. Matsuhisa et al. eds., Seibundo 2018); T. Maeda and A. Pardieck, 'ADR in Japan's Financial Markets & The Rule of Law' 10 *Northeastern University Law Review* 400 (2018); and 'Executing Contracts in Japan', 40 *Journal of Japanese Law* 183 (2015). He is also the author of *Shoken Torihiki Kanyu no Ho Kisei: Kaiji Gimu, Setsumei Gimu o Koete [Regulating the Solicitation of Securities Transactions: Beyond Disclosure and the Duty to Explain]* (Commercial Law Centre, 2001).

Kenji Saigusa (LLB/LLM *Waseda*, LLM *Harvard*) is Professor of Law at Waseda University in Japan. His academic interests lie in contract and tort law. His research mainly compares Japanese and U.S. law.

His recent publications include chapters in books on contract law and consumer law, as well as many articles on topics such as misrepresentation and standard form contracts, including: '*Yakkan no Henko* [Unilateral Modification of Standard Form Contract Terms]' 89(3) *Horitsu Jiho* 69 (2017); '*Sakugo to Fujitsuhyoji* [Mistake and Misrepresentation]' in *Saikenho Kaisei no Ronten to Kore Kara no Kento Kadai [Issues in the Obligations Law Reform and Topics For Future Consideration]*, 1 (N. Segawa ed., 147 *NBL Bessatsu*, Shoji Homu 2014).

The Authors

Table of Contents

List of Abbreviations

ADR	Alternative dispute resolution
ALA	Agricultural Land Act
ALBL	Act on Land and Building Leases
CISG	United Nations Convention on Contracts for the International Sale of Goods
GPA	Agreement on Government Procurement
Hanji	Hanrei-Jiho (Cases-News Report)
Hanta	Hanrei-Taimuzu (Cases-Times)
Investment Act	Acceptance of Investment, Money Deposits and Interest Rates Regulation Act
IRRA	Interest Rate Restriction Act
Kaminshu	Kakyusaibansho Minji-Saibanreishu (Report on civil cases of the lower courts)
Kinho	Kin-yu Homu Jijo (Situation of financial law)
Kinsho	Kin-yu Shoji Hanrei (Financial and commercial cases)
LLP	Limited Liability Partnership
LLPA	Limited Liability Partnership Act
Minroku	Taishin-in Minji-Hanketsuroku (Report on civil cases of the Great Court of Cassation) (1896 – 1921)
Minshu	Saikosaibansho Minji-Hanreishu (Report on civil cases of the Supreme Court) (1947–current)

List of Abbreviations

Minshu	Taishin-in Minji-Hanreishu (Report on civil cases of the Great Court of Cassation) (1922–1946)
MLIRA	Money Lending Industry Regulation Act
Model Law	1985 UNCITRAL Model Law on International Commercial Arbitration
MOJ	Ministry of Justice
PAA	Public Accounting Act
PBC	Pawnbroker Business Act
PRAMC	Perfection Requirements for the Assignment of Movables and Claims Act
Shimbun	Horitsu-Shimbun (Newsletter for lawyers)

Preface

This volume provides an analysis of contract law in Japan as reformed in 2017. The law of obligations, including contract law, in the Japanese Civil Code of 1896 had remained largely intact for over 120 years until this reform took place. The amendments cover the law of obligations, but exclude the law of torts and the law of restitution from their scope. Thus, this was basically a contract law reform. It is a result of an extensive drafting process that stretches over eleven years (or eight years, depending on what one counts as the drafting process). The reform attempts to modernise Japanese contract law, to incorporate case law developments into the Civil Code and to promote the global convergence of contract law.

The reformed Civil Code will come into effect on 1 April 2020. This volume aspires to be the first English-language overview of contract law in Japan that provides up-to-date accounts of the reform of 2017.

Some notes on how to use this volume are in order:

- The provisions of the Japanese Civil Code cited in this volume are, unless otherwise indicated, those of the Civil Code as revised in 2017. Accounts of the provisions prior to the 2017 Reform are included only when the authors considered it significant to highlight the change.
- Article numbers cited in brackets, without indication of which law they refer to, are those of the Civil Code as revised in 2017. When citing provisions of other laws, the title of the law is indicated unless it is obvious from the context.
- There is no official English-language translation of provisions of the Japanese law. However, the 'Japanese Law Translation' website maintained by the Japanese Ministry of Justice, available at http://www.japaneselawtranslation.go.jp, offers semi-official translations of many laws. The translations of Japanese laws and terminology used in this book are mostly taken from that website, including its regularly updated Standard Legal Terms Dictionary downloadable through 'Dictionary Search'. Where unavailable or otherwise appropriate, we have used our own translations. Unfortunately, an English-language translation of the Civil Code as revised in 2017 was not available as we completed writing this book. After its completion, a German-language translation coordinated by Professor Keizo Yamamoto was published in Issue 45 of the *Journal of Japanese Law* (2018) pp. 183–305.
- Non-official English-language translations of some Supreme Court judgments are available at the Supreme Court of Japan's website. In order to save space, we

have not indicated URLs to every Supreme Court judgment cited in this volume. They are easily searchable by accessing http://www.courts.go.jp/app/hanrei_en/search?

- The style used in this volume does not incorporate macrons or such like in romanised Japanese words to indicate long vowel sounds. Readers of Japanese should already know those sounds, while non-readers do not really need to be told about them.

As this volume belongs to the *International Encyclopaedia of Laws/Contract Law* series, it follows the structure of the other monographs in the series in order to make functional comparison across different jurisdictions possible. This means that the volume does not follow the sequence of the provisions as they appear in the Civil Code. This has the effect of bringing to light for the authors some interesting insights about how to view contract law. These will be more fully developed in our future writings.

This volume has had a long gestation period. We are grateful to Kluwer for their patience in allowing us to follow the reform process, and to Professor Jacques Herbots for giving us the opportunity to write this book.

We are also grateful to Wenkai Lyu, Beverly Pargungao, Matthew Power, Ganesh Vaheisvaran and especially Kirsten Gan for editorial and research assistance. We also acknowledge funding from JSPS KAKENHI Grant Numbers JP15H01917, JP16K13326, JP17K03482, Sydney Law School, as well as the hosting provided to Nottage for sabbatical research at Hokkaido University (2011) and Kyoto University (2014, courtesy of Professor Keizo Yamamoto).

November 2018

Hiroo Sono
Luke Nottage
Andrew Pardieck
Kenji Saigusa

General Introduction

§1. Japan and Its Legal System: General Background

1. The Japanese legal system has been successively influenced mainly by Chinese, German and American law. However, it is now a unique hybrid system paying keen attention to a variety of foreign legal systems and international legal instruments, with its own rich legal history.[1]

2. In the seventh century, a new imperial state introduced a codification inspired by Chinese law to centralise power, but political and legal pluralism soon re-emerged until Japan was unified under the Tokugawa Shogunate (1603–1867). Tokugawa era law was again predominantly administrative law, used to maintain national unity. Detailed rules and precedents did emerge concerning loans, commercial notes and security interests, in parallel with significant economic development, but ideologically the law was not available to citizens as 'judiciable rights'.[2] To maintain stability, the Shogunate also largely closed off the country to the outside world until 1853, when American navy (black) ships arrived to call for cross-border trade. Related political turmoil led to the 'Meiji Restoration' in 1868. The new government promoted a stronger imperial system and modernisation of the legal system, to revise 'unequal treaties' concluded by the late Tokugawa rulers with the US and European powers, including extraterritorial jurisdiction over their nationals in Japan. The Meiji Government sent officials around the world to study modern Western law. It was first attracted primarily by French law, but ultimately enacted six major codes drawing more on German law towards the end of the nineteenth century, including the Meiji Constitution (promulgated by the Emperor in 1889) and a Civil Code (Act No. 89 of 1896).[3]

---

1. *See* further M. Abe and L. Nottage, 'Japanese Law' in *Elgar Encyclopedia of Comparative Law*, 462 (J. Smits ed., 2nd ed., Edward Elgar 2012); L. Nottage, 'Comparative Law in and for Japan' in *Oxford Handbook of Comparative Law*, forthcoming (M. Reimann and R. Zimmerman eds., 2nd ed., Oxford University Press 2019).
2. D. F. Henderson, *Conciliation and Japanese Law: Tokugawa and Modern* (University of Washington Press 1965).
3. *See* generally H. Ishikawa, 'Codification, Decodification, and Recodification of the Japanese Civil Code', 10 *U. Tokyo J. L. & Pol.* 61 (2013). Major parts of an earlier Civil Code inspired much more by French law, with the advice of Professor Gustave Boissonade from France, were passed in 1890 but never came into effect. *See,* e.g., K. Mukai and N. Toshitani, 'The Progress and Problems of Compiling the Civil Code in the Early Meiji Era', 1 *Law in Japan* 25 (1967).

3. Anglo-American law was also studied, and impacted especially some legislation on commercial law in early modern Japan, but it had a much more significant influence during the US-led Occupation (1945–1952) after Japan lost World War II. As well as a whole-scale revision of the Constitution enacted in 1946, significant reforms were made to criminal and civil procedure (including more adversarial proceedings), corporate law and family and succession law (within the Civil Code, after parts or 'Books' covering general provisions, property law and the law of obligations). New legislation was also enacted in fields such as competition and securities law.[4] Another wave of 'Americanisation' has followed since the early 1990s, following an economic slowdown, more political fragmentation and transformations in the legal profession.[5]

4. The contract-related provisions of the Civil Code provisions were reviewed semi-officially from 2006 and officially from 2009. Over 2009–2015, a Working Group of the Legislative Council under the aegis of the Ministry of Justice developed a detailed and comprehensive set of proposals to reform the contract law-related provisions of the Civil Code. A driving force behind this reform initiative, and a prior (predominantly) academic 'Reform Commission' that met 260 times between October 2006 and April 2009, was Professor Takashi Uchida who retired from the University of Tokyo in 2008 to work until 2014 as a senior Ministry official. Of the thirty-seven members of the Working Group, about half were legal academics, a quarter were judges (including five seconded to the Ministry) and the rest were *bengoshi* lawyers or representatives of other stakeholder groups (consumer, union or business groups). The main aims were to make the Civil Code more 'transparent' and accessible (incorporating important case law developments), more modern and compatible with new technologies and socio-economic circumstances (including an ageing and consumer services-based society), and more aligned with the contract law regimes in influential jurisdictions abroad (including a revised German Civil Code and EU law instruments) and found in international instruments (such as CISG and the UNIDROIT Principles of International Commercial Contracts). The Working Group released an Interim Report on 11 March 2013,[6] and a

4. *See* generally, e.g., R. Frank, 'Law of Obligations' in *History of Law in Japan Since 1868*, 227 (W. Rohl ed., Brill, 2005), reviewed by L. Nottage at 'Book Review: Roehl, W (ed) A History of Japanese Law Since 1868', 11 *J. Japanese L.* 283 (2007).
5. R. D. Kelemen and E. C. Sibbitt, 'The Americanization of Japanese Law', 23 *U. Pa. J. Int'l Econ. L.* 269 (2002). But querying the extent of such transformations, *see*, e.g., D. H. Foote, *Law in Japan: A Turning Point* (University of Washington Press 2007), reviewed at L. Nottage, 'Book Review: Daniel H Foote (ed.), Law in Japan: A Turning Point', 25 *J. Japanese L.* 261 (2008); J. O. Haley, 'Heisei Renewal or Heisei Transformation: Are Legal Reforms Really Changing Japan?', 19 *J. Japan L.* 5 (2005); T. Tanase, *Law and the Community: A Critical Assessment of American Liberalism and Japanese Modernity* (Edward Elgar 2010); *Who Rules Japan? Popular Participation in the Japanese Legal Process* (L. Wolff et al. eds., Edward Elgar 2015).
6. For an analysis of the Interim Report, the Working Group's membership and summary of deliberations, *see* S. Kozuka and L. Nottage, 'Policy and Politics in Contract Law Reform in Japan' in *The Method and Culture of Comparative Law*, 235 (M. Adams and D. Heirbaut eds., Hart 2014) with a longer version at http://papers.ssrn.com/sol3/papers.cfm?abstract_id=2360343 (accessed 21 Jun. 2018), and Ministry of Justice, *Civil Code Reform*, http://www.moj.go.jp/ENGLISH/ccr/CCR_00001.html (accessed 21 Jun. 2018). *See also* A. Kamo, 'Crystallization, Unification, or Differentiation? The Japanese Civil Code (Law of Obligations) Reform Commission and Basic Reform Policy (Draft

Final Report was adopted by the Legislative Council on 24 February 2015. This formed the basis for a reform Bill approved by Cabinet on 31 March 2015 and submitted to the national Diet on the same day. The Bill passed the Diet on 26 May 2017 and was promulgated on 2 June 2017. This reform will enter into force on 1 April 2020.[7]

§2. To What Legal Family Does Japan Belong?

5. Despite the post-War changes to Japanese law, the six codifications remain central and many fundamental legal institutions (such as the judicial system, outlined at Introduction to the Law of Contract §2 below) remain closer to the European Civil Law tradition. German law, and more recently European Union (EU) law, remains an influential reference point in Japanese private law. However, Japanese law reformers and commentators increasingly refer also to Anglo-American law as well as international instruments, including the United Nations Convention on Contracts for the International Sale of Goods (CISG) in effect with respect to Japan from 1 August 2009 (Treaty No. 8 of 2008).[8]

6. It has also been suggested, partly in response to those (particularly from the United States (US)) who perceive major differences between Japanese and American law, that both legal systems in general[9] as well as their contract law regimes (including underlying theories of contract law[10]) share a greater openness to 'substantive reasoning' compared to the more 'formal reasoning' patterns characteristic

---

Proposals)', 24 *Colum. J. Asian L.* 171 (2010); T. Uchida, 'Contract Law Reform in Japan and the UNIDROIT Principles', *Uniform Law Review* 705 (2011); N. Kano, 'Reform of the Japanese Civil Code: The Interim Draft Proposal of 2013', 36 *J. Japanese L.* 249, 259 (2013).

7. For details on the law reform process and commentary on the 2017 Reform provisions, by Ministry of Justice officials (in Japanese), *see Ichimon Itto Minpo (Saikenkankei) Kaisei [Questions and Answers: Civil Code (Obligations) Reform]* (T. Tsutsui and H. Muramatsu eds., Tokyo: Shojihomu, 2018). Other helpful books include Y. Shiomi, *Minpo (Saikenkankei) Kaiseihono Gaiyo [An Outline of the Revised Civil Code (Obligations)]* (Kinzai 2017); *Shokai Kaisei Minpo [Detailed Explantion of the Revised Civil Code]* (Y. Shiomi et al. eds., Shojihomu 2018). For a summary of key amendments in English, *see* S. Yoshida and P. Cassidy, 'Top 10 Major Revisions to the Civil Code: From the Viewpoint of the Transportation and Shipbuilding Industries' *Higashimachi LLP* (Newsletter) (2017) http://www.higashimachi.jp/column/images/column205.pdf (accessed 27 Jun. 2018) and M. Dernauer, 'The 2017 Reform of the Law of Obligations in Japan: Impetus, Rulemaking Process, and Outcome' *ANJeL Research Publication* (April 2018) via https://sites.google.com/prod/view/anjel-network/research (accessed 17 Jun. 2018); T. Yoshimasa, 'The Reform of the Japanese Contract Law – From the Perspective of Self-responsibility' *J. Japanese L.* (2018, forthcoming).
8. *See* generally H. Sono, 'Japan's Accession to the CISG: The Asia Factor', *25 J. Japanese L.* 195 (2008) and H. Sono, 'Japan's Accession to and Implementation of the United Nations Convention on Contracts for the International Sale of Goods (CISG)', 53 *Japanese Yearbook of International Law* 410 (2010).
9. L. Nottage, *The Japanisation of American Law? Substantive Similarities, Compared to Formal Anglo-New Zealand Law* (Sydney Law School Research Paper No. 10/80, August 2010) at http://ssrn.com/abstract=1663456 (accessed 21 Jun. 2018).
10. L. Nottage, 'Tracing Trajectories in Contract Law Theory: Form in Anglo-New Zealand Law, Substance in Japan and the United States', 4 *Yonsei L. J.* 175 (2013) http://ssrn.com/abstract=2270889 (accessed 21 Jun. 2018).

of the stricter Anglo-Commonwealth law variant within the common law tradition. Both Japanese and American law are more willing to entertain moral, economic, political, institutional or other considerations within legal reasoning patterns, for example by recognising a general principle of 'good faith' in performing contractual obligations.[11] However, the extent and contents of such considerations can vary, with Japanese law (in this respect and others) putting somewhat greater emphasis on maintaining continuity within contractual relationships than US law, perhaps in line with persistently more long term or 'relational' contracting in Japanese business practice (as outlined further in General Introduction §8 below).[12]

§3. PRIMACY OF LEGISLATION?

7. Consistently with the historical influence of continental European codifications and basic legal institutions on modern Japanese law, Japan shares the civil law tradition's relative emphasis on the primacy of legislation over case law applications by the judiciary. It also starts from the premise that the Civil Code should not have 'gaps': any apparent lacunae can and should be filled by generalising from the principles explicit or implicit within the Code.[13] However, this is subject to the principle that more specific legislation overrides more general legislation (such as a Code).[14] In fact there have been growing statutory incursions related to contract law especially since World War II. There is also a long tradition and large volume of contract case law developed by the Japanese courts, which has had a major impact in practice (as outlined in General Introduction §1 and §4).

§4. THE POSITION OF THE JUDICIARY

8. As in Germany, for example, the judiciary mainly comprises career judges. Almost all are selected after completing a one-year training program at the Legal Training and Research Institute (run by the judiciary) for those who have passed the difficult National Legal Examination that candidates must pass to be able to work as judges in courts of general jurisdiction (numbering 2,775 in 2017), public prosecutors (1,964) or practising lawyers in private practice (*bengoshi*: 38,980, including 411 registered foreign lawyers). Those who graduate from the Institute and are admitted as judges generally remain with the judiciary, administered by the General

---

11. L. Nottage, 'Form and Substance in US, English, New Zealand and Japanese Law: A Framework for Better Comparisons of Developments in the Law of Unfair Contracts', 26 *Victoria U. Wellington L. Rev.* 247 (1996); L. Nottage, 'Economic Dislocation in New Zealand and Japan: A Preliminary Empirical Study', 26 *Victoria U. Wellington L. Rev.* 59 (1997).
12. *See*, e.g., J. O. Haley, 'Relational Contracting: Does Community Count?' in *Japan: Economic Success and Legal System* 167 (H. Baum ed., de Gruyter 1997).
13. *See* generally J. Merryman et al., *The Civil Law Tradition: Europe, Latin America, and East Asia, Cases and Materials* (Michie Company 1999).
14. *See* generally, e.g., S. Kozuka, 'Project for a Reform of the Contract Law in Japan and its Impact on Franchise Agreements' (March 2014), available at http://papers.ssrn.com/sol3/papers.cfm?abstract_id=2408038 (accessed 21 Jun. 2018).

Secretariat of the Supreme Court of Japan, until mandatory retirement age of 65 (or 70 for the 15 Justices of the Supreme Court).[15]

9. Japan does not have a doctrine of *stare decisis*, with lower courts being bound by law applied to the same material facts by a superior court. However, case law has had a large and growing influence in practice due to the career judiciary system (including rotation of judges among courts often every three years), a shared vision of the 'rule of law' that emphasises uniformity and predictability of outcomes,[16] and a strong interest in case method among jurists even before World War II.[17]

10. The Japanese judiciary has also played a major role in law reform projects, serving on deliberative councils or committees as representatives of the Supreme Court and/or other government departments (notably the Ministry of Justice) where elite-track career judges may be seconded for 2–3 years or occasionally even longer. This is evident in the first comprehensive revision of the contract law provisions contained in the Civil Code, since it was enacted fully in 1896. Of the 39 members of the Legislative Council's Working Group, which met regularly over 2009–2015 to propose significant reforms (as mentioned in General Introduction §1 above), there were six judges as well as three representatives from the Ministry of Justice who were in fact judges seconded by the Supreme Court of Japan.[18]

11. In terms of formal court structure,[19] the Supreme Court of Japan is the highest body of the judicial branch, dealing primarily with appeals filed against judgments from eight High Courts (with six branch offices), as well as judicial administration (of the career judiciary). Under the post-War Constitution, which includes a Bill of Rights, the Supreme Court can declare government (in)action and legislation to be unconstitutional, although it has only declared statutory provisions

---

15. Japan also has many other legal professionals, with narrower scope of (transactional rather than court litigation) practice compared to *bengoshi*, including patent attorneys (11,057), judicial scriveners (22,283) and administrative scriveners (46,205). *See* Japan Federation of Bar Associations, *White Paper on Attorneys* (2017) available at https://www.nichibenren.or.jp/en/about/whitepaper.html (9 Jul. 2018), pp. 17, 23, and 29. *See* further Abe and Nottage, *supra* n. 1.
16. *See,* e.g., Foote, *supra* n. 5. This vision is also shared by public prosecutors, including those representing the government in civil or public law cases: L. Nottage and S. Green, 'Who Defends Japan?: Government Lawyers and Judicial System Reform in Japan', 13 *Asian-Pacific L. & Pol. J.* 129 (2011). Before World War II public prosecutors were equal partners with the judges within the predecessor to today's Ministry of Justice, and even today some judges are still seconded to represent the government in civil or public law litigation.
17. Nottage, *supra* n. 10.
18. Some commentators have speculated that their involvement has been influential and motivated to legitimise 'judge-made law', even in a traditionally Civil Law tradition legal system, by perhaps pressing for the 2017 revisions to the Civil Code: (a) to include more detailed provisions (reflecting case law developments) on aspects of contract law which are relatively uncontroversial, but (b) more 'general clauses' or open-ended provisions otherwise – leaving the judges more discretion to be able to mould judgments in light of evolving social circumstances. *See* Kozuka and Nottage, *supra* n. 6.
19. *See* further Abe and Nottage, *supra* n. 1.

unconstitutional on nine occasions since 1947.[20] The Chief Justice and fourteen Justices of the Supreme Court, exceptionally, do not all need to have passed the National Legal Examination and qualified as judges, prosecutors or *bengoshi*. By convention, five (including the Chief Justice) are such career judges, but five are *bengoshi*, and the rest are prosecutors, law professors and/or former government officials.[21]

12. The eight High Courts in major cities (with six branch offices) are intermediate appellate courts with jurisdiction mainly over appeals against judgments rendered by District Courts or Family Courts, with all judges having passed the National Legal Examination. All High Court cases are handled by a collegiate body consisting of three judges, with no dissenting opinions (unlike the post-War Supreme Court). The 50 District Courts (with 203 branch offices) have general jurisdiction and deal with most of the first instance civil, criminal, and administrative law cases, mostly with a single judge but with a three-member bench for more complex matters (also then without dissenting opinions). District Courts also have jurisdiction over appeals against civil judgments from 438 Summary Courts, where sole judges (often former Ministry of Justice officials, who do not need to have passed the National Legal Examination) deal with disputes up to JPY 1,400,000 in value.[22]

§5. Distinction Between Public Law and Private Law

13. Japan follows the German rather than the French tradition in not distinguishing between contracts concluded by the government or public authorities compared to those involving private parties. For more on this, *see* Part II, Chapter 11. Nor are there separate administrative courts, although governmental (in)action can often first be challenged within the relevant government department before being appealed to the regular Japanese courts.[23]

14. However, the public law does impact on private law relations in Japan. One issue is whether and how constitutional rights guaranteed to citizens can apply to relations between them. Under the 'Indirect Application Theory' prevalent among commentators and recognised by case law, this should be resolved by applying the general provisions in private law, including those limiting party autonomy in contracting due to public policy and good morals (Article 90 Civil Code) or providing

20. The most recent, and the first dealing with the Civil Code, held unconstitutional a provision (then part of Art. 900(iv) proviso) giving children born out of wedlock a lesser share of their parents' estate than their legitimate half siblings: Supreme Court, 4 Sep. 2013, Minshu 67-6-1320. Three months after the decision, on 5 Dec. 2013, the relevant part of Art. 900(iv) was deleted from the Civil Code. *See* generally, e.g., S. Matsui, 'Constitutional Precedents in Japan: A Comment on the Role of Precedent', 88 *Washington U. L. Rev.* 1669 (2011).
21. For the Court's current composition, *see* http://www.courts.go.jp/english/about/justice/index.html (accessed 21 Jun. 2018).
22. For diagrams and further information, *see* http://www.courts.go.jp/english/judicial_sys/index.html (accessed 21 Jun. 2018).
23. *See*, e.g., Nottage and Green, *supra* n. 16, with examples (e.g., regarding patents or competition law) and further references.

damages for harm caused by negligence (Article 709 Civil Code), interpreted in light of the spirit of the post-War Constitution. Some argue that tort law and contract doctrines releasing parties from contractual obligations due to fraud are more specific private law protections enacted by the legislator consistently with the constitutional requirements to recognise the creation and implementation of property rights.[24]

15. A more common question concerns the effect on contracting parties if one violates provisions set out in administrative laws or related regulations (*torishimari hoki*). Traditionally, the prevailing view was that the contract generally remains valid. However, it could be void under Civil Code Article 90 as a provision related to public policy (*kojo*), depending on:

(a) the legislative purpose behind the administrative law provision;
(b) the extent of the society's ethical censure of the violation;
(c) the need to ensure security of transactions;
(d) good faith between the parties.

16. More recently, some influential academic opinion rejects the premise underlying this approach, and instead views private and public law as mutually reinforcing and serving common purposes, including both maintaining transactional security and protecting parties that are unfairly disadvantaged. To advance such purposes within public law, this opinion is more amenable to finding private law consequences from violations of administrative regulations.[25] Such an approach may have growing resonance with respect to consumer contracts (outlined further at General Introduction §7 below).[26] It is also significant given the emergence of hybrid private and public contracting patterns in Japan's slowly deregulating and rapidly ageing society.[27]

---

24. K. Yamamoto, 'The Role of Private Law in a Constitutional System', 1 *Kyoto J. L. & Pol.* 45, 46 and 58 (2013). *See also*, e.g., Tokyo High Court, 22 Jun. 2011, Hanji 2116 invalidating a multi-tiered dispute resolution clause in a commercial contract, partly in reference to constitutional law but mainly in light of specific legislation enacted to promote out-of-court mediation: L. Nottage and A. Monichino, 'International Commercial Arbitration Developments in Model Law Jurisdictions: Japan Seen from Australia', 1 *Int'l Arb L. Rev.* 34 (2013).
25. K. Yamamoto, 'Civil Law - Contract Law – Nullity of Contracts (Juristic Acts) Due to a Violation of Mandatory Public Law Provisions', in *Business Law in Japan – Cases and Comments*, 5, 11 (M. Baelz, M. Dernauer, C. Heath and A. Petersen-Padberg eds., Kluwer 2012). (discussing the judgment of the Supreme Court, 4 Sep. 1997, Minshu 51-8-3619 regarding a securities dealer's loss indemnification contract with a customer).
26. *See* generally M. Dernauer, *Verbraucherschutz und Vertragsfreiheit im japanischen Recht [Consumer Protection and Freedom of Contract in Japan]* (Mohr Siebeck 2006); and, with respect to consumer credit contracts, A. Pardieck, 'Japan and the Moneylenders: Activist Courts and Substantive Justice', 17 *Pac. Rim L. & Pol'y J.* 529 (2008). *See also* the discussion of 'Illegal Contracts', below at Part I Ch. 2 §3.
27. *See* generally T. Ryan, 'Demographic Transition and Transformation of Regulation and Law in Japan' (Ph.D Thesis, Australian National University 2010); T. Ryan, 'Administering Welfare in an Ageing Society' in *Who Rules Japan? Popular Participation in the Japanese Legal Process,* 108 (L. Wolff, L. Nottage and K. Anderson eds., Edward Elgar 2015).

§6. Distinction Between Civil Law and Commercial Law (Commercial Contracts)

17. The Japanese Commercial Code (Act No. 48 of 1899), which was even more heavily influenced originally by German law, includes provisions on Commercial Transactions (now in Book II)[28] relating to the following types of contracts:

(a) Sales (*Baibai*)
(b) Accounts Current or Netting (*Kogo Keisan*)
(c) Anonymous Partnerships (*Tokumei Kumiai*)
(d) Brokerage (*Nakadachi Eigyo*)
(e) Commission Agencies (*Toiya Eigyo*)
(f) Freight Forwarding Businesses (*Unso Toriatsukai Eigyo*)
(g) Transportation Businesses (*Unso Eigyo*)
(h) Deposits (*Kitaku*).

18. These more specific provisions apply in lieu of corresponding Civil Code provisions (Article 1 Commercial Code), for example regarding sales, if:

(a) Transactions are commercial per se (including transactions to acquire for value movables, immovables or securities with the intention of transferring them for profit, or the transfer of them so acquired: Article 501 Commercial Code).
(b) Transactions are commercial because effected as a business (including manufacturing or processing for others, money-changing or other banking and insurance services: Article 502 Commercial Code).
(c) Incidental commercial transactions carried out as a business (Article 503 Commercial Code) by a 'merchant' (defined in Article 4(1) as a person or entity effecting commercial transactions on its own behalf as a business).

19. If there is no specific provision in the Commercial Code, 'commercial usage' will apply, otherwise the Civil Code (Article 1(2) Commercial Code). However, commercial usage is nowadays limited to certain banking and finance transactions,[29] and it differs from the much broader notion of commercial practices that is quite often referred to by Japanese courts when interpreting the Civil Code.[30]

20. The priority of the provisions in the Commercial Code (as the more specific legislation) over those in the Civil Code also extended to provisions beyond the specific types of contracts listed in both laws prior to the 2017 Reform. For example,

---

28. Other Books or parts cover General Provisions, and Merchant Shipping and Insurance. The original Book II, on Companies, was frequently amended from 1990s and eventually separated out as the Companies Law (No. 86 of 2005): *see* generally *Corporate Governance in the 21st Century: Japan's Gradual Transformation* (L. Nottage, L. Wolff, K. Anderson eds., Edward Elgar 2008).
29. *See,* e.g., T. Otori, 'Shokanshuho [Commercial Customary Law]' in *Enshu Shoho (Sosoku, Shokoi) [Seminar on Commercial Law (General Provisions and Commercial Transactions)]* 55 (T. Otori et al., eds., Seirinshoinshinsha, 1971).
30. *See* generally, e.g., V. Taylor, 'Continuing Transactions and Persistent Myths: Contracts in Contemporary Japan', 19 *Melbourne U. L. Rev.* 352 (1993); Haley, *supra* n. 12.

the extinctive prescription period for claims arising from commercial transactions was five years (former Article 522 Commercial Code), whereas the general extinctive prescription period under the Civil Code was ten years (former Article 167 Civil Code). This difference was eliminated in the 2017 Reform when the Civil Code adopted a shorter prescription period. *See* Part I, Chapter 6 §8. Likewise, the difference in the statutory interest rate (which applies absent contrary agreement), which existed between the Civil Code and Commercial Code prior to the 2017 Reform, was also eliminated. Prior to the 2017 Reform, the statutory interest rate was five percent per annum under the Civil Code (Article 404), but this became instead six percent for an obligation arising out of a commercial transaction (Article 514 Commercial Code). *See* paragraph 21.

21. There were some discussions about incorporating (updated versions of) Commercial Code provisions related to contracts into the revised Civil Code.[31] The 2017 Reform did not do so to a significant degree, but some differences between the Civil Code and the Commercial Code were eliminated. One example is the rules on extinctive prescription periods as briefly noted above in paragraph 20. Another example is the discrepancy between the default statutory interest provision in the Commercial Code (six percent per annum) further highlighted the issue of whether five percent per annum was nowadays an appropriate rate for non-commercial contracts under the Civil Code. In the end, the 2017 Reform adopted a variable interest rate, to be reviewed every three years after the revision comes into force but starting with three percent per annum, which will be applied both to civil and commercial claims.[32] Furthermore, when reviewing the Civil Code provisions on strict liability for latent defects under contracts of sale (*kashi tanpo sekinin*), the official reform Committee considered the specific limitation periods provided in the former Articles 566(3) and 570. In the 2017 Reform, an approach was adopted similar to the prevailing interpretation of a similar provision in the Commercial Code (Article 526): the claim need not be lodged within one year of becoming aware of the non-conformity but the plaintiff must give notice of the discovered non-conformity within that period (Article 566 of the 2017 Reform).[33]

31. Cf. Thailand's combined Civil and Commercial Code, enacted in 1925 drawing partly on advice from a leading Japanese expert of civil law at the time. *See* further Nottage, *supra* n. 1.
32. *See* Kano, *supra* n. 6, 259, on an earlier draft of the variable interest rate proposal.
33. Prior case law, under pre-2017 Reform law, establishes first that exercise of the buyer's right to claim strict liability for latent defect need not involve bringing court proceedings in order to fulfil the special time limitation of one year from the time the buyer became aware of the defect (Supreme Court, 20 Oct. 1992, Minshu 46-1129). Second, however, the buyer's right to claim strict liability for latent defect is subject to the general extinctive prescription period of 10 years provided by Civil Code Art. 167 (Supreme Court, 27 Nov. 2001, Minshu 55-6-1311), calculated from the time of delivery (on which opinions had been split. *See* K. Nakata, 'Civil Law – Contract Law – Purchase Contract – Extinctive Prescription for Damage Claims Under the Warranty against Defects' in *Business Law in Japan – Cases and Comments*, 49 (M. Baelz, M. Dernauer, C. Heath and A. Petersen-Padberg eds., Kluwer 2012).

§7. Distinction Between Civil Law and Consumer Law (Consumer Contracts)

22. The Civil Code traditionally has not recognised the specific role and status of consumers. However, separate statutes to protect consumers in particular situations began to be enacted at the national level especially from the 1960s, when the government also passed a framework or 'Basic Law' encouraging financing and enactment of consumer protection measures by local authorities.[34] Examples of such statutes included the Instalment Sales Act (Act No. 159 of 1961), the Door-to-Door Sales Act (Act No. 57 of 1976), now renamed the Act on Specified Commercial Transactions, and the Investment Advisory Services Business Act (Act No. 74 of 1986) that was merged into the Financial Instruments and Exchange Act (Act No. 25 of 1948) in 2007. These include 'cooling-off' periods to allow consumers to withdraw from contracts concluded under high-pressure situations. Consumer protection statutes also usually imposed disclosure and other requirements on suppliers, as also under the Act on Sales etc. of Financial Instruments (Act No. 101 of 2000), which attracted regulatory sanctions but not necessarily private law consequences if violated (*see* generally General Introduction §5 above).

23. Enactment of consumer protection statutes slowed over the 1980s, as the Japanese economy boomed and some steps were taken towards deregulation. For example, although the Money Lending Industry Regulation Act (Act No. 32 of 1983) was enacted given growing social concerns about loan sharks, non-deposit-taking consumer lenders were still able to conclude contracts with borrowers that included extra 'grey zone' interest. This grey zone arose because the earlier and more generally applicable anti-usury statute (Interest Rate Restriction Act, Act No. 100 of 1954) rendered void any interest beyond specified rates, while allowing extra grey zone interest if certain criteria were met, subject to an upper limit beyond which lenders were subject to criminal sanctions under the separate Acceptance of Investment, Money Deposits and Interest Rates Regulation Act (Act No. 195 of 1954).[35]

24. From the mid-1990s, however, economic stagnation combined with accelerating deregulation prompted renewed calls for consumer protection initiatives. To offset reduced scope for ex ante public regulation of product safety, ex post compensation under the private law was strengthened by introducing strict liability on

34. L. Nottage, 'Consumer Rights' in *Japanese Consumer Dynamics*, 31 (P. Haghirian ed., Palgrave Macmillan 2010). Statutes enacted in 1921 had codified protections developed by courts to protect lessees of land or buildings, limiting lessors' rights to limit the duration of leases, with leases all but automatically renewable unless the lessor could establish 'just cause'. However, the combined Land Lease and House Lease Act (Act No. 90 of 1991) provided for non-renewable 'fixed term land leases' for ground rent if the agreed term was at least fifty years and the lease was created by notarial deed (*kosei shosho*). *See* Haley, *supra* n. 12, 146.

35. *See* further Pardieck, *supra* n. 26; S. Kozuka and L. Nottage, 'The Myth of the Careful Consumer: Law, Culture, Economics and Politics in the Rise and Fall of Unsecured Lending in Japan', in *Consumer Credit, Debt and Bankruptcy: Comparative International Perspectives*, 199 (J. Niemi eds., Hart 2009).

manufacturers and specified intermediaries for defective products, under the Product Liability Act (Act No. 85 of 1994) inspired by EU (and earlier American) law.[36] EU law on unfair terms also prompted enactment of the Consumer Contract Act (Act No. 61 of 2000), but the latter's provisions on substantive control of the contents of consumer contracts were relatively limited, as were additional procedural controls over the pre-contractual negotiation process.[37]

25. After a slow start, Japanese courts have generally interpreted these two statutes quite expansively,[38] in the wake also of amendments from 2006 to the Consumer Contract Act allowing certified consumer organisations to bring injunction suits.[39] The Supreme Court also favoured consumers through various interpretations of the Money Lending Industry Regulation Act, culminating in a 2006 judgment disallowing grey zone interest as not having been 'voluntarily' agreed by borrowers in the (usual) event of the consumer credit contract including an acceleration clause, requiring the borrower to repay the whole amount owed if in default of the loan.[40] This had a major impact on the industry and prompted revisions to the Money Lending Industry Regulation Act and the two related laws, abolishing the grey zone interest provision and introducing responsible lending requirements.[41]

---

36. L. Nottage, *Product Liability and Safety Law in Japan: From Minamata to Mad Cows* (Routledge Curzon 2004).
37. *See* generally, e.g., T. Matsumoto, 'Privatization of Consumer Law: Current Developments and Features of Consumer Law in Japan at the Turn of the Century', 30 *Hitotsubashi J. L. & Pol.* 1 (2002). *See also* T. Uchida and V. Taylor, 'Japan's Era of Contract' in *Law in Japan: A Turning Point*, 454, 455 (D. H. Foote ed., University of Washington Press 2007) (describing both statutes as illustrating a broader 'shift towards personal responsibility' in Japanese contract law). They also identify a 'shift towards efficiency maximisation', illustrated for example by further revisions in 1999 to the Land and House Lease Act (Act No. 90 of 1991) extending provisions for non-renewable leases to residential property (*ibid.*, 460). Illustrating a third trend, 'escaping state intervention' (*ibid.*, 464), they point to initiatives facilitating e-commerce legislation such as the Electronic Signatures and Verification Act (Act No. 102 of 2000) and the Special Provisions to the Civil Code Concerning Electronic Consumer Contracts and Electronic Acceptance Notice Act (Act No. 95 of 2001).
38. Nottage, *supra* n. 36; Nottage, *supra* n. 34; and S. Kozuka, 'Judicial Activism of the Supreme Court in Consumer Law: Juridification of Society Through Case Law?' 27 *J. Japanese L.* 81 (2009).
39. M. Okino, 'Recent Development in Consumer Protection in Japan', 4 *U. Tokyo Soft. L. Rev.* 10 (2012); H. Sono, 'Private Enforcement of Consumer Law: A Sketch of the Japanese Landscape', 63 *Hokkaido J. New Global L. & Pol.* 63 (2012). Injunction suits were also permitted for certain violations of the pre-contractual negotiation process set out in the Unjustifiable Premiums and Misleading Representations Act (Act No. 134 of 1962) and the Specific Commercial Transactions Act (Act No. 57 of 1976, successor to the Door-to-Door Sales Law). Certified consumer organisations can also bring damages and other claims on behalf of consumers under the Special Provisions on Civil Court Procedures for Collective Recovery of Property Damage to Consumers Act (Act No. 96 of 2013): *see* also M. Madderra, 'The New Class Actions in Japan', 23 *Pac. Rim L. & Pol'y J.* 795 (2014).
40. Supreme Court, 13 Jan. 2006, Minshu 60-1. *See* further Pardieck, *supra* n. 26; S. Matsui, 'Cloudy Weather, with Occasional Sunshine: Consumer Loans, the Legislature, and the Supreme Court of Japan', 22 *Pac. Rim L. and Pol'y J.* 555 (2013).
41. Kozuka and Nottage, *supra* n. 35, 199.

26. Against this backdrop, leading up to and during the official deliberations on reforming the Civil Code from 2009, debate emerged over incorporating the concept of the consumer more organically into the Code's structures and basic principles. Unlike contemporary German law, however, this idea was abandoned.[42] Instead, the law reform Committee first considered incorporating into the revised Code some provisions from Article 4 of the Consumer Contract Act dealing with consumer's rescission rights for misrepresentation etc. These notions were also not adopted in its Interim Report of 2012, but the latter proposed several provisions for the revised Civil Code that either applied only to consumers, or to all contracting parties but with greatest potential for assisting consumers.[43] One proposal suggested that 'the disparity in the quality and quantity of information and negotiating power between consumers and business' should be taken into account when applying Article 1(2), the Civil Code provision on 'good faith'. Another proposal was a general provision on duty to disclose information. It is easy to see that the main application of this rule will be to consumer contracts.[44] None of these proposals were adopted in the 2017 Reform. However, with respect to the addition of a very limited rule on standard terms, *see* below Part I, Chapter 3, §1, III.

§8. CONTRACT LAW 'IN ACTION': COMPARING JAPAN

I. The Traditional View

27. As the Japanese economy rebounded from the 1960s, foreign importers (mainly of manufactured goods) and exporters (mainly of raw materials) started to become interested in Japanese contract law and practice. A translation in 1972 of a work by Japan's leading professor of civil law and legal sociology, Takeyoshi Kawashima, was particularly influential.[45] He argued that Japanese contracting was characterised by oral or shortly worded agreements, not readily enforced (let alone litigated) when impediments to performance arose, except sometimes in some situations involving unequal relationships (such as between borrower and lender). These characteristics were linked to Kawashima's broader thesis that post-War society in Japan remained functionally diffuse and 'pre-modern', despite the overlay of modern Western law, although he predicted that Japan would gradually modernise.[46] This view paralleled the broader argument by his colleague at the University of Tokyo, Yoshiyuki Noda, that the 'Japanese do not like law'.[47]

42. Kano, *supra* n. 6, 259 (2013).
43. H. Sono, 'Integrating Consumer Law into the Civil Code: A Japanese Attempt at Re-codification', in *Codifying Contract Law: International and Consumer Law Perspectives*, 107 (M. Keyes and T. Wilson eds., Ashgate 2014).
44. *Ibid.*, 119.
45. T. Kawashima (C. Stevens trans.), 'The Legal Consciousness of Contract in Japan', 7 *Law in Japan* 1 (1974).
46. *Ibid.* Cf. also generally Tanase 2010, *supra* n. 5.
47. Y. Noda, *Introduction to Japanese Law* (Tokyo University Press 1976).

II. Contemporary Perspectives

28. Such perspectives resonated strongly in the West over the 1970s and 1980s, in an era of cultural relativism when many Western commentators lost confidence in their institutions and were inspired by (perceived) alternatives in successful economies such as Japan.[48] Examples consistent with this view of Japanese socio-economic ordering were widely reported in the international media, such as Japanese importers' successful calls to renegotiate a fixed-price long-term supply contract for sugar from Australia.[49]

29. Especially from the early 1990s, after the collapse of Japan's 'bubble economy', Western observers began revisiting this conventional wisdom. John Haley argued generally that rather than an inherent or social aversion to law itself, institutional barriers prevented Japanese citizens from accessing the courts to enforce their rights: 'the Japanese cannot like law'. Frank Upham suggested that such barriers, but also parallel alternative dispute resolution (ADR) mechanisms developed especially under government leadership to resolve pressing social problems (such as environmental pollution), were maintained by an elite comprising bureaucrats, conservative politicians and big business: 'the Japanese are made not to like law'. Adopting instead a 'law and economics' approach, J Mark Ramseyer argued that 'the Japanese like the law', in that they negotiate settlements and otherwise structure their affairs in the shadow of a legal system which is very predictable (at least compared to the US or in some fields, such as traffic accident dispute resolution). They therefore can obtain outcomes that track legal entitlements without needing to incur the costs and delays associated with filing and prosecuting cases through the courts.[50]

30. During this phase of major reassessments of the role of law in contemporary Japan in general, empirical and theoretical studies emerged focused on Japanese contract law and practice.[51] From extensive multi-country surveys of law and business students, Masanobu Kato and others found that Japanese responses to scenarios like the Australian 'sugar case' renegotiation were often quite similar to those on the part of many Western respondents.[52] Smaller-scale survey and interview research largely confirmed such findings, in the context of other long-term contracts

48. L. Nottage, 'Planning and Renegotiating Long-Term Contracts in New Zealand and Japan: An Interim Report on an Empirical Research Project', *New Zealand L. Rev.* 482 (1997).
49. Outlined in R. M. March, *The Japanese Negotiator: Subtlety and Strategy Beyond Western Logic* (Kodansha 1988). *See also* L. Nottage, 'Contract Law, Theory and Practice in Japan: Plus ça Change, Plus c'est la Même Chose?', in *Asian Laws Through Australian Eyes*, 316 (V. Taylor ed., Law Book Company 1997).
50. *See* Abe and Nottage, *supra* n. 1 (with further references to leading works by Haley, Upham and Ramseyer). *See also* generally J. M. Ramseyer, *Second-Best Justice: The Virtues of Japanese Law* (University of Chicago Press 2015).
51. Cf. also generally J. O. Haley, 'Rethinking Contract Practice and Law in Japan', 1 *J. East Asia and Int'l L.* 1 (2008), http://ssrn.com/abstract=1131327 (accessed 21 Jun. 2018).
52. M. K. Young et al., 'Japanese Attitudes Towards Contracts: An Empirical Wrinkle in the Debate', (2003) 34 *Geo. Wash. L. Rev.* 789 (2003).

for example between Japanese and New Zealand companies, albeit with some other significant differences in contract design and implementation.[53]

31. In a detailed analysis of Japanese case law, Veronica Taylor also introduced to Western audiences the important role played by Japanese courts in developing the Civil Code's general provision on good faith (Article 1(2)) to limit the scope for terminating long-term distributorship and franchise contracts.[54] John Haley emphasised a broader tendency for Japanese judges to apply or adapt the law to maintain long-term relationships among contracting parties, for example in employment contracts and leases.[55] Both studies questioned Kawashima's conventional view that the law remained irrelevant to socio-economic ordering in Japan. Taylor and Takeshi Uchida went further in emphasising how legislators and policymakers also began making the private law more relevant, through statutory interventions (beginning with the Product Liability Act in 1994, impacting on contractual claims more broadly).[56] They linked such transformations to the Judicial System Reform Council's recommendations in 2001 to move Japan away from ex ante public regulation, towards more indirect ex post socio-economic ordering through enhancing and redress mechanisms for citizens or corporations affected by violations of rights under private law, as well as a shift towards a more complex service-based and internationalised economy.[57]

32. Taylor also translated in 1993 an excerpt from a book by a Kyoto University professor that also queried Kawashima's arguments that contract law continued to play a marginal role in Japan, emphasising instead how contracts were often detailed in writing for certain transactions (e.g., involving land) and how such practices were also recognised by the courts and/or the legislator.[58] The tendency towards ever more detailed contractual documentation, even in domestic transactions, has accelerated into the twenty-first century. Nonetheless, it has been argued that there still exist 'layers of the law' in Japan.[59] While primary ordering of relationships and services is often based on complex, legalistic contracts and regulation, secondary ordering is often based on Japanese analogues to equity or reasonableness. For example, leases may be so detailed that they address liability for a broken toilet paper holder. Yet, if challenged in court, leases may be rewritten to reflect current economic circumstances or 'common sense in society' (*shakai*

---

53. Nottage, *supra* n. 48. Cf., e.g., R. Lewi, 'Japanese Perspectives on Long Term Contracts', in *Long Term Contracts*, (K. Dharmananda and L. Firios eds., Federation Press 2013).
54. Taylor, *supra* n. 30.
55. J. Haley, *The Spirit of Japanese Law* (University of Georgia Press 1998). *See also* generally F. Upham, 'Stealth Activism: Norm Formation by Japanese Courts', 88 *Washington University Law Review* 1493 (2011); J. Haley, 'The Role of Courts in "Making" Law in Japan: The Communitarian Conservatism of Japanese Judges', 22 *Pac. Rim L. & Pol'y J.* 491 (2013).
56. *See also* generally Nottage, *supra* n. 34; and Part I Ch. 4 below.
57. Uchida and Taylor, *supra* n. 37. *See also,* e.g., V. Taylor, 'Japanese Commercial Transactions and Sanctions Revisied: Sumitomo v UFJ', 8 *Washington University Global Studies Law Review* (2009).
58. S. Michida (V. Taylor trans), 'Contract Societies: Japan and the United States Compared', 1 *Pac. Rim L. & Pol'y J.* 199 (1992).
59. A. Pardieck, 'Layers of the Law: A Look at the Role of Law in Japan Today', 22 *Pac. Rim L. & Pol'y J.* 599 (2013).

tsunen). Employment contracts may start with indemnification requirements and end with termination rights, but if they are litigated, the courts will look for 'just cause'. Volumes of regulation govern when a nuclear reactor may operate, but the final decision is based on a 'gentlemen's agreement' and local consensus. As a result, negotiation occurs first in the shadow of detailed rights and obligations, and, if contested, then in the shadow of law, equity and local consensus.

33. Other commentators have also analysed the complex mix of private law and public regulation impacting on the design and implementation of contractual relationships, especially in Japan's rapidly ageing society.[60] It is therefore important for those seeking to understand contemporary Japanese contracting to take seriously the statutory provisions and case law developments, and sometimes detailed contractual documentation, while being aware that other community norms can still play major roles in implementing performance and resolving disputes both in and outside the courts.

60. *See,* e.g., Ryan 2010, *supra* n. 27 and Ryan 2015, *supra* n. 27. *See also* generally H. Baum, M. Baelz and M. Dernauer (eds)., 'Self-regulation in Private Law in Japan and Germany', Special Issue No 10 of the *J. Japanese L.* (2018), https://shop.wolterskluwer.de/recht/europa-voelkerrecht-auslaendisches-recht/59243000-self-regulation-in-private-law-in-japan-and-germany.html (accessed 2 Jul. 2018).

Introduction to the Law of Contracts

§1. Definition of 'Contract'

34. Although there is no express definition of 'contract' in the Civil Code, it is usually understood to mean the coincidence of valid 'declarations of will' or intention (*ishi hyoji no gatchi*).[61] Book I deals with certain defective declarations of will and their potential effects on third parties: 'mental reservations' (concealment of true intention) by the person making the declaration (Article 93), 'fictitious declarations' or shams (Article 94), mistaken declarations (Article 95) and declarations arising from fraud or duress (Article 96).

35. Declarations of will are part of the more abstract concept of 'juristic acts' (*horitsu koi*), derived from German law to mean acts directed at achieving a specific legal effect, such as in relation to rights enforced through the legal system. A contract is therefore a (major) example of juristic acts, but so are unilateral acts such as making a gift or will, and joint acts of incorporation. Article 90 states that: 'A juristic act with any purpose which is against public policy is void'. The Civil Code distinguishes between juristic acts that are null and void (Article 119), and those that are voidable and therefore valid until rescinded (Article 121).

36. Japan has experienced a 'dual reception' of modern Western civil law. The Civil Code not only incorporated a structure and many provisions derived from early drafts of the German Civil Code. From the turn of the twentieth century until World War I, but to lesser extent even until World War II, Japanese scholars referred to interpretations of the German Code to address issues that emerged under the Japanese Code, for example by filling perceived gaps through application of a general principle of good faith (even though this was only expressly added to the Japanese Code in Article 1(2) from 1947).[62] This further 'theory reception' also influenced pre- and post-War court practice, for example the 'doctrine of changed circumstances' providing relief (including court adjustment of long-term contracts) from unexpected supervening events.[63] However, some of these early applications and

61. *See*, e.g., H. Nakata, *Keiyakuho [Contract Law]*, 17–21 (Yuhikaku 2017). However, *see also* E. Hoshino, *Minpo Gairon [Outline of Civil Law]* vol. 4, 3 (Ryoshofukyukai 1975), which attempts to define contract as a 'promise, the enforcement of which is protected by law'.
62. Z. Kitagawa, 'Japanese Civil Law and German Law: From the Viewpoint of Comparative Law' in *The Identity of German and Japanese Law in Comparative Perspectives*, 11, especially 16–42 (Z. Kitagawa and K. Riesenhuber eds., Walter de Gruyter 2007).
63. Nottage, *supra* n. 11.

theories sat awkwardly with the actual wording and/or legislative history of Japan's Code provisions, which sometimes were still derived from French law (such as Article 415 on the scope of damages claimable for breach of contract).[64]

37. From the 1960s, important new academic theories emerged that drew on a closer analysis of the Civil Code's wording and legislative history, a broader comparative law analysis and studies of contracting practices and case law, which often in turn impacted on court practice.[65] Court came to recognise, for example, reliance-based damages for breaking off pre-contractual negotiations in bad faith.[66] The judiciary also became more active and confident in developing new doctrines not expressly provided in the Code, such as certain security interests.[67] The national legislator also enacted many specific laws impacting on commercial and consumer contracts, both specifically (regulating for example door-to-door sales) and generally (such as regulating unfair terms), as mentioned in General Introduction §6 and §7 above.

38. The most recent development is the reform of the law of obligations in 2017, as mentioned in General Introduction §1 above. The reform passed the Diet on 26 May 2017 and will enter into force on 1 April 2020.

§2. Classification of Contracts

39. Like other Civil Codes in the continental European tradition, the Japanese Code provides specific provisions for thirteen types of contracts:

(1) Gifts (*Zoyo*)
(2) Sales (*Baibai*)
(3) Exchanges (*Kokan*)
(4) Loans for Consumption (*Shohi Taishaku*)
(5) Loans for Use (*Shiyo Taishaku*)
(6) Leases (*Chintaishaku*)

---

64. Z. Kitagawa, 'Damages in Contracts for the Sale of Goods', 3 *Law in Japan* 43 (1969).
65. *See*, e.g., the work of Zentaro Kitagawa, Eiichi Hoshino and Ichiro Kato, outlined in Nottage, *supra* n. 10, and in much greater detail in G. Rahn, *Rechtsdenken und Rechtsauffassung in Japan [Legal Thought and Conceptions of Law in Japan]* (CH Beck 1997). *See also*, e.g., E. Hoshino, 'The Contemporary Contract', 5 *Law in Japan* 1 (1972).
66. S. Kawakami, 'Japan' in *Pre-Contractual Liability: Reports to the 13th Congress, International Academy of Comparative Law*, 207 (E. Hondius ed., Kluwer 1991). On the more recent litigation between major banking groups regarding a merger and acquisition negotiation subject to express clauses on exclusive and good faith negotiations, *see* Taylor, *supra* n. 57; K. Takahashi, *Walford V Miles in Japan: Lock-in and Lock-out Agreements in Sumitomo v. UFJ*, *J. Bus. L.* 166 (2009), and J. Westhoff, 'Civil Law – M&A – Binding Nature of Letter of Intent – Obligation to Negotiate in Good Faith – Confidentiality Clause – Injunctive Relief Business Law', in *Business Law in Japan – Cases and Comments*, 25 (M. Baelz, M. Dernauer, C. Heath and A. Petersen-Padberg eds., Kluwer 2012).
67. J. O. Haley, 'The Preliminary Contract for Substitute Performance: A Reflection of Japanese Judicial Approach', 7 *Law in Japan* 133 (1974).

(7) Employment (*Koyo*)
(8) Contracts for Work to be Done (*Ukeoi*)
(9) Mandates (*I'nin*)
(10) Deposits (*Kitaku*)
(11) Partnerships (*Kumiai*)
(12) Life Annuities (*Shushin Teikikin*)
(13) Compromises (*Wakai*).

40. However, on the one hand, the provisions on employment contracts and life annuities are now almost completely displaced by labour law and new mechanisms for income security governed by specific legislation.

41. On the other, innovative types of commercial relationships have emerged over the twentieth century, such as distributorships and franchise contracts,[68] for which the Civil Code does not incorporate specific provisions – even following the revision process that concluded in 2017. The thirteen traditional types of contracts are set out in Book III, Chapter 2, Sections 2–14 of the Civil Code, placed after general contract law provisions (found in Book I and Book III, Chapter 2, Section 1 Articles 521–548), which have been extended by courts and commentators to the new types of commercial relationships.

42. The thirteen traditional types of contract have generally been further classified from different viewpoints as follows:

I. Consensual Contract (*Dakusei Keiyaku*) Versus Real Contract (*Yobutsu Keiyaku*)

43. Consensual contracts are those that require the mere agreement of the parties to enter into force, whereas real contracts require handing over of a thing to enter into force. In principle, contracts are consensual contracts under Japanese law (Article 522(2)).

44. Prior to the 2017 Reform, loans for use, loans for consumption and deposits were classified as real contracts, meaning that the lender is not obligated to lend, or the depositary is not obligated to take the deposit, until the agreed subject matter is provided. Under the 2017 Reform, loans for use and deposits are classified as consensual contracts which means that the lender can be obligated to lend, and depositary can be obligated to take the deposit (Articles 593 and 697). However, unless these contracts are put into writing, the lender or depositary is given a right to cancel the contract before the borrower receives the object of loan, or the depositor deposits a thing with the depositary (Articles 593-2 and 657-2(2)). Loans for consumption remains a real contract under the 2017 Reform, but a new provision is

68. *See*, e.g., Taylor, *supra* n. 30; Kozuka, *supra* n. 14; S. Kozuka, 'The Impact of Japan's Contract Law Reform on Franchise Agreements', 20 *Int'l Franchising* 24 (May 2016).

added that provides that a loan for consumption in writing has full force even before the lending is carried out (Article 587-2(1)).

II. Contract for Value (*Yusho Keiyaku*) Versus Gratuitous Contract (*Musho Keiyaku*)

45. Contracts for value involve economic exchange, whereas gratuitous contracts do not. This classification is important because the provisions for sales contracts apply *mutatis mutandis* to other contracts of value (Article 559).

46. Most of the typical contracts are classified as contracts for value. Contracts not for value are gifts, loan for use, loan for consumption, mandates and deposits. Generally, the binding force of contracts not for value is limited in the sense that the parties can either cancel the contract before performance unless the contract is in writing (Articles 550 (gift), 593-2 (loan for use), 657-2(2) (loan for consumption)) or cancel at any time (Article 651 (mandate)). However, for loan for consumption, mandate and deposits, the parties may agree to make it an economic exchange, by agreeing to pay interests on the loan or by agreeing to pay for the service provided by that mandatary or the depositary.

III. Bilateral Contract (*Somu Keiyaku*) Versus Unilateral Contract (*Henmu Keiyaku*)

47. Bilateral contracts are contracts where both parties owe obligations arising from the contract against each other, whereas unilateral contracts are contracts where only one party owes an obligation.

48. Most of the typical contracts are classified as bilateral contracts. Under the 2017 Reform, unilateral contracts are gifts and loans for consumption if not in writing. A loan for consumption not in writing is a unilateral contract because the contract enters into force only when the borrower receives the object of the loan (Article 587). (The term 'unilateral contract' is used differently than in common law, where it means that one party promises something in exchange for the other carrying out an act, such as a promise of reward for returning a lost pet.)

49. The distinction between bilateral and unilateral contracts focuses on the existence of an obligation and a counter-obligation. This is different from the distinction between contracts for value and not for value, which focuses on the existence of economic exchange. All bilateral contracts are contracts for value, but unilateral contracts can be for value as well. If the parties to a loan for consumption, not in writing, agree on payment of interest, that is an agreement for economic exchange. But since the lender does not owe an obligation to lend (Article 587), only the borrower is obligated to return the object and pay the interest. This makes it a unilateral contract for value.

50. Rules on simultaneous performance (Article 533) and cancellation for breach (Articles 541 and 542) are relevant only with respect to bilateral contracts.

§3. Contract and Torts

51. A further classification is between commercial and general contracts, discussed in the General Introduction §6 above. Although German law had a major influence on the Japanese Civil Code's basic structure, many provisions and especially their interpretations (especially during the first half of the twentieth century), the Code differed significantly by adopting a general provision providing for tort liability for negligence. Inspired instead by French law, Article 709 simply provides: 'A person who has intentionally or negligently infringed any right of others, or legally protected interest of others, shall be liable to compensate any damages resulting in consequence.' This has meant, for example, that Japanese courts have not needed to expand contractual liability, as in Germany,[69] to provide relief for harm suffered by a party to pre-contractual negotiations that were broken off before a contract could be concluded. The Supreme Court of Japan has held that such pre-contractual liability should be considered tortious in nature, at least for the purpose of the limitation period applicable to the claim.[70] However, the precise juridical basis of pre-contractual liability is still unclear from case law and commentary in Japan (as outlined in Part 1 Chapter 1 §3 below).

52. Failed pre-contractual negotiations, workplace accidents and medical malpractice are prominent examples where the plaintiff may be able to frame the claim under contract or tort law. Like German law but unlike French law,[71] Japanese civil procedure allows the plaintiff to choose which avenue to pursue. The choice will depend on differences in remedies (detailed below in Part I, Chapter 6) in the following respects under contract law as opposed to tort law:

(a) burden of proof regarding negligence: the defendant must prove lack of fault (e.g., in supplying medical services);
(b) comparative negligence: the plaintiff's negligence impacts on both 'liability for damages' and the 'amount thereof' (Article 418, cf. Article 722(2));
(c) prescription periods: this difference has diminished after the 2017 Reform. Prior to the Reform, contract claims were extinguished after ten years (former Article 167(1)), rather than three years from the time the victim becomes aware of the harm and the tortfeasor or twenty years from the time of tort for torts (Article 724). After the 2017 Reform, the length of prescription period for contract claims are changed to five years from the time the obligee becomes aware that its right can be exercised, or ten years from the time the right can be exercised (Article 166(1)). Further, with respect to infringement to life or limb the ten-year period is extended to twenty years (Article 168);

69. Cf. generally B. Markesinis, *The German Law of Contract and Restitution* (Clarendon 1997).
70. Supreme Court, 27 Nov. 2012, Hanji 2175.
71. *See* generally B. Nicholas, *The French Law of Contract* (Oxford University Press 1996).

(d) point of time for calculating damages for delay: from when the plaintiff makes its claim (Article 412(3)), rather than when the tort was committed;
(e) solatium (*isharyo* or general damages for pain and suffering): unavailable in contract claims except where a 'personality interest' is infringed (e.g., to life, limb, liberty or honour) or where recovery of economic value is not sufficient to compensate for the pain and suffering (e.g., loss of a pet);
(f) lawyers' fees: only claimable in tort suits (or where a damages claim is brought as a contractual claim but the non-performance also amounts to tort).[72]

53. Following the amendments to the contract law-related provisions of the Civil Code, it has been suggested that the tort provisions may also be subject to formal review.[73]

§4. CONTRACT AND RESTITUTION

54. Largely following German law, within the continental European Civil Law tradition, Book III of the Japanese Civil Code recognises two main types of obligation (apart from tort) that arise even without a contractual obligation, although sometimes in contracting contexts. One is the management of another's affairs without mandate. If someone begins to do so (e.g., repairing an absent neighbour's property after a storm), he or she must do so in accordance with the nature of the situation and by means best suiting the interests of the other (Article 697). Necessary expenses can then be claimed in reimbursement (Article 702(1)).

55. The most important in practice is restitution for unjust enrichment. Generally, *see* Part II, Chapter 13. For the situation when contracts are terminated, *see* Part I, Chapter 6, §4, IV.

56. Further, the Supreme Court has spoken with respect to the possibility of claiming restitution of a value conferred on someone under a contract, against a third person (e.g., owner of the item whose value was increased). If someone (X) benefits from another's property or services without legitimate ground and therefore causes loss to that person (Y), the former must make corresponding restitution (Article 703). In its judgment of 16 July 1970, the Supreme Court of Japan extended this concept to require the plaintiff (X), who had repaired a bulldozer for Z that was leased from the owner Y, to claim restitution of the repair fee from Y due to the latter's unjust enrichment.[74] However, following some academic criticism, in a judgment of 19 September 1995, the Supreme Court narrowed the scope of such obligations. The repairer (Y) of a building under a contract for services concluded

---

72. H. Kihara, *Tort Law in Japan* 27 (Kluwer 2015). Indeed, lawyers' fees are claimable (albeit within 'reasonable', in fact typically low, limits) if the plaintiff is successful in the tort claim, but is not liable for the defendant's lawyers' fees if the claim is unsuccessful (as in Anglo-Commonwealth law).
73. *See*, e.g., Y. Shiomi, 'Kikakuno Shushi [Proposal Outline]', in *Fuhokoihono Rippotekikadai [Legislative Challenges for Tort Law]* 1 (Gendai Fuhokoiho Kenkyukai ed., Shojihomu 2015).
74. Supreme Court, 16 Jul. 1970, Minshu 24-7-909.

with its lessee (Z), who became insolvent, can claim restitution from the owner (X) 'only when the owner received the benefit without paying any price under the lease contract between the owner and the lessee as a whole'.[75]

§5. Contract and the Law of Property

57. Book II of the Civil Code sets out 'property rights' (such as rights of possession and ownership) as well as 'real security rights' (such as rights of retention).[76] Despite the generally strong influence of German law overall, Book III on obligations differs in not requiring registration (or transfer of possession) for a transfer of property to take effect. Declarations of will or intention by the parties are sufficient (Article 176). However, to claim rights against third parties, registration is necessary for immovable property (Article 177) and delivery is necessary for movables (Article 178). These provisions derive from French law, as incorporated into Japan's Old Civil Code, although that never came into force.[77]

§6. Contract and Trusts

58. Japanese law has recognised trusts in general for almost a century, since enacting the Trust Act (Act No. 62 of 1922) and the Trust Business Act (Act No. 65 of 1922). The latter originally was the primary focus, establishing a strict regulatory regime. Moneylenders, real estate brokers, investment and other services providers calling themselves 'trust' companies had proliferated during the Taisho era (1912–1926) due to strong economic growth and the still undefined term 'trust' borrowed from the West. However, the Trust Law established basic principles derived from and similar to Anglo-American trust law, including the concept of legal ownership of trust property remaining with the beneficiaries.

59. Until around 1950, this legislative framework supported trusts that mainly pooled large amounts of capital that were invested individually or jointly into public bonds or loans (similar to today's large floating-rate bank deposits). After enactment of the Loan Trust Act (Act No. 195 of 1952), money trusts became popular for long-term smaller investments, benefitting from tax-free treatment of trust income (similar to funds in bank deposits). Guarantees of principal, not offered in

---

75. Supreme Court, 19 Sep. 1995, Minshu 49-5-2805. This means a more case-by-case assessment, depending for example on the actual duration of the lease contract, although the scope of unjust enrichment remains wider than under German law: M. Fujiwara, 'Civil Law – Case to Seek Return of Money Equivalent to Unjust Enrichment – *Actio de in rem verso*', in *Business Law in Japan: Cases and Comments*, 55 (M. Baelz, M. Dernauer et al. eds., Kluwer 2012). Statutory liens (*sakidoritokken*) for repairers or builders (Arts 320 and 326–327) are limited to immediate contracting parties.
76. On recent reforms to security interests law in Japan, *see*, e.g., S. Kozuka and N. Fujisawa, 'Old Ideas Die Hard? Reform of Secured Transactions Law in Japan and its Impact on the Banking Practice', 31 *T. Jefferson L. Rev*. 293 (2009).
77. *See* General Introduction §1 above.

other countries, also remained available. This period also saw the gradual emergence of company pension, charitable and other types of trusts adding some asset management functions to investment and financing functions.

60. Since the 1980s, new types of asset management trusts have become a further mainstay for licensed trust banks: business trusts (especially land trusts), managing trusts (securities trusts) and convertible trusts (asset liquidation trusts). This has been underpinned by the ageing population and diversification of asset holdings, creating opportunities for trust banks (allowed partially from 1992 and fully from 2002) to bring to bear their asset management expertise while insulating assets from insolvency risks.[78]

61. Reforms to the Trust Business Act in 2004 liberalised rules on engaging in commercial trusteeship, relaxed duties on such trustees and expanded permitted types of trust property, while strengthening disclosure obligations. This deregulatory impetus carried over to amendments to the Trust Act in 2006, for example allowing 'self-declared trusts' (where the settlor is also the trustee), 'limited liability trusts' protecting trustees and 'beneficiary security-issuing trusts' (where trust income, e.g., from receivables, constitutes a beneficial interest use to find tradable securities issued to investors). Some commentators remain disappointed, however, that the potential for non-commercial trusts was not adequately addressed during this reform process, including civil trusts (such as the 'self-benefit trust' where the settlor is also the beneficiary) and charitable trusts.[79]

§7. Good Faith and Other General Principles

62. Freedom of contract is a general principle of the Civil Code. The 2017 Reform expressly provides for the freedom to agree on the terms of a contract (Article 521(2)), freedom whether or not to enter into a contract (Article 521(1)), as well as freedom from formal (writing) requirements (Article 522(2)).[80] There is some overlap between the provision on freedom to agree on the terms of the contract and Article 91, which states that: 'If any party to a juristic act manifests any intention which is inconsistent with a provision in any laws and regulations not related to public policy, such intention shall prevail'.

63. However, Article 1 states that:

(1) Private rights must conform to the public welfare.

---

78. M. Arai, 'Japan', in *Trusts in Prime Jurisdictions*, 233, 234 (A. Kaplan ed., Globe Business Publishing 2010).
79. T. Ryan, 'The Trust in an Ageing Japan: Has Commercialisation Precluded the Trust from Reaching its Welfare Potential', 7 *Asian J. Comp. L.* 197, 204 (2012). Also not clarified was the scope of an analogue to the common law 'constructive trust', recognized by the Supreme Court of Japan to have been established between a local government (as settlor) and a construction company (trustee) regarding the latter's advance payment into a bank: 17 Jan. 2002, Minshu 56-1-20.
80. But *see* Michida, *supra* n. 58; and Part 1 Ch. 1 §2 (formal requirements) and §3(I) (pre-contractual liability) below.

(2) The exercise of rights and performance of duties must be done in good faith.
(3) No abuse of rights is permitted.

64. Exercising rights in conformity with public welfare, and not abusing rights, are particularly important with respect to property rights.[81] But the principle of good faith has come to play a major role in Japanese contract law, more like German than French law.[82] To a lesser extent, so has Article 90, which provides: 'A juristic act with any purpose which is against public policy is void.'[83]

65. The general principle of good faith – in both the formation and performance of contracts – emerged through early twentieth century 'theory reception' from German law, then partial recognition through pre-War case law in Japan.[84] It was expressly acknowledged in 1947 by adding Article 1(2) to the Civil Code, and has been increasingly applied by the courts especially since the 1960s.[85]

66. The good faith principle has come to have particular relevance for establishing liability for failed pre-contractual negotiations,[86] providing relief for certain types of contractual unfairness (both generally, for example, in residential lease and employment contracts,[87] and in some contracts with consumers[88]), and in limiting scope for termination of contracts (both for breach, as in distributorships or franchise contracts,[89] or situations of unexpected supervening events[90]).

---

81. *See also* Art. 29(2) of the Constitution.
82. B. Jazulot, *La bonne foi dans les contrats: Etude comparative de droit français, allemand et japonais [Good Faith in Contracts: Comparative Study of French, German and Japanese Law* (Dalloz 2001).
83. *See,* e.g., General Introduction §5 (public law) above and Part 1 Ch. 2 §3 (illegality and public policy) below.
84. *See* above Introduction to the Law of Contracts §1.
85. *See,* e.g., T. Uchida, 'The New Development of Contract Law and General Clauses: A Japanese Perspective', in *Proceedings of the Symposium: Dutch and Japanese Laws*, 119 (ICCLP et al. eds., International Center for Comparative Law and Politics, University of Tokyo 1993).
86. *See* Kawakami, *supra* n. 66, and Part I, Ch. 1 §3 below.
87. Haley, *supra* n. 55, 138.
88. *See* Nottage, *supra* n. 11; and Kozuka, *supra* n. 38; and generally General Introduction §7 above.
89. *See also* V. T'Hooft, 'Japanese Law and the Unilateral Termination of Distribution Agreements: The Breakdown of Distribution Keiretsu', in *Yearbook of Law and Legal Practice in East Asia*, 137 (A. De Roo and R. Jagtenberg eds., Kluwer Law International 1996). *See* further Part I, Ch. 5 below.
90. P. Waer, 'Frustration of Contracts in Japanese Law: The Doctrine of Changed Circumstances', 20 *Law in Japan* 187 (1987); Nottage, *supra* n. 11 and Nottage, *supra* n. 48; Nottage et al. 2008, *supra* n. 28; F. Bennett, 'Civil Law – Contract Law – Doctrine of Frustration – Change of Circumstances', in *Business Law in Japan: Cases and Comments*, 17 (M. Baelz, M. Dernauer et al. eds., Kluwer 2012). *See also* further Part I, Ch. 5 below.

§8. Style of Drafting

67. Western commentators, especially from common law tradition jurisdictions, have often been surprised at the comparatively short written contracts used by Japanese parties. However, this arises partly because the Japanese language (incorporating Chinese characters) can express concepts more succinctly say than the English language, and also because the background Civil Code lessens the need to spell out default rules and principles.[91] Empirical research into supply contracts in Japan shows that the extent to which framework contracts are used (incorporating various types of clauses to address future contingencies, such as force majeure clauses), and which side typically drafts such framework contracts (sellers or buyers), differs significantly nowadays depending on the business sector.[92] There have also long-existed areas where more detailed written contracts are used within Japan, for example in relation to land, and this tendency seems to have has been accelerating in recent decades – even if the specific provisions are still often not determinative when disputes arise in or outside of court.[93] There are also newer transaction types, such as franchises, construction contracts or corporate Mergers and Acquisitions, where extensive contractual documentation is common (with readily available commentaries or guidance) and violations may more likely lead to major litigation.[94]

68. For cross-border contracts, moreover, Japanese parties have often agreed to more detailed contracts, especially when drafted in English and/or with a governing law other than Japanese (which is quite common in practice, along for example with an arbitration clause specifying a seat outside Japan).[95] Indeed, some Japanese jurists and businesspeople have recently complained about the tendency for contracting parties in other parts of Asia to draft shorter contracts and/or not to abide

91. Taylor, *supra* n. 30.
92. For, e.g., S. Kitayama, *Keizokuteki Torihiki ni kansuru Kokunai Chosa on Kekka (1) [Results from a Domestic Survey of Continuous Transactions (Part 1)*, 627 N.B.L. 11 (1998) and H. Nakata, *Keiyaku to Kankei – Keizokuteki Torihiki no Chosa Kekka (Jo) [Contracts and Relationships: Continuous Transactions Survey Results (Part 1)* 631 N.B.L. 6.
93. Michida, *supra* n. 58; Pardieck, *supra* n. 59. For some frustration from Japanese commentators, with backgrounds in legal practice, regarding the Japanese courts' tendency in some fields to not give sufficient weight to the provisions set out by the parties, *see*, e.g., M. C. Chino, N. Kashiwagi and A. Okada, 'Contract and Tort', in *Japanese Business Law*, 173 (G. P. McAlinn ed., Kluwer Law International 2008).
94. *See* respectively V. Taylor, 'Contracts with the Lot: Franchises, Good Faith and Contract Regulation', *New Zealand Law Review* 459 (1997); A. Kaiser, 'The Construction Contract in Japan from a German Perspective', 36 *J. Japanese L.* 217 (2013); Taylor, *supra* n. 57.
95. On international arbitration clauses and practices, *see*, e.g., M. Richter, 'Attitudes and Practices of Japanese Companies with Respect to International Commercial Arbitration: Testing Perceptions with Empirical Evidence', 5 *Transnat'l Disp. Mgmt.* (2011) at http://www.transnational-dispute-management.com/article.asp?key=1762 (accessed 21 Jun. 2018); T. Nakamura and L. Nottage, 'Arbitration in Japan', in *International Commercial Arbitration in Asia*, 223 (S. Ali and T. Ginsburg eds., 3rd ed, Juris 2013).

readily by their provisions, which is quite ironic given that similar criticisms were often levelled at Japanese parties by Western commentators in the 1970s and 1980s.[96]

69. The main source remains the Civil Code (Act No. 89 of 1896), especially:

(a) Book I: Chapter I (General Provisions) Article 1, Chapter V (Juristic Acts), Chapter VII (Prescription).
(b) Book III (Claims [relating to Obligations]): Chapter I (General Provisions), Chapter II (Contracts) including Section 1 (General Provisions, Articles 521–548), Section 2 (Gifts, Articles 549–554), Section 3 (Sales, Articles 555–585) and subsequent Sections for ten other contract types.

70. The 2017 Reform was based on the Act to Amend Part of the Civil Code (Act No. 44 of 2017). That statute amends the Civil Code (Act No. 89 of 1896). When the 2017 Reform comes into effect on 1 April 2020, some of the article numbers will be renumbered from the current Civil Code. References to article numbers in this monograph are to the renumbered article numbers, unless otherwise indicated.

71. Semi-official English translations of the currently applicable Civil Code and the Commercial Code have become freely available via the Ministry of Justice's website[97] and so have various other specific statutes impacting directly on contracting under Japanese law. These include the:

(a) Interest Rate Restriction Act;
(b) Act on Land and Building Leases;
(c) Real Estate Brokerage Act (Act No. 176 of 1952);
(d) Act on Specified Commercial Transactions (formerly the Door-to-Door Sales Act);
(e) Instalment Sales Act;
(f) Consumer Contracts Act;
(g) Act on Special Provisions to the Civil Code Concerning Electronic Consumer Contracts and Electronic Acceptance Notice (Act No. 95 of 2001);
(h) Product Liability Act (albeit mainly relevant to claims by users of unsafe products against manufacturers and certain others with whom not in direct contractual relationships);
(i) CISG (for certain cross-border commercial sales of goods).

---

96. *Cf*, e.g., R. March, *The Japanese Negotiator: Subtlety and Logic Beyond Western Logic* (Kodansha 1988).
97. Searchable via http://www.japaneselawtranslation.go.jp/?re=02 (accessed 21 Jun. 2018). For a guide to online resources in English on Japanese Law generally, *see* H. Baum, L. Nottage, J. Rheuben and M. Their, *Japanese Business Law in Western Languages: An Annotated Selective Bibliography* (2nd ed., William S. Hein & Company 2013).

72. Note that the CISG is directly applicable in Japan, and therefore the authentic treaty texts in six United Nations official languages should be referred to. The government's Japanese language translation is not officially binding.[98]

73. Full translations of some Supreme Court judgments related to contract law are available via its website, while some case summaries are available elsewhere online or in printed works.[99]

---

98. Sono 2010, *supra* n. 8.

99. *See*, respectively, http://www.courts.go.jp/app/hanrei_en/search; http://www.tomeika.jur.kyushu-u.ac.jp/ (accessed 21 Jun. 2018) and), *Business Law in Japan: Cases and Comments* (M. Baelz, M. Dernauer et al. eds., Kluwer 2012).

Part I. General Principles of the Law of Contract

Chapter 1. Formation

§1. Agreement and Quid Pro Quo (Reciprocity)

74. Contracts are generally formed by agreement of the parties, through their respective manifestations or expressions of intention coinciding (*ishihyoji no gatchi*).[100] Exceptionally, valid formation of contracts may require writing (*yoshiki keiyaku*, such as guarantee contracts: Article 446[101]) or delivery of the subject matter (*yobutsu keiyaku*,[102] such as loans for consumption under Articles 587–592: only formed when the amount agreed to be borrowed is received), or notarisation.[103]

75. Usually, party agreement and contract formation are evidenced by the offeror making an offer, which is accepted by the offeree. However, this can also follow if agreement is evidenced in other ways.[104] One situation is if 'facts arise that ought to be regarded as a manifestation of intention of acceptance', in situations 'where no notice of acceptance is required due to the offeror's manifestation of intention or usage of trade' (Article 527). Such acceptance by conduct is known as

100. *See* Introduction to the Law of Contracts §1 above (definition of contract).
101. *See* §2. I.B below.
102. *See* Introduction to the Law of Contracts §3 above (classifications of contract).
103. *See* respectively Part II, Ch. 10 and § 2. II.B below.
104. Draft Proposal No. 28(1) of the Ministry of Justice (MOJ)'s 'Annotated Interim Recommendations for Reforming the Civil Code (Law of Obligations) [*Minpo (Saiken Kankei) no Kaisei ni kansuru Chukan Shian (Gaiyo-tsuki)*]' (March 2013, reprinted in *NBL Bessatsu* No. 143, 122) states that a contract is concluded when an offer is accepted, but the commentary notes that this does not imply that a contract cannot be concluded by other appropriate means of indicating agreement. *See also* draft proposal [3.1.1.07] of the (mainly private) study group, which has heavily influenced the Ministry's official deliberations, the Japan Civil Code (Law of Obligations) Reform Commission (2009, at http://www.shojihomu.or.jp/saikenhou/English/draftproposals.html#Book3ch1 (accessed 21 Jun. 2018)). It states in relation to 'Agreement forming the contract' that: '(1) A contract comes into existence when an agreement has been reached on the matters that should be stipulated in light of the intention of the parties and the nature of the contract.'

'contract formation by realising intentions' (*ishijitsugen*).[105] Second, under Japanese law, a contract can be validly formed by cross-offers, such as when a buyer dispatches an offer to purchase a product at a specified price and time while a seller happens to dispatch simultaneously an offer to supply at the same price and time. An exception is where one such party lacks the intention to form a contract, unless the other party reasonably interprets the former's declaration to constitute a valid offer.[106]

I. Offer and Acceptance

76. The original Japanese Civil Code did not define 'offer' or 'acceptance'.[107] However, commentators generally understand an offer to mean a manifestation of intention to be contractually bound if and when the other party manifests acceptance,[108] and this is reflected in Article 522(1) as revised in the 2017 Reform. An offer takes effect when it reaches the other party (Article 97(1) – the general 'receipt principle'). Thus, it can be withdrawn until it reaches the offeree because it has not taken effect, but after it reaches the offeree, in principle, offers cannot be revoked unless the offereor reserves the right of revocation (Article 523(1) & 525(1)). *See* paragraphs 81 and 82.

77. Article 529 clarifies that 'a person who places an advertisement to the effect that any person who performs a defined act will be given a set reward … shall be obligated to give the reward to the person who has performed the act'. The 2017 Reform preserved this approach for such prizes, but adds that the obligation arises 'whether or not the party performing the act knew about the advertisement'.

78. Otherwise, whether public statements – such as other advertisements through the media or price labels on displayed goods – amount to offers, or instead

105. Y. Shiomi, *Saiken Kakuron I: Keiyakuho/Jimu Kanri/Futou Ritoku [Law of Obligations I: Contracts and Unjust Enrichment]*, 18 (3rd ed., Shinseisha 2017), giving the example of a regular customer requesting by fax another delivery of a 10-kg rice pack, which the local store drops off at the home when the customer happens to have stepped out.

106. *Ibid.*, giving as the example of the exception a person raising her hand to send off a friend on the other side of the road – not reasonably interpreted by a passing taxi as an offer to conclude a transportation contract.

107. Cf. *Commentary on the UNIDROIT Principles of International Commercial Contracts* (S. Vogenauer ed., 2nd ed., Oxford University Press 2015), 266 (by Luke Nottage) and 185 (by Ross Anderson).

108. Y. Shiomi, *Shin Saiken Soron I [New Obligations in General I]*, 15 (Shinzansha, 2017), suggesting therefore that a taxi displaying an 'available' sign would generally be expressing an offer, so that a taxi refusing a customer to get in the taxi after the customer indicated acceptance would be in breach of contract.

merely 'invitations to make offers', will depend on specific (categories of) facts in light of the above-mentioned general test.[109] One commentator suggests, for example:[110]

> If the contract is a sales contract and the proposal is concrete, such a proposal is more likely to be deemed an offer than it would be in the case of a sole-distributor contract. There are several reasons for this. In a sales contract, the most important preparatory step is for the seller to check the solvency of the buyer; a concrete proposal in the form of a sales contract to a party with good credit can be construed as an offer without fear of harm to either party. In the case of a sole-distributor contract, however, not only the solvency of the partner but also other qualities, such as salesmanship, size of the distribution network, business reputation, etc, are also important. This means that even a concrete proposal to a party with established credit should sometimes be construed as a first step in the negotiations to determine the suitability of a business partnership.

79. Draft Proposal No. 28(2) of the Ministry of Justice's *Annotated Interim Recommendations for Reforming the Civil Code (Law of Obligations)* stated that an offer must be able to 'indicate the contents of the contract' as soon as it is accepted. The commentary adds that the offer, in contradistinction to an 'invitation of an offer' (or willingness to entertain offers), must propose matters sufficient to be able to determine the contents of the contract.[111] This language was not codified in the 2017 Reform, but the same is implied in Article 522 which provides that 'a contract is formed when one party manifests an intention to conclude a contract, indicating its contents (an offer), which is accepted by another party'.

80. Conversely, an acceptance is understood to be a manifestation of intention to be contractually bound by the terms of the offer. Thus, if 'the offeree has accepted the offer by adding any condition or by making *any other modification*, it shall be deemed that the offeree has refused the offer and has made a new offer' (Article 528).[112]

---

109. *Ibid. See also* generally T. Uchida, *Minpo II [Civil Code II]*, 31 (3rd ed., Tokyodaigaku Shuppankai 2011), criticising Art. 2(2) of the Specified Commercial Transactions Act (Act No. 57 of 1976) which regulates distance sales (*tsushin hanbai*) defined as supplying goods and services after 'receiving offers', which implies that catalogues posted out to customers must merely constitute invitations to place offers.
110. M. Kato, 'Contract Law' in *Business Law in Japan*, 77, 92 (L. Nottage ed., CCH Japan 2008).
111. Ministry of Justice, 'Annotated Interim Recommendations for Reforming the Civil Code', *supra* n. 104, 122.
112. Uchida, *supra* n. 109, 32, emphasising the strictness of the Civil Code's mirror image rule in Art 528, despite potential for a 'battle of the forms' whereby each party attempts to transact based only on its own standard form contract. Cf. H. Dogauchi, 'Outline of Contract Law in Japan' (last updated 2010), available from www.tomeika.jur.kyushu-u.ac.jp/transaction/contract.html#part1 (accessed 21 Jun. 2018), Part 1.3.1.3:

> Nevertheless, in theory - with reference to article 19 of the UN Convention on Contracts for the International Sale of Goods – even if the 'acceptance is modified' when the modifications are

81. If the offeror specifies a period for acceptance, and the offer reaches the offeree, the offeror cannot revoke the offer within that period unless it reserves the right to revoke it (Article 523(1)). In order for the contract to be formed, the offeree's acceptance must be received within the specified period (pursuant to the general 'receipt principle', *totatsushugi*, under Article 97(1)), so even a withdrawal of a dispatched acceptance will be effective if the withdrawal arrives before the notice of acceptance. If the acceptance is not received within the specified period, the offer lapses (Article 523(2)).[113] If an acceptance is received by the offeror outside the period specified in the offer, he may treat it as a counter-offer (Article 524), which can be accepted by the original offeror to conclude the contract.[114]

82. If the offeror does not specify a period for acceptance, Japanese law distinguishes between contract formation arising from negotiations where parties are physically present and those negotiating at a distance. For the former, the offer can be revoked at any time if the parties are continuing their negotiations in each other's physical presence (Article 525(2). If the offeror does not receive acceptance during such a period, the offer loses effect, unless the offeror manifests its intention to keep the offer in effect (Article 525(3)).

83. For the latter, negotiation at a distance, the offeror may not revoke the offer until the expiry of a period that is reasonable for the offeror to receive notice of acceptance, unless the offeror has reserved the right of revocation (Article 525(1)). Under the original Civil Code, if the offeree dispatches such a notice of acceptance, it then cannot be withdrawn because the contract was formed at the time of dispatch (the 'dispatch principle', *hasshinshugi*, under former Article 526(1) and thus an exception to the general principle in Article 97(1)). However, this provision was deleted in the 2017 Reform, thus reinstating the 'receipt principle' under Article

---

not major the contract shall be formed with the modified terms of acceptance, unless the offeror objects. Even if such a rule is not clearly adopted, in a situation in which both parties think a contract has been formed and act according to that assumption, notwithstanding that the offer and acceptance are not in agreement, the court can be expected to recognize the formation of contract by construing the intent of the parties to find terms consistent with fairness between the parties.

The 2017 Reform makes no change to Art. 528 and does not contain any further provisions dealing specifically with the 'battle of forms'.

113. Y. Shiomi, *Saiken Kakuron I: Keiyakuho/Jimu Kanri/Futou Ritoku [Law of Obligations I: Contracts and Unjust Enrichment]*(2nd ed., Shinseisha 2009), dealing with pre-2017 Reform law, 15 criticised many commentators who extend the former Art. 526(1) (which provided that contracts between parties at a distance are formed upon dispatch of acceptance) to situations involving offers specifying a period for acceptance as well as those which do not, thus rendering ineffective any withdrawal of an acceptance even if received by the offeror before the acceptance is received. He notes that the Japan Civil Code (Law of Obligations) Reform Commission (2009) proposed moving generally towards the 'receipt principle', prevalent in most overseas jurisdictions. In fact, as mentioned *infra*, that principle was indeed adopted in the 2017 Reform.

114. Prior to the 2017 Reform, there was a provision providing exceptionally for a late arrival of notice of acceptance which would normally have arrived on time to be deemed to have arrived in time under certain conditions (former Art. 522). That provision was deleted in the 2017 Reform.

97(1): contract is formed at the time the notice of acceptance reaches the offeror.[115] Accordingly, the notice of acceptance can be withdrawn until the contract is formed by the offeror receiving the acceptance.

84. What else happens after the expiry of a period that is reasonable for the offeror to receive notice of acceptance? One view is that the offer remains in effect until the offeror then declares it to be revoked. The predominant view, however, finds this unpersuasive in light of the nature of an offer and the circumstances of both parties. Instead, extending the approach found in Article 508(1) of the Commercial Code, most commentators conclude that after the expiry of this period, plus a further reasonable period, the offer lapses and loses effect so it can no longer be accepted. [116]

85. Prior to the 2017 Reform, Article 4 of the Act on Special Provisions to the Civil Code Concerning Electronic Consumer Contracts and Electronic Acceptance Notice (Act No. 95 of 2001) provided that the provisions of the Civil Code regarding the dispatch principle for notice of acceptance (Articles 526(1) and 527) do not apply where the offeree manifests acceptance through electronic means (such as fax, telephone or e-mail). Thus, the general 'receipt' principle set out in Article 97 applied. If, for example, an e-commerce supplier seeks to enforce a claim based on a contract with a consumer, it will have to prove that a contract was validly formed – including through the notice of acceptance having been received (rather than merely having been dispatched).[117] However, that provision was deleted in the 2017 Reform as under the revised rule, the receipt principle will generally apply to notices of acceptance as well. The Act will be renamed Act on Special Provisions to the Civil Code Concerning Electronic Consumer Contracts.

86. Lastly, Article 526 provides an exception to Article 97(2), which maintains the effect of manifestations of intention even if the person subsequently dies or loses the capacity to act. An offer loses effect in such cases where the offeror has expressed a contrary intention or the offeree 'has come to know of the fact of the offeror's death or loss of capacity to act' before it dispatches notice of acceptance.

II. Intention to Create Legal Relations

87. The Japanese Civil Code, commentaries and case law contain no such separate criterion for validly forming a contract, but an intention to create legal relations is implicit in the notions of offer and acceptance, as well as agreements evidenced

115. Y. Yamashita, 'Formation of Contract in Japan' in *Studies in the Contract Law of Asia Vol. II: Formation and Third Party Beneficiaries* 247 (M. Chen-Wishart et al. eds., Oxford University Press 2017).
116. Nakata, *supra* n. 61, 88.
117. Shiomi, *supra* n. 113, 16.

by other means (as outlined in Part II above). Nor is there much discussion or practice around 'honour clauses' or 'gentlemen's agreements', where the parties reach an agreement but expressly state that they do not intend it to be legally binding.[118]

88. One commentator does give the example of a person taking a ride on a city bus as a situation where a contract intuitively does seem to be formed, yet it is hard to pinpoint agreement through offer and acceptance, especially if the person takes the ride while declaring that 'I have no intention to enter into a contract or pay the listed ticket price, because public transport should be free.' The person might still be contractually bound if there exist a set of socially recognised circumstances surrounding the transaction, despite the manifested lack of intention, as asserted by some proponents of 'fact-based contractual relationship theory' (*jijitsuteki keiyaku kankei riron*).[119] However, most commentators generally reject this theory as conflicting with the classical 'will theory' of contract.

89. Conversely, even if there is clear agreement, a contract may not be formed if the courts perceive it as not warranting mobilisation of the enforcement machinery of state law. The dividing line is delicate, especially as the Japanese Civil Code adopts the principle of consensualism (*dakuseishugi*) by allowing for a promise to be enforced as a contract even without a counter-promise or counter-performance (as explained further in Part I, Chapter 1, §1(III) below). In 1935, however, the Great Court of Cassation (*Taishin-in,* predecessor to the Supreme Court of Japan) remitted a case to the Osaka District Court where the latter had enforced a man's promise to make a gift to a female entertainer to secure her financial 'independence'.[120]

90. An intention to assume contractual obligations is considered more likely if, for example, a party uses its registered seal to formalise an agreement despite the general principle that contracts can be concluded without writing (as explained further in §2 of this chapter below, especially I.A).

III. Consideration

91. Japanese contract law contains no requirement of 'consideration' (bargained for exchange, or a promise given as a 'price' for another promise, or quid pro quo) to limit the scope of agreements deserving of legal protection as contracts, as in the common law tradition, or the requirement of *cause* in the French law tradition, which serves a similar purpose (at least in theory) of indicating the seriousness of the agreement. Rather, Japanese contract law follows the German law tradition,

118. Cf., e.g., Vogenauer, *supra* n. 107, 270.
119. Uchida, *supra* n. 109, 16.
120. 25 Apr. 1935, Shimbun 3835-5 [1], discussed by Uchida, *supra* n. 109, 15 (noting that the District Court then undertook a detailed fact inquiry and again found there was a valid and enforceable gift contract in the particular circumstances).

which permits 'a free inquiry whether the promise was intended to be legally binding or whether it fell outside the legal sphere as being a mere social courtesy or act of friendship'.[121]

92. By extension, for example, 'firm offers' (specifying a period for acceptance) have legal effect (as discussed in Part I, Chapter 1, §1(I) above). By contrast, in Anglo-Commonwealth law, the offeror would generally be able to revoke such an offer even within the specified period, unless the offeree provided something (legally) valuable in exchange, such as some amount of money as part of an 'option contract'.

A. Analogues?

93. To a limited extent, the Japanese Civil Code does provide parties with ways to demonstrate their seriousness in entering into agreements, thus enhancing contractual enforceability through the court system. For example, Article 557 states that: 'When the buyer delivers earnest money to the seller, the buyer may cancel the contract by forfeiting his or her earnest money or the seller may cancel the contract by reimbursing twice its amount, until either party commences performance of the contract.' Second, the category of 'real contracts' (*yobutsu keiyaku*, such as loans for consumption) also provides indicia of seriousness and enforceability by requiring delivery of the subject matter (such as the amount agreed to be loaned) before the contract is validly formed. However, in the 2017 Reform, the rules on real contracts have been significantly curtailed (*see* Part II, Chapters 2 (deposit) and 10 (loan for consumption and loan for use). Third, writing or other formal requirements can serve similar functions, although these are also comparatively limited in Japanese law (as outlined in §2 of this chapter below).

B. Gratuitous Promises

94. With no doctrine of consideration under Japanese law, promises can be enforced as 'gratuitous contracts' (*musho keiyaku*) involving no counter-promise or counter-performance. Unilateral contracts (*henmu keiyaku*), where only one party undertakes an obligation, are often also gratuitous contracts. For example, Article 549 provides that: 'Gifts shall become effective by the manifestation by one of the parties of his or her intention to give his or her property to the other party gratuitously, and the acceptance of the other party thereof.' However, non-gratuitous contracts (*yusho keiyaku*) are not necessarily always bilateral contracts (*somu keiyaku*). An example is an interest-bearing loan for consumption, which is a non-gratuitous but unilateral contract.[122] Because gratuitous promises may be perceived as ethical

121. *See* generally K. Zweigert and H. Koetz, *Introduction to Comparative Law*, esp 81 (2nd ed., Clarendon Press 1984); and S. Takenaka, 'La theorie de la cause vue du Japon ["Cause" Theory Seen from Japan]' in *Droit japonais, droit francais,* 137 (Beatrice Jazulot ed., Shulthess 2014).
122. *See* above Introduction to the Law of Contracts §3 (classifications of contracts).

or moral matters, and can be enforced through the state's legal enforcement mechanisms, there needs to be social consensus that they deserve recognition as contracts; often that is lacking, so the contractual effect of gratuitous promises needs to be approached carefully.[123]

C. Natural Obligations

95. This concept, derived originally from Roman law, has become accepted in Japanese civil law (*shizen saimu*).[124] An example is the Great Court of Cassation's judgment in 1935, outlined in Part I, Chapter 1, §1.II above, where the possibility was acknowledged that there could be a contractual obligation to make a gift that would not be enforceable by the promisee, but which would be deemed validly performed if and once the gift was made.

IV. Modifications of the Contract

96. Again, because there is no doctrine of consideration or the 'pre-existing rule' as in the common law tradition,[125] under Japanese law, modification of a contract is possible by one party simply agreeing to undertake a greater obligation, even if the other party does not promise or provide more in return.

97. Furthermore, Article 519 provides that: 'If an obligee manifests his or her intention to release an obligation to the obligor, such obligation shall be extinguished.' In addition, Articles 513–518 provide for novation (*kokai*) of contracts. (For release and novation, *see* Part I, Chapter 5, §1 below.)

§2. Formal and Evidential Requirements

98. In Japan, the principle of freedom of contract is often understood to mean 'freedom from form' or writing requirements, and this was expressly affirmed by a new Article 522(2) after the 2017 Reform. The Civil Code therefore lays down only a few such requirements or even incentives for parties to formalise their contracts in writing (as outlined in Part I, Chapter 1, §2.I.B below). However, other specific legislation may require contracting parties (especially suppliers in regulated industries) to formalise their contracts in various ways. Whether this has private law consequences depends on the express or (more often) implied legislative intention.[126] Further legislation may require notarisation of contracts (*see* below Part I, Chapter

123. Uchida, *supra* n. 109, 15.
124. Cf. also the provision for extra 'grey zone' interest, which could be retained by the lender if the consumer 'voluntarily' agreed to pay it, until the moneylending legislation was amended in 2006: *see* generally Pardieck, *supra* n. 26.
125. Zweigert and Koetz, *supra* n. 121, 74.
126. *See* above General Introduction §5 (public law).

1, §2.II.B) for them to be effective, such as fixed-term leases for interests in land or certain guarantee contracts. Even fifteen years ago one commentator remarked that in practice 'it is frequently quite difficult to prove formation of contracts without documentation', noting also a broader tendency towards using increasingly detailed written contracts in various types of transactions.[127]

99. Nonetheless, informal agreements have given rise to some well-known cases decided by Japanese courts. In 1957,[128] the Tokyo District Court enforced an offer made and accepted orally between very large Japanese corporations, for a major sale and purchase of imported soya beans. A leading early commentary in English made this case famous as an example of a supposed preference among Japanese for informality in contract negotiations.[129] In 1962,[130] the Kobe District Court also upheld the New Zealand exporter's claim that a contract had been formed by an exchange of telexes and letters. It rejected the Japanese importer's defence to the effect that the parties only intended to be legally bound by a formal 'confirmation note'. Shinichiro Michida approves the 1957 judgment for upholding a bargain that the parties probably intended as binding[131] and would probably have done the same for the 1962 judgment.

100. Michida and Veronica Taylor have stressed, however, that Japanese courts have been reluctant to find agreements for the sale of land to be legally binding until registration of title and formalisation of documentation.[132] Michida and the anonymous author of the Headnote to a 1975 judgment of the Tokyo High Court further suggest that this follows from a 'custom' (*kanshu*) as to such formalisation.[133] Pursuant to Article 92 of the Civil Code, that would create a rebuttable presumption (subject to proof of the parties' contrary intention) against the validity of such contracts until all the documentation has been finalised. Yet, a closer analysis shows that this decision does not go that far.[134] Nor do any relevant judgments over at least the

127. Dogauchi 2004, *supra* n. 112, Part 1.3.1.1 and *see* generally above General Introduction §9 (style of drafting).
128. Tokyo District Court, 31 Jul. 1957, Kaminshu 8-1366.
129. T. Kawashima, *supra* n. 45. *See also* R. M. March, *The Japanese Negotiator: Subtlety and Strategy Beyond Western Logic*, 111 (Kodansha 1988); H. Yamada, *Different Games, Different Rules: Why Americans and Japanese Misunderstand Each Other*, 67 (Oxford University Press 1997). The latter cites S. Michida, *Keiyaku Shakai – Amerika to Nihon no Chigai o Miru [Contract Societies: Looking at Differences between America and Japan]* (Yuhikaku 1987), ironically since this book argues that informality in contracting is *not* common at least in sales for real property.
130. Kobe District Court, 10 Dec. 1962, Hanji 320. A partial translation of the judgment can be found in *Comparative Law: Law and the Legal Process in Japan*, 444 (3d ed, K. L. Port et al. eds., Carolina Academic Press 2015).
131. Michida, *supra* n. 58, 199, 200, 207 (1992).
132. *Ibid.*, 213; Taylor, *supra* n. 30, 352, 359. On registration, necessary to give effect against third parties (although not for validity of the contract between the parties), *see* above Introduction to the Law of Contracts, §6.
133. Tokyo High Court, 30 Jun. 1975, Hanji 790-63.
134. L. Nottage, 'Form, Substance and Neo-Proceduralism in Comparative Contract Law: The Law in Books and the Law in Action in England, New Zealand, Japan and the U.S.', Ch. 2 (PhD Thesis, Victoria University of Wellington, 2001), available from http://hdl.handle.net/10063/778 (accessed 21 Jun. 2018).

last eighty years. 'Practices' (*kanko*) of formalising land sales, for instance, instead constitute one factor among many in determining the intentions of the parties in all the particular circumstance of each case. The same approach is apparent in case law regarding informal leases.[135] This is even more apparent for cases in other types of contracts, including even a ship sale agreed 'subject to details'.[136]

I. Formal Requirements

A. *Contracts under Seal?*

101. Japanese contract law has no analogue to the concept of contracts under seal in the common law tradition, where it is important partly because of the doctrine of consideration impacting on contract formation.[137] Other functions of contracts rendered under seal, namely to facilitate proving their contents, are partly served in Japan by notarisation (Part I, Chapter 1, §2.II.B below).

102. Nonetheless, Japan has a long history of using seals in lieu of signatures to conduct both private transactions and business with the government. Article 228 of the Code of Civil Procedure (Act No. 109 of 1996) recognises both signatures and the use of a seal as valid forms of evidencing the party's intention: 'A private document, if it is signed or sealed by the principal or his or her agent, shall be presumed to be authentically created.' However, use of a seal in lieu of or in conjunction with a signature remains common in practice. '*Hanko*', the common term used for seals, are used for everything from registering receipt of a package, to registering a marriage, to executing a contract.[138] The seals, more formally referred to as *inkan*, come in a variety of shapes and sizes and their usage varies. Both individuals and companies will often have and use at least three different seals: (1) a registered seal (*jitsuin*) for 'important' documents and transactions; (2) a common seal (*mitomein* or *sanmonban*) for 'regular' transactions; and (3) a bank seal (*ginkoin*) for bank transactions.

103. Individuals and companies typically purchase a seal for registration that has an individual's surname or the name of the company hand-carved onto it. Individuals register their personal seals with the local government office; legal entities register theirs with the local Ministry of Justice office. Local ordinances prescribe the

135. *See*, e.g., Tokyo High Court, 23 Apr. 1981, Hanta 452-106.
136. *See* Tokyo District Court, 30 May 1986 Hanji 1234-100.
137. Cf. above Part I, Ch. 1 §1.3. Contracts formalised under seal, in the common law, do not need to satisfy the further requirements of the doctrine of consideration.
138. N. Daimon, *Keiyakusho, Inkan, Ryoshusho, Tegata, Kogitte no Horitsu Chishiki* [Legal Understandings of Contracts, Seals, Receipts, Bills and Notes] 36 (Sanshusha 2008).

size of the seal and registration process for individuals; Ministry of Justice regulations do the same for company seals.[139] Following registration, the users will receive a Seal Registration *(inkan torokusho)* document and, thereafter, may request the local government office to issue a Proof of Seal Registration (*inkan toroku shomeisho*) confirming registration of the seal, the owner's name, address and an imprint of the seal.[140]

104. Use of a registered seal, or its Proof of Seal Registration, is required by law for some transactions, e.g., to execute a notarised will or to register real property.[141] More commonly, use of a registered seal is required in practice when executing 'significant' contracts. Some parties will demand or expect use of a registered seal. Some parties, and some government filings, will require a party to attach to the contract, or filing, a Proof of Seal Registration issued within the past three or six months. The intent in each case is to confirm the intent of the parties by requiring use of government-registered seals and, at the same time, minimise the risk of fraud.

105. Any seal that is not registered is classified as a common seal, or *mitomein*. Common seals will also show the name of the individual or company, but they are often mass-produced seals and, hence, more easily duplicated. Apart from those few instances where required by law, the choice of whether to use a common seal or a registered seal in a transaction is left to the discretion or demands of the parties. Article 228 of the Code of Civil Procedure does not afford greater evidentiary weight to the use of a registered seal, but practice does: people believe that a registered seal carries greater weight. Its use suggests that the transaction is a more serious undertaking and the parties' intent to be bound is confirmed and evidenced by their use of a registered seal.

106. The bank seal (*ginkoin* or *todokedein*) is a seal that has been registered with the bank at which the individual or company does business. Assuming the account has not been opened with a signature, banks will require a bank-registered seal to change address, execute promissory notes, tender checks and conduct other business with the bank. For business entities, the bank seal is often smaller in size than its registered seal in order to distinguish between the two.[142]

---

139. *See*, e.g., Kobe City Seal Ordinance No. 52 of 1972, Art. 4, http://www.city.kobe.lg.jp/information/data/regulations/rule/reiki/reiki_honbun/k302RG00000197.html (accessed 21 Jun. 2018); Commercial Business Registration Rules], Ministry of Justice Ordinance No. 23 of 1964, http://law.e-gov.go.jp/htmldata/S39/S39F03201000023.html (accessed 21 Jun. 2018).
140. *See*, e.g., Shinagawa-shi, *Inkan Touroku Shomeisho no Seikyu no Hoho [Ways to Seek Proof of Registered Seals]*, http://www.city.shinagawa.tokyo.jp/hp/page000001500/hpg000001424.htm (last visited 24 Jul. 2013).
141. *See*, e.g., Nihon Koshonin Rengokai [Japan National Notaries Association], *Igon*, http://www.koshonin.gr.jp/index2.html (last visited 24 Jul. 2013); Property Registration Rules, Ministry of Justice Ordinance No. 18 of 2005.
142. Daimon, *supra* n. 138, 48.

107. A business entity will register and use as its official seal the seal of its representative director. Also called a *maruin* because of its round shape, the representative director's seal commonly consists of two concentric circles with the name of the company identified on the outer ring of the seal and the inner circle identifying it as the seal of the representative director. Larger companies will utilise additional seals: seals for corporate officers (*yakushokuin*), department heads (*buchoin*) and branch managers (*shitenchoin*) and the like for those with a grant of authority to bind the company.[143]

108. The signature block of a contract in Japan may take different forms. It may include only signature lines (*jisho*). It may include a signature line and space for affixing a personal or company seal (*shomeiouin*). Or it may consist of the printed names of the parties, with space for affixing a personal or company seal (*kimeiouin*). Each is legally valid, though some practitioners suggest that use of a printed name plus seal is more common because, in the event of a dispute, a party's use of a seal is, in fact, accorded greater evidentiary weight.[144] Its use is deemed stronger proof of the party's intent to be bound.

109. Apart from the use of the seal on the signature block of the contract, the parties' seals are often used in preparing the contract for execution. Contracts may be printed on looseleaf paper and stapled together or bound. If the contract is bound, the individual pages are fixed with an adhesive along the left-hand margin, and the parties' seals are then affixed to the intersection between each set of pages in the booklet (*keiyakuin*). The intent is to prevent, after execution, substitution of any pages to the original contract. Similarly, where the contract is executed with multiple originals, the original copies are laid on top of each other so that a small portion of the top, front page of each contract is showing, and the parties' respective seals are affixed to the intersection so that a portion of each seal is visible on each copy of the contract (*wariin*). If contested, the originals can then be confirmed by lining up the seal imprints. Finally, seals are also used to denote acceptance of handwritten changes made to the printed contract (*teiseiin*). If language in a contract is crossed-out or modified, the parties will affix their seals to that portion of the contract as opposed to initialling any of the changes.[145]

B. 'Solemn' Contracts

110. Since 2004 amendments, the Civil Code requires a contract of guarantee to be in writing to be effective. If concluded by recording the contents electronically, it is deemed to have been in writing (Article 446(2)–(3)). (*See* Part II, Chapter 8.)

111. Otherwise, even a gift contract is effective without any writing or formal requirement. However, an incentive to formalise gift contracts follows from Article

143. *Ibid.* 48.
144. *Ibid.* 40.
145. *Ibid.* 55.

550: 'Gifts not in writing may be revoked by either party; provided, however, that this shall not apply to any portion of the gift for which performance has been completed.' A similar rule was added to loan for use and gratuitous deposits. (*See* Part II, Chapter 2 §2 and Chapter 10 §2.)

II. Evidential Requirement: Proof

112. Despite the paucity of writing requirements in the Japanese Civil Code, commentators and case law have recognised their various functions, including providing better evidence of the parties' intentions.[146] Courts have therefore often drawn an inference, in the particular circumstances, that parties do not intend to be contractually bound by their land sale agreements unless and until all documentation has been finalised (as mentioned above).[147]

A. *The Parol Evidence Rule*

113. Japanese law does not have a direct equivalent to this rule in Anglo-American common law, whereby if the parties have indicated their intention to embody their agreement in writing (usually through an 'entire agreement' clause), no extrinsic evidence can be adduced in court to vary or contradict the written stipulations.[148] However, entire agreement clauses are sometimes now found in Japanese contracts (even for domestic transactions), and some lower court case law has given strict effect to such a clause.[149]

B. *Function of Notaries Etc.*

114. Under Japanese law, notarising a contract gives it greater evidentiary weight, and it may allow for summary enforcement of a debt.[150] Notaries in Japan

146. *See*, e.g., Nakata, *supra* n. 61, 138 (also noting other functions such as *channelling* parties' behaviour to achieve goals, and causing them to take more *precautions* before entering into major transactions).
147. Michida, *supra* n. 58; Nottage, *supra* n. 134.
148. *See* generally Zweigert and Kotz, *supra* n. 121, 91. On other important aspects of the parol evidence rule, namely principles of interpretation precluding reference to pre-contractual negotiations or subsequent conduct of the parties to determine the meaning of contracts, *see* below Part I, Ch. 3 §2 (contract interpretation).
149. Tokyo District Court, 13 Dec. 1996, Hanta 938-160; Tokyo District Court, 25 Dec. 2002, Hanji 1964-106. The High Court in New Zealand also faced such a clause in an international joint venture contract dispute, expressly governed by Japanese law, and appears to have given it some effect (albeit as part of a complex assessment of the price to be paid by one party for a minority shareholding): *Multiply Ltd v Old Mill Farm Ltd & Ors; Millbrook Country Club Ltd v Multiply Ltd & Anor* (1995) 7 NZ Company Law Cases 260, 746.
150. M. K. Young and C. Hamilton, 'The Legal Profession', in *Japan Business Law Guide*, (M. Matsushita ed., CCH Australia Ltd 1988), Ch. 7, para. 7–900. Basic information in English regarding

are public servants appointed by the Ministry of Justice. They are limited in number (506 as of 2009) and they are typically retired judges, prosecutors or, sometimes, retired attorneys.[151]

115. For a notary to notarise a contract, all parties to the contract, or their agents, must appear in person before the notary, provide proof of person, with their registered seal and Proof of Seal Registration, and request that the document be notarised. The document is authenticated when notarised, and the notarised date (officially attested date) is then recognised conclusively as the date of the execution for the purposes of establishing when rights and obligations incidental to the execution of the contract arise.

116. Following amendments in 2000 to the Notary Act, 'e-Notarisation' of certain documents is possible. Parties may authenticate electronic documents including contracts and articles of incorporation by completing the documents, along with the required electronic signatures and submitting an online request to the Japan National Notaries Association's e-Notarisation Centre. However, completion of the process still requires the party or her agent to appear before a local notary to attest to the document. The local notary then attaches a digital certificate to it, saves it to a CD or other storage medium and provides that to the requesting party.[152]

117. Where the contract requires the payment of money, e.g., a promissory note or a settlement and release, and the obligor agrees to compulsory execution, the notary will prepare an Acceptance of Execution (*shikko judaku bunsho* or *shikko nindakuyakkan*). The document is then, in the event of breach, treated similarly to a court judgment. It creates an established debt (*saimu meigi*) and allows the creditor to place a lien on the debtor's bank account or otherwise seek compulsory payment of the debt without first obtaining a judgment from the court.

118. Certain documents must be notarised in order to be legally enforceable. They include articles of incorporation, contracts for the lease of land for more than 50 years, the lease of a commercial building for more than 30 years but less than fifty 50 years without the right of renewal and contracts voluntarily establishing a legal guardianship.[153]

119. Consulting a notary is generally free, but the notarisation is not. Fees are fixed by law and vary depending on the document to be notarised.[154] The fees for

---

notarising contracts can also be found at the Japan National Notaries Association, 'How to Make Good Use of Japan's Notaries', http://www.koshonin.gr.jp/pdf/en.pdf (accessed 21 Jun. 2018).

151. T. Sugawara, *Nihon no Koushounin Seido* [The Notary System in Japan] (1 Sep. 2010), http://www.e-hoki.com/column/jpn/112.html (accessed 21 Jun. 2018).

152. N. Koushounin Rengoukai, *Denshi Koushounin Seido no Go-Annai* [Introduction to the e-Notary System], http://www.koshonin.gr.jp/index2.html (accessed 21 Jun. 2018).

153. *See,* e.g., Company Act (Act No. 86 of 2005), Art. 30(1); Land and Building Leases Art (Act No. 90 of 1991), Arts 22 & 23; Voluntary Legal Guardianship Act (Act No. 150 of 1999), Art. 3.

154. Fees range from JPY 5,000 for a contract valued at JPY 1 million or less; to JPY 43,000 for contracts ranging from JPY 50 million to JPY 100 million; with separate fees schedules for contracts

notarising a contract are generally assessed based on the value of the contract. Once notarised, the notary maintains the original copy of the document for twenty years (Article 27 Ordinance for Enforcement of the Notary Act (Ordinance of the Attorney-General's Office No. 9 of 1949)).

III. Burden of Proof

A. *'Obligation of Means' Versus 'Obligation of Result'*

120. This conceptual distinction is not expressly stated in the Civil Code, but is discussed in some Japanese commentaries. Whether an obligation is one of means or one of result must be determined in light of the aim of the contract. However, in general, for example, in services contracts, the obligation of a contractor undertaking a contract for work (*ukeoi keiyaku*) to complete the work (under Article 632) is considered an 'obligation of result' (*kekka saimu*) or an obligation based on the principle of compensation liability (*hosho sekinin*), because it incorporates a guarantee to achieve the interests assumed by the contract. As such, it is irrelevant whether or not the contractor has taken due care in assessing completion of the work, and the burden of proof is consequently lessened for the other party.[155] This differs from medical contracts in which a physician agrees to treat a patient.

§3. Liability During Negotiations

121. Japanese civil law has developed quite extensive scope for pre-contractual liability. Case law applying the Civil Code has recently become particularly extensive regarding information duties. A related line of case law emerged from the 1970s to cover situations where a party to negotiations breaks off negotiations (Part II below).[156] Although extensively discussed during the Civil Code Reform discussions over 2006-2014, sufficient consensus could not be reached to include recommendations in the Final Report or provisions in the Amendment Bill in 2015, which was passed in 2017.[157]

---

of greater value. Fixed fees are established for other types of documents, e.g., JPY 11,000 for a contract establishing a legal guardian, and for incidental charges such as providing notarised copies. Nihon Koushounin Rengoukai, *Tesuuryou* [Fees], http://www.koshonin.gr.jp/index2.html (accessed 21 Jun. 2018).

155. Shiomi, *supra* n. 105, 243. For these services contracts, requiring proof of fault to establish liability, *see* below Part II, Ch. 1.

156. *See also* generally Kawakami, *supra* n. 66; and C.J. Milhaupt, 'A Relational Theory of Japanese Corporate Governance: Contract, Culture, and the Rule of Law', 37 *Harvard Int'l L. J.* 41 (1996) (noting that prior dealings with bank customers can heighten the chance of courts imposing 'lender liability' if agreements under negotiation are not renewed or forthcoming).

157. Earlier recommendations and discussions may however inform the future development of case law regarding pre-contractual liability: *see* generally K. Yamashiro, 'Keiyaku Kosho Dankai no Hoteki Sekinin [Legal Liability at the Stage of Negotiating Contracts]' in *Saikenho Kaisei no Ronten to Kore Kara no Kento Kadai [Issues in the Obligations Law Reform and Topics For Future Consideration]*, 139 (N. Segawa ed., 147 *NBL Besstatsu*, Shoji Homu 2014).

122. Parties also sometimes expressly agree to 'lock-out' clauses or assume other obligations during negotiations. This growing practice, at least in some sectors, has resulted recently in some high-profile contract law litigation. In 2004, the UFJ Holdings and Sumitomo Trust & Banking concluded a 'basic agreement' for the possible sale of the former's trust banking business to Sumitomo, which provided that neither party would provide information or negotiate with a third party regarding its subject matter, and that the parties would negotiate in good faith if a matter arose not covered in the agreement or its provisions were ambiguous. UFJ announced that it was terminating this agreement to conclude a full merger with another bank. Sumitomo filed successfully in the Tokyo District for an injunction to prevent UFJ from negotiating further with the other bank. The Tokyo High Court reversed, finding that trust had broken down between the parties so that Sumitomo's right fell away. The Supreme Court also ruled in favour of UFJ, holding that the right subsisted but could not be enforced by the injunction because Sumitomo would not be irreparably harmed if it were not granted.[158] Sumitomo then sued UFJ for JPY 100 billion in the Tokyo District Court. On 13 February 2006 it declined to award those expectation damages, holding that although there was breach of the agreed duty to negotiate (at least until a final agreement could no longer reasonably expected), the basic agreement did not oblige the parties necessarily to conclude a final agreement, and no such duty arose directly or by analogy through Article 130 (where a party prevents fulfilment of conditions).[159] Sumitomo appealed, seeking instead JPY 10 billion based on reliance damages, but accepted on 21 November 2006 a JPY 2.5 settlement from the successor company to UFJ (which by then had merged with the other bank).[160]

I. Pre-contractual Liability

123. Without expressly assumed obligations, Japanese civil law has considered various principles for attributing liability for breach of duties to provide information (*joho teikyo gimu*) or explanations (*setsumei gimu*) arising during negotiations prior to concluding a contract, typically in situations of information asymmetries between the parties (such as in business-to-consumer transactions).[161] Such duties can involve either positive duties to provide important information (e.g., in specified documentary form), or prohibitions on providing wrong or misleading information (e.g., prohibiting a determinative opinion, guarantee of a benefit or concealment of important information). Often these are imposed by specific legislation, with

158. Supreme Court, 30 Aug. 2004, Minshu 58-6-1763.
159. Tokyo District Court, 3 Feb. 2006, Hanji 1928-3.
160. *See* Westhoff, *supra* n. 66 including full citations and translated excerpts from the Supreme Court judgment; and generally Takahashi, *supra* n. 66, 166, contrasting *Walford v. Miles* [1992] 2 A.C. 128 (H.L.).
161. For further details, *see* M. Dernauer, 'Civil Law – Tort Law/Contract Law – Liability for a Breach of Pre-contractual, Contractual and Non-contractual Information Duties – Liability of Experts – Claims for Damages', in *Business Law in Japan: Cases and Comments,* 70 (M. Baelz, M. Dernauer et al. eds, Kluwer 2012). *See also* above General Introduction §7 (consumer law).

administrative or criminal sanctions for breach; whether and how contract law consequences follow depends on express or (more often) the implied intention of the legislator.[162]

124. Under the Civil Code, courts rarely upheld liability for an induced mistake in motive for entering in the contract (Article 95), fraudulent misrepresentation (where fraudulent intent must be proven: Article 96) or a broader theory of lack of intent or defective agreement (*goi no kashi*, advocated by some commentators). Japanese courts have never referred directly in this context to the doctrine of *culpa in contrahendo*, although it was introduced from Germany by Japanese academic commentators (as the theory of 'negligence in concluding contracts', *keiyaku teiketsu-jo no kashitsu*) from the 1920s. There it became widely invoked, based on the general principle of good faith, and *culpa in contrahendo* has been codified in Articles 280(1), 311(2) and 241(2) of the German Civil Code since amendments in effect from 2002. Instead, Japanese courts have generally developed pre-contractual liability awarding damages (rather than actual rescission of the contract) often with reference also to the principle of good faith in Article 1(2). In most judgments, the Japanese courts list multiple breaches of both pre-contractual and post-contractual duties, and decide on an overall view whether liability should be imposed.[163] It was not clear until recently whether such damages' claim is a contractual remedy for non-performance under Article 415 or under the general negligence provision in Article 709 (derived from French rather than German law). The Supreme Court clarified this point by holding in 2011 that this is a tort law claim as there can be no non-performance of a contract when the contract is not formed.[164]

125. Case law mainly arises in four contracting situations: real estate transactions, franchises, investment products and medical services.[165] In real estate sales involving professional sellers, the seller must anyway inform the buyer about important matters pursuant to Article 35 of the Building Lots and Buildings Transaction Business Act (Act No. 176 of 1952), as a matter of administrative law. But in 1977, the Tokyo High Court established a similar civil law duty, as an ancillary obligation (*fuzui gimu*) to the sales contract, to investigate and explain the situation, where a seller of an apartment knew or ought easily to have known that a building might be built on a neighbouring property.[166] The Supreme Court upheld a claim for pain and suffering (*isharyo*) based on the principle of good faith, where the public entity seller had not provided explanations sufficient for the buyer to decide on

162. *See* above General Introduction §5 (public law). Arguing that Japanese law suffers consequently from an 'information overload', *see* F. Christian, 'From Information Overflow to Incapacitation: Comparing German and Japanese Consumer Protection', 27 *J. Japanese L.* 170–181 (2009).
163. Dernauer 2012, *supra* n. 161; *see* above Introduction to the Law of Contract §4 (torts). Shiomi, *supra* n. 105, at 4–7 considers pre-contractual liability through a tort law lens, but acknowledges that the prevailing academic view in Japan (influenced by German law on this point) has tended to see it through a contract-based approach.
164. Supreme Court, 22 Apr. 2011, Minshu 65-3-1405.
165. Uchida, *supra* n. 109, 26–29.
166. Tokyo High Court, 31 Mar. 1977 (albeit the duty was held not to be breached, on the facts).

appropriateness of a subdivision price.[167] The Court also upheld liability of the owner/seller of an apartment, as well as its wholly owned subsidiary company engaged for the sales transaction, where the buyer was not informed about a fire door and that a switch that operated it automatically (but was difficult to locate) was not on.[168] The Court awarded damages in tort against the agent for failing to inform the buyer about the switch's whereabouts and how to operate the fire door mechanism, marking a rare reported case of liability found for one breach of a pre-contractual information duty. The Supreme Court also confirmed that the owner was liable for breach of an ancillary obligation derived from the sales contract; the lower courts had established liability for a latent defect (former Articles 566 and 570) and non-performance (Article 415).[169]

126. More recently, judgments upholding pre-contractual liability for breaches of information duties are also found with respect to franchisors,[170] and especially suppliers of investment products. In 1996, for the first time, the Supreme Court found an insurance company liable in tort for non-disclosure when soliciting a contract for variable insurance.[171] It also found a financial institution seeking to use real estate more flexibly had violated a good faith duty to explain about relevant building standards legislation.[172] The Supreme Court has also upheld liability on various bases where investment brokers have solicited customers for commodity transactions without adequately explaining that conflict of interests could arise.[173] The Supreme Court has even recognised tort liability on securities companies for soliciting transactions contrary to the 'suitability principle', although such a 'know-your-customer' rule is also a regulatory requirement under Article 40 of the Financial Instruments and Exchange Act (Act No. 25 of 1948).[174]

127. Information duties can also arise in the context of medical service contracts, including not only duties of explanation (*setsumei gimu*) concerning the

---

167. Supreme Court, 18 Nov. 1989, Minshu 58-8-2225.
168. Supreme Court, 16 Sep. 2005, Hanji 1912-8. A fire caused by the buyer subsequently killed him and spread throughout the building.
169. *See* below Part I, Ch. 6 (remedies). Dernauer 2012, *supra* n. 161, 69 remarks that the Supreme Court may have envisaged breach of the seller's ancillary obligation to constitute liability for non-performance (Art. 415), but it could also have been liability for tort (Arts 707 and 715): Japanese courts 'often do not precisely distinguish between contractual information duties and information duties based on the law of torts if the information duty in question relates to a situation after the contract has been concluded … The basis for kinds of information duties is … [Art. 1(2)]'.
170. *See*, e.g., Sapporo High Court, 31 Jan. 2006, Hanta 1235-217; and generally Taylor, *supra* n. 94; t'Hooft, *supra* n. 89.
171. Supreme Court, 28 Oct. 1996, Kinho 1469.
172. Supreme Court, 12 Jun. 2006, Hanji 1941.
173. Supreme Court, 16 Jul. 2009, Minshu 63-6-1280 (based on contractual non-performance); Supreme Court, 18 Dec. 2006, Hanta 1318-90 (accepting the appellant's argument that the claim should be based on tort, and remanding the case to the trial court).
174. Supreme Court, 14 Jul. 2005, Minshu 59-6-1323. On this legislation (previously the Securities and Exchange Law), *see* generally C. Wisenbaker, 'Japan's Financial Instruments and Exchange Law: Hercules or Hydra?', 38 *Ga. J. Int'l & Comp. L.* 473 (2010).

ongoing treatment but also to solicit informed consent for risky procedures.[175] One commentator argues that doctors should also be subject to a somewhat broader 'duty to advise' (*jogen gimu*).[176]

II. Breakdown of Negotiations

128. If negotiations do not result in a contract, and there are no prior agreements that could give rise to injunction or damages proceedings as in the *Sumitomo v. UFJ* litigation outlined at Part 1, Chapter 1, §3 above, case law and commentators have come to recognise that a party should be liable to compensate for the actual damages incurred by another in reliance on the strong inducement of the former that a contract would be concluded, yet this trust is betrayed.[177] This principle emerged originally in various lower courts. For example, where one party gave another the impression that it was the preferred contractor to produce a film and failed to inform the other that the contract was going to be decided through a tender process, resulting in the other filming in vain, the Tokyo District Court awarded damages for the costs incurred.[178] The Tokyo High Court also upheld a claim against a general trading company (Mitsui & Co) when it did not go through with a joint venture agreement, involving purchasing half the shares of a Brunei company that held shares in Indonesian companies with logging concession rights.[179]

129. The Supreme Court recognised the principle in a case where a developer relied on a dentist's expressed intention to purchase premises in the building, by modifying its design to make it suitable for dental practice. The dentist did not object to the developer's proposal to include the extra cost in the price offered for the premises and continued to negotiate, but ultimately did not go through with the

175. *See* generally also Y. Tejima, 'Recent Developments in Informed Consent Law in Japan', 36 *Kobe U. L. Rev.* 45 (2002); 37 *Kobe U. L. Rev.* 45 (2003); Y. Tejima, 'Recent Developments Concerning a Doctor's Legal Duty of Explanation after Medical Treatment in Japan', 40 *Kobe U. L. Rev.* 87 (2006).

176. Uchida, *supra* n. 109, 29–30. He also notes that in contexts like medical services, involving rights to personhood (*jinkakuken*), violations should allow for damages for pain and suffering (*isharyo*), whereas otherwise only pecuniary losses should be compensated. In a case arising from the Kobe Earthquake of 1995, the Supreme Court held (9 Dec. 2003, Minshu 57-11-1887) that an insured who had not taken out earthquake insurance cover due to non-disclosure and lack of explanation could not claim a solatium. (The insured probably would not have taken out cover even if the information had been properly given, as the likelihood beforehand of an earthquake in Kobe had been considered low, limiting scope to claim pecuniary damages).

177. Uchida, *supra* n. 109, 22.

178. Tokyo District Court, 29 May 1978, Hanji 925.

179. Tokyo High Court, 17 Mar. 1987, Hanji 1232-110 (partially translated in *Law and Investment in Japan* (2nd ed., Y. Yanagida et al. eds., Harvard University Press 2000) 255-261). The parties had entered into a preliminary agreement specifying the share sale price, the closing date and timing for entering into the joint venture agreement, which was sent from Mitsui the following month, whereupon the counterparty leased office space for the joint venture in Singapore. He was arrested seven months later by the Malaysian government so negotiations were suspended for a year until he was released, whereupon Mitsui resumed negotiations for several months.

purchase, so the developer was awarded the costs of the modification.[180] The Supreme Court also upheld a claim against a party ordering construction works by a subcontractor (not in a direct contractual relationship), who had been strongly led to believe by the former that it would be awarded a contract for a specific aspect of the construction.[181]

130. Case law and commentaries generally only acknowledge reliance damages for breaking off negotiations.[182] They can include items such as actual expenses incurred while negotiating and preparing for the contract, interest on loans from third parties in preparing for the contract, but also the lost chance of concluding another favourable contract because the defendant gave the impression that it would conclude the contract in question. Conversely, awarding expectation damages (putting the plaintiff in the position it would have been in if the contract had been duly concluded) seems contradictory since no contract was ever concluded. Developing this line of reasoning, it is generally thought that reliance damages awarded for breaking off negotiations should not exceed such expectation damages.[183]

---

180. Supreme Court, 18 Sep. 1984, Hanji 1137. *See also* Supreme Court, 27 Feb. 2007, upholding the claim of a game developer against a defendant who generated a strong expectation that it would ensure the game was eventually sold to a US firm.
181. Supreme Court, 27 Feb. 2007, Hanji 1964.
182. On classification of damages, *see* generally below Part I, Ch. 3 §7.
183. Shiomi, *supra* n. 105, 7.

Chapter 2. Conditions for Substantive Validity

§1. Capacity of Parties

131. Article 3-2 of the Civil Code provides that a contract or other juristic act such as a will is void if a party to it is proved not to have had sufficient intelligence or mental capacity to understand his or her legal rights and duties of the juristic act when he or she performed it.

132. As summarised in the following Parts I to IV, the Civil Code also lists four types of person whose contract or other juristic act can be rescinded solely because of his or her so qualified status, if he or she wants to invalidate it, without requiring any further specific proof of his or her incapacity at the time of each juristic act.

I. Minors

133. Under the Civil Code, the age of majority is currently twenty. However, it will be eighteen after 1 April 2022 (Article 4), as a result of an amendment to the Civil Code that was promulgated on 20 June 2018 (Act No. 59 of 2018). This amendment corresponds to the change of the voting age from 20 to 18, which took place in 2016.

134. To make a contract or other juristic act, a minor needs the approval of a parent or other legal representative. If a minor makes his or her juristic act without such approval, the parent or other legal representatives as well as the minor may rescind the juristic act because of him or her being a minor. Because minors are likely to be exploited for their immaturity in the free market, the Civil Code protects their interests by allowing parents or other legal representatives to rescind their juristic acts even to the detriment of the other party.

135. The following four cases are exceptions for when a minor can perform juristic acts without the approval of his or her legal representative. There is no need for him or her to be protected in these cases. Rather, there is a need to ensure stable transactions so that his or her daily life can run more smoothly.

136. First, he or she does not need the approval of his or her representatives in order to acquire the rights only and get his or her duties simply exempted (the proviso of Article 5(1)). Second, a minor does not need the approval of his or her individual dispositions of certain property for which he or she has already obtained the comprehensive approval of a legal representative, for example in the case of an allowance being provided (Article 5(3)). Third, a minor is regarded as a person of full age within the scope of business when his or her legal representative gives his or her approval for running it (Article 6). Fourth, a minor is also regarded as a person of full age when he or she gets married.

II. Adult Wards under Guardianship

137. If a person constantly lacks the capacity to discern right and wrong due to his or her mental disability, a family court may qualify him or her as an adult ward upon his or her request, or on the request of his or her certain relatives, including his or her spouse, or a public prosecutor, and so on, and then may appoint a guardian for him or her. An adult ward or his or her guardian may rescind his or her contract or any other juristic act, except for a juristic act related to the purchase of daily housing items (Articles 7 to 9). A rescission can be made even when an adult ward performs his or her juristic act with the approval of his or her guardian because an adult ward is completely incompetent in any case.

III. Persons under Curatorship

138. An adult ward, who does not have any capacity at law, is protected, but sometimes a person who has limited capacity also needs help. If a person has extremely insufficient capacity to discern right and wrong due to his or her mental disability, a family court may, similarly, upon the request of that person and others, declare him or her to be under curatorship. The Civil Code allows such a person or his or her curator to rescind the following juristic acts if he or she performs it without the approval of his or her curator: (a) receiving or using any principal, (b) making a contract of loan or becoming a guarantor, (c) performing any juristic act to obtain or relinquish a right regarding real estate or other valuable property, (d) taking any procedural action, (e) making a gift or, any settlement, agreeing to arbitrate, (e) accepting or renouncing any succession, (f) refusing an offer of a gift, renouncing any bequest, accepting an offer of a gift with a burden or any bequest with a burden, (g) making any new construction, renovation, expansion or major repair or (h) making a lease contract with a term exceeding three years in the case of a lease of a house or a certain period in the case of a lease of others specified in Article 602, unless any of those juristic acts listed here relate to the purchase of daily housing items (Articles 11 to 13).

IV. Persons under Assistance

139. A family court may designate a curator for a person with an extremely insufficient capacity to discern right and wrong, while the court may appoint an assistant for a person who has such an insufficient capacity due to mental disability (Articles 15 and 16). For assistance to be given, the consent of the person subject to it is required (Article 15(2)).

140. A person receiving assistance or his or her assistant can rescind any particular juristic act or acts listed under (a) to (h) above for a person under curatorship for whom a court has ruled needs the approval of his or her assistant, if he or she makes it without approval.

141. In cases under (I) to (IV), rescission of a juristic act by a person with limited capacity, such as a minor or a person under guardianship, curatorship or assistance, is allowed, either within five years of the time when the juristic act was able to be ratified or within twenty years of the time when the juristic act was made, whichever comes earlierArticle 126). Until then, the other party can deprive such a person with limited capacity of the right of rescission if he or she does not receive a reply, within a certain period he or she fixes of one month or more after asking a person with limited capacity, or a legal representative, curator or assistant for such a person, to express whether to ratify the juristic act (Article 20).

142. Because a contract or other juristic act is deemed to be void from the beginning when it is rescinded (Article 121), the result should be that a party needs to make restitution for all of what he or she has received in order to restore the other party to the original position as if it had not existed. However, the Civil Code requires a minor or a person under guardianship, curatorship or assistance only to make this restitution to the extent of his or her actual enrichment from his or her contract or other juristic act (the proviso of Article 121).Therefore, if a seller rescinded a contract to sell his or her car for reason of being a minor, he or she would not need to return to the buyer any more than the current remaining amount of the price which he or she received from the buyer, while he or she would require the buyer to return the car or if the car had been completely destroyed for some reason, its whole value in money.

143. The Civil Code denies a minor or a person under guardianship, curatorship or assistance the right to rescind a contract or other juristic act for his or her lack of or limited capacity if he or she uses a trick to make the other party believe that he or she is a person with full capacity contrary to the truth, because in such a case he or she would not deserve this limited scope of restitution to current actual enrichment specifically provided in a favourable way to him or her as an effect of the rescission (Article 21).

§2. Defects of Consent

144. For a contract or other juristic act to be validly formed, a party must express his or her consent to it. Under this consent theory, an expressed consent must agree with the intention of a party to have such a legal effect. But sometimes it does not match. Moreover, sometimes it might appear to agree, but an expressed consent may not, in fact, be the true intention of that party for some reason. In a case where consent is lacking or defective, as shown in the following Parts I to IV, the effect of that juristic act is so questionable that it needs careful consideration.

I. Concealment of True Intention

145. If an expressed consent of a party to a contract or other juristic act does not reflect the true intention of that party, such consent must properly be void, so that under consent theory, the juristic act would be invalid. But the Civil Code provides that such consent shall be considered to be valid if a party who expresses it knows that it is not his or her true intention (Article 93(1)). It aims to protect the other party who believes that the consent reflects the true intention of the expressing party, rather than the expressing party who himself or herself knowingly creates a false impression by such a misleading consent.

146. However, this provision does not apply if the other party knows or has reason to know that an expressed consent is not in agreement with the true intention of an expressing party. This is because the other party, with such knowledge, does not need protection, so that an expressed consent can, in turn, be considered to be void simply in accordance with consent theory (the proviso of Article 93(1)). Nevertheless, an expressing party in such a situation is not allowed to claim that his or her consent is void against a third party who, without the knowledge that it is different from the true intention of an expressing party, enters into a new legal relation with that other party to the contract or other juristic act which he or she has made (Article 93(2)). It is fair that a party knowingly expressing consent that is different from his or her true intention should be protected rather than the other party with knowledge of it, but it is unfair that such an expressing party should be protected rather than an innocent third party.

II. Fictitious Expression of Intention

147. In some situations, a party may express a fictitious consent in order to simulate a contract or other juristic act in collusion with another party who knows that the consent is not a true intention of the expressing party. For example, a debtor A, facing the possibility that his or her creditor will attach his or her property for execution, might make a pretense of selling his or her property to the other party [B], who also makes a pretense of buying it, so that A can avoid its possible attachment by creating the appearance that the property is no longer his or her own.

148. In line with consent theory, the Civil Code provides that such consent is void because it is not the true intention of an expressing party, thereby invalidating the simulated contract or other juristic act. But a party A who express a fictitious consent may claim its voidness against the other party B with whom an expressing party colludes (Article 94(1)), while the Civil Code does not allow him or her to assert it against a third party C who, being ignorant of the fact that an expressed consent, does not correspond to the true intention of that expressing party A, and enters into a new legal relation with that other party B (Article 94(2)).

149. In this case, it would seem to follow that a third party C would end up having no ownership of the property that A colludes with B to make a pretense of selling to B because A's fictitious consent is considered to be void, so that the ownership of that property is, in fact, not transferred to B from A.

150. But this is unfair. A party who expresses a misleading fictitious consent should not be protected to the detriment of a party who believes such consent is real. This is why Article 94(2) provides that the voidness of a fictitious consent does not go beyond the relation between A and B, and thus permits the ignorant party, C, to insist on his or her ownership of that property.

151. The idea behind this is called apparent theory, by which a party liable for the appearance that his or her expressed consent agrees with his or her true intention shall assume the legal effects as if that consent was real in order not to impair the reliance of a third party on the appearance. As matter of a fact, Article 94(2) applies by analogy in practice beyond the scope originally expected in the Civil Code, so that it also covers cases where A is somehow liable for the appearance of consent even if no collusion is involved between A and B. Those expanded cases include cases where A's fictitious consent is later approved by B who did not notice it when it was expressed,[184] where B makes a pretense of buying A's property without the consent of A but A later approves such an apparent situation[185] and where A's gross negligence contributes to the appearance that his or her property is actually sold to B even if A did not notice his contribution.

152. An example of the last kind of cases is where A, after being requested by B, signs a contract to sell his or her land to B without understanding or even reading it, and then C buys it from B, assuming the sales contract between A and B is real. In this case, the Supreme Court admits C's ownership of the land through application by analogy of Article 94(2), although it relies on Article 110 together with Article 94(2), to hold that it is not enough for a third party C to be just ignorant of the situation as Article 94(2), reads, but it is necessary for him to have no fault in being ignorant, as Article 110 states.[186]

153. The expansion of Article 94(2) is important in a practical way in the transaction of a real property, where Article 192, which is similar to the principle of the bona fide purchaser in common law, does not apply. It is expected to virtually function as a substitute of that principle in these transactions as well. It enables an innocent third party C to have ownership of property from its apparent owner B who looks to but does not in fact acquire it from its real owner A, either with or without collusion between the previous two—the first real and the second apparent—owners A and B

---

184. Supreme Court, 18 Mar. 1966, Minshu 20-3-451.
185. Supreme Court, 22 Sep. 1970, Minshu 24-10-1424.
186. Supreme Court, 23 Feb. 2006, Minshu 60-2-546.

III. Mistake

154. If consent is expressed by mistake, the Code permits an expressing party to rescind such consent in some circumstances[187]. The Civil Code categorises mistakes according to two types. One type is the mistake in which an expressed consent does not correspond to the intention of an expressing party, which is a so-called mistake in expression (Article 95(1)(i)). Among the examples is the case where a party intends to buy a machine for USD 1,000, but expresses to the other party his or her consent to buy it for JPY 10,000 by mistake in his or her writing an offer, and the case where he or she intends to buy machine A for USD 1,000, but expresses to the other party his or her consent to buy machine B for USD 1,000, mistakenly believing that machine B is the same as machine A. This type of mistake is in common with the other two articles, Articles 93 and 94, where it has already been mentioned that consent is lacking in the true sense because the expressed consent does not agree with the true intention of the party. On the other, Article 95 is different from these in that an expressing party gives such consent while being ignorant of the disagreement.

155. Another type of mistake is one that occurs in recognition of certain facts on the basis of which a party expresses consent to a contract or other juristic act, a so-called mistake of facts (Article 95(1)(ii))[188]. For example, a guarantor expresses consent to a contract of guarantee with a creditor, mistakenly believing that there is another guarantor for the same debtor, but, in fact, there is not. In this type of mistake, consent is not lacking but certainly exists, although it is defective in the sense that the current consent would not be expressed if the party had not misunderstood certain facts.

156. In line with consent theory, the validity of consent expressed under either mistake in expression or mistake of facts is questioned because of a lack or defect of intention. But it is not fair to the other party for consent to be always rescinded for a mistake because, in some cases, an expressing party should be liable for his or her own mistake. This is why the Civil Code sets the following requirements for consent to be rescinded because of a mistake, so that a transaction should not be too precarious.

157. First, consent can be rescinded either in the case of a mistake in expression or a mistake of facts only if the mistake under which consent to a contract or other

187. Before the 2017 Reform, the original Civil Code provided that mistake renders consent void, not rescindable. It is argued that consent must not be theoretically void at least in the case of mistake of facts, because consent expressed by such mistake corresponds to the intention of an expressing party, although that intention was not his or her true one as it was distorted by such mistake. Moreover, since any person would be allowed to claim at any time that consent is void, it is criticized that in either type of mistake, it is enough, for the purpose of protecting an expressing party, for consent to be only rescinded by that party within certain time. This leads to the change from voidness to rescission with regard to the effect of mistake.

188. Traditionally, this has been called mistake in motive in legal discourse.

juristic act is expressed is so important in terms of the purpose of that juristic act and the socially accepted reason as to justify the result of the juristic act being invalidated as a whole (Article 95(1)).

158. Second, an expressing party can only rescind his or her consent in the case of either type of mistake if the mistake is not due to his or her gross negligence (Article 95(3)). This reflects the idea that the other party should be more protected than a blameworthy expressing party. But the requirement of no gross negligence is not needed where the other party knows of the mistake on the part of an expressing party or where the other party also expresses consent to a contract or other juristic act under the same mistake as an expressing party does. In those situations, it is not necessary to be considerate to the other party.

159. Third, as far as a mistake of facts is involved, it must be indicated that consent is expressed on the basis of certain facts which an expressing party misunderstands (Article 95(2))[189]. The requirement of indication is added to set a higher hurdle for rescission in case of a mistake of fact rather than a mistake in expression. In the former, the consent of an expressing party is just defective, while, in the latter, the consent of that party is lacking in the true sense. Without such an indication, the involved risk of misunderstanding remains with an expressing party, which means that he or she is not allowed to rescind that contract or other juristic act made by mistake[190].

---

189. Indication can be made not only explicitly but also implicitly. In a case where a divorcing husband expressed concern to his wife about whether she could afford to pay tax after receiving real property from him as part of the distribution of property in a divorce, the Supreme Court held that he implicitly indicated to her his assumption that contrary to fact, the tax will be imposed on her, not him. The Court thus found mistake of facts (mistake in motive) in the husband's expression of consent to such distribution. Supreme Court, 4 Sep. 1989, Kagetsu 41-11-75.

190. The 2017 Reform does not aim to change the case law on mistake but rather to clarify its framework. The case law, however, cannot be easily explained. Although some courts seem to consider that it is sufficient for an expressing party to unilaterally indicate, explicitly or implicitly to the other party, that his or her consent is expressed on the basis of certain facts, most courts generally hold that an expressing party's indicated assumption needs to be shared by the other party and thereby form the content of a contract or other juristic act. Consider, for example, where loans were made pursuant to a guarantee contract concluded between a credit guarantee association and a bank, and where it later turns out that the principal debtor falls within the category of anti-social forces such as organized crime groups. Contrary to Government guidelines to request severing any relation with those forces, the Supreme Court has held that the association's misperception about the status of the principal debtor does not constitute a mistake such as to invalidate its consent and thus the guarantee contract. According to the Supreme Court, an expressing party's wrong assumption of certain facts – which is a motive in expressing his or her consent – does not constitute an operative mistake even if it has been expressed to the other party unless it forms the content of a contract or other juristic act (Supreme Court, 12 Jan. 2016, Minshu 60-1-1). The same reasoning can be also found in a contemporaneous judgment of the Supreme Court, 12 Jan. 2016, Hanji 2327-21). This suggests that the unilateral indication of an expressing party's assumption of certain facts is not enough to find mistake. The revised Article 95 expressly states that as a requirement of mistake, the expressing party needs to have indicated to the other party that his or her consent is made on the basis of certain facts, but it still leaves to the court whether that expressing party's indicated assumption of certain facts must be shared by the other party and thereby form the content of a contract or other juristic act.

160. If all of those requirements mentioned above are met, an expressing party can claim that consent be rescinded for a mistake against the other party, but he or she is not allowed to do so against a third party who has a new legal relation without any fault and being ignorant of the fraud, so that such an innocent third party can be protected in a way similar to Article 94(2) (Article 95(4)).

IV. Fraud

161. An expressing party can get into a mistake under which consent is expressed not only by himself or herself but also by another person's fraud. For example, in the case of a mistake, consent expressed under fraud is also defective, so that it can be rescinded (Article 96(1)).

162. For fraud to be found, the act of a person to deceive an expressing party and the intent of that person to do so must be proved. Silence could constitute fraud if the person has a duty to disclose in accordance with good faith.

163. The requirement of rescission for fraud, unlike that of rescission for a mistake, is neither the importance of the mistake, nor the gross negligence of the expressing party and nor the indication that consent is expressed on the basis of certain facts. Considering that an intentional misleading act is involved in fraud, the Civil Code allows consent expressed under fraud to be rescinded more easily than one expressed simply under a mistake.

164. Fraud is typically committed by the other party to a contract or other juristic act, but it is sometimes committed by any person other than a party to it, where an expressing party can rescind his consent only if the other party to a contract or other juristic act knows or has reason to know of the fraud (Article 96(2)).

165. Under Article 96(3), an expressing party may claim that consent be rescinded for fraud against the other party to a contract or other juristic act, although he or she is not allowed to do so against a third party who has entered a new legal relation without any fault at being ignorant of the situation, likewise as in Article 95(4).

V. Duress

166. Duress is the threat of violence or other harm to compel another person to express consent to a contract or other juristic act. Article 96(1) permits consent expressed under duress and under fraud to be rescinded because such consent is also defective in the sense that consent is different from one which would be expressed without being subject to duress.

167. Article 96(1) covers both cases of duress and fraud, but 96(2) and 96(3) of the article only apply to a case of fraud, not to that of duress. Thus, there are two differences between them. First, although duress can also be committed by any person other than a party to a contract or other juristic party, Article 96(2) does not allow consent under duress to be rescinded even if the other party to it knows or has reason to know of the fact that an expressing party was subject to duress when he or she expressed consent. Second, an expressing party may claim consent under duress to be rescinded against anyone, including a third party, without any fault in not knowing of the duress. These two differences come from the idea of the Civil Code giving greater protection to an expressing party in a case of being subject to duress than in a case of being subject to fraud with relation to an innocent third party. Some blame can be imputed to an expressing party under fraud, who should be more cautious, while an expressing party under duress cannot be blamed at all.

VI. Special Rules under the Consumer Contract Act

168. Under consent theory, a party is bound to his or her consent to a contract or other juristic act as long as the true intention is voluntarily expressed through such consent. The Civil Code ensures this by providing for mistake, fraud and duress.

169. However, these are not enough to police the inappropriate ways of inducing a party to express consent to an undesirable contract or other juristic act. In particular, a consumer is vulnerable to aggressive or oppressive solicitations of business, so the Consumer Contract Act was enacted in 2000 to regulate consumer contracts more restrictively than the Civil Code. Amendments in 2018 expanded the substantive scope of protection (as explained in paragraph 173 below), and collective redress procedures were improved from 2006 (*see* General Introduction, §7, paragraph 25).

170. The Consumer Contract Act clarifies that a consumer may rescind a contract [1] if a business, intentionally or with gross negligence[191], only represents advantageous facts and fails to inform a consumer of disadvantageous fact (even without representing any false fact at all) as to the quality or the price of goods or services and other important subjects normally affecting a consumer's decision on whether to make such a contract (Articles 4(2) and 4(5)). A consumer is also entitled to rescind a contract [2] if a business, either intentionally or innocently, misrepresents any fact as to such important subjects or as to the circumstances[192] normally requiring a consumer to make such a contract in order to avoid the risk of his or her life or property being in danger (Articles 4(1)(i) and 4(5)), while under the Civil

191. The 2018 amendments of the Consumer Contract Act, in effect from 15 Jun. 2019, further allows rescission of a contract if misrepresentation is made with gross negligence (if not intentionally).

192. An example is where a business tells a consumer, without measuring, that the floor under their house is affected by humidity, in order to induce him or her to make a contract to install under-floor ventilation. Such a business's statement is not as to the quality of service contracted for itself. Yet it will be a sufficient reason for the consumer to rescind a contract because it is a misrepresentation as to the circumstances normally requiring a consumer to make such a contract, in order to avoid the risk of his or her house suffering damage.

Code, a party may only rescind a contract for fraud for intentional misrepresentation of such facts (Civil Code Article 96). Moreover, he or she is allowed to rescind a contract [3] if a business tells a consumer that a prediction it states is certain about future prices and other uncertain subjects that will change in the future, so that a consumer mistakenly believes the prediction (Articles 4(1)(ii) and 4(5)). By contrast, under the Civil Code, no party is legally responsible for whatever prediction is made.

171. A consumer may rescind a contract in the situations listed above in [1] to [3] under the Consumer Contract Act even if it is impossible or at least difficult for him or her to be protected for mistake or fraud under the Civil Code.

172. Furthermore, the Consumer Contract Act supplements duress in the Civil Code by providing for the following situations [4] to [11]. He or she may also rescind a contract [4] if a business continues to remain at the residence of a consumer even after he or she has requested it to leave, [5] if a business does not let a consumer leave a place of solicitation even after he or she has requested to leave, or [6] if a business knowingly makes a contract to sell goods or provide a service of a quantity, time or period that considerably exceeds what the consumer would normally need in his or her daily situation (Article 4(4)). In these situations, a consumer is not subject to any exactly defined duress, but his or her consent cannot be voluntarily expressed because he or she is somehow being pressured.

173. In order to protect consumers likely to feel pressured into making a contract, the Consumer Contract Act was amended in 2018,[193] enabling such consumers to rescind a contract in the following further situations:

- [7] if a business stirs up the excessive anxiety of a socially inexperienced consumer about his or her marriage, career or educational advancement, as well as his or her face or body shape, telling him or her that the goods or services contracted for are necessary for him or her to realise his or her wish about those personally important subjects (Art. 4(3)(iii));
- [8] if a business knowingly takes advantage of the fact that a socially inexperienced consumer has some romantic feelings towards the sales staff, telling him or her that their relationship will end unless he or she makes a contract (Art. 4(3)(iv));
- [9] if a business stirs up excessive anxiety of a consumer without enough ability to judge due to his or her old age or mental disorder about his or her health or living conditions, telling him or her that the current standard of those subjects will be difficult to keep without the goods or services contracted for (Art. 4(3)(v));

193. This amendment aims at least in part to give more protection to young consumers as the age of majority has been lowered from twenty to eighteen. Thus, a young consumer is typically thought of as a socially inexperienced consumer covered by situations [7] or [8].

[10]if a business stirs up excessive anxiety of a consumer, telling him or her, according to spiritual forces, that he or she will be pursued by misfortune without the goods or services contracted for (Art. 4(3)(vi)); or

[11]if a business starts performing its own obligation or unrequested preparation for such performance before a contract is made, telling a consumer that it is extremely impossible or needs his or her compensation to make restitution (Art. 4(3)(vii)-(viii)).

174. In all situations [1] to [11], the Consumer Contract Act has a provision similar to Article 96(3) of the Civil Code, whereby a third party ignorant of the situation can be protected (Article 4(5)). An agent or the intermediary entrusted by a business to make a contract with a consumer shall also be treated in the same way as the business itself under the Consumer Contract Act (Article 5).

§3. Other Conditions for Validity

175. A party to a contract or other juristic act is free to determine its content. It is a common idea that unless there is any defect of consent, a contract or other juristic act should be respected as it is in accordance with the autonomy of a party. However, there are some limits on such freedom. Those limits to regulate the contents of a contract or other juristic act are summarised in the following Parts I and II under the Civil Code, and Part III under the Consumer Contract Act.

176. For a contract or other juristic act to be enforceable, its content needs to be at least legal and definite. Otherwise, the state cannot be expected to enforce it. But its content does not have to be possible to perform when it is formed. Thus, initial impossibility, like supervening impossibility, is just treated as non-performance, which presupposes the validity of an already formed contract or other juristic act.

I. Illegality and Public Policy

177. According to Article 91, a party to a contract or other juristic act may determine its content unless it conflicts with mandatory provisions. As opposed to default provisions, mandatory provisions are those which may not be overridden by the agreement otherwise made between the parties. For example, Article 1 of the Interest Rate Restriction Act provides that the legal maximum rate of interest for a loan contract is 20% for a principal of less than JPY 100,000, 18% for a principal of JPY 100,000 or more but less than 1,000,000 and 15% for a principal of JPY 1,000,000 or more, and that a loan contract shall be void in relation to the portion which exceeds those legal interest rates. A contract or other juristic act shall be void to the extent that it is contrary to the mandatory provisions even if it is voluntarily made, so that its content would be modified in a way that fits such provisions.

178. The conflict of a contract or other juristic act with mandatory provisions does not form the only ground for its unenforceability. According to Article 90, a contract or other juristic act is also void when it is contrary to public policy. Certainly, the violation of laws can constitute the violation of public policy, but it is not always necessarily so. For example, the Supreme Court held that if a person without a license required under the Food Sanitation Act purchases meat to sell to his or her customers, the purchase contract is still valid regardless of fact that the Act is violated, because this Act is a mere regulatory law.[194] The traditional idea is that, based on the distinction between public and private laws, the violation of regulatory laws needs to be only subject to an administrative sanction, but does not have anything to do with private rights and duties.

179. Thus, the character of a law that a contract or other juristic act violates is taken into consideration to discern whether public policy is violated for the application of Article 90, but so too are other factors, such as the maliciousness of the violation of the laws and the equity between the parties to a contract or other juristic act. In fact, the Supreme Court has found a contract to be unenforceable in another case where a person knowingly sold snacks with ingredients prohibited under the same regulatory law, the Food Sanitation Act, considering that an administrative sanction was not sufficient for such a malicious violation of the law.[195] Moreover, it is also argued that a contract or other juristic act should be void for violation of mere regulatory laws at least before any obligation of either party is performed, because as a result of it being made unenforceable at such a stage, each party would be released from his or her obligation equally and fairly. In sum, the violation of laws does not always invoke the application of Article 90, but may trigger it in some cases after all three factors mentioned above are considered.

180. A contract or other juristic act can violate public policy without violating laws. For example, it can violate public policy and thus be found void if it is grossly immoral, such as a contract to maintain a relationship with a lover in exchange for some reward. It is also found to be contrary to public policy and, as such, considered void if it seriously threatens the freedom of the individual, such as a non-compete clause with an unreasonably long duration. Article 90 is expected to play a role as a wild card just in case, but due to its abstract nature, it is difficult to describe to which cases it actually applies.

II. Gross Disparity

181. Although courts are generally reluctant to intervene in a contract for reason of the unfairness of its content, they have been willing to regulate it if it is so one-sided as to give an excessive advantage to one of the parties. Such a contract of gross disparity between the parties allows courts to find it or its terms to be unenforceable as a matter of public interest under Article 90 because they can no longer leave it as a matter of private interest, but rather can consider it unacceptable enough

194. Supreme Court, 18 Mar. 1960, Minshu 14-4-483.
195. Supreme Court, 23 Jan. 1964, Minshu 18-1-37. *See* also generally General Introduction §5.

to find it to be a violation of public policy. Among those examples are a loan contract with abominably high interest and an unreasonably high amount of liquidated damages clause.

182. However, courts usually do not allow such a contract or its terms to be void for the reason of gross disparity alone. Some procedural unfairness needs to be involved. Unless, in the process of a contract being formed, a party takes advantage of the other party's urgent need, imprudence and inexperience in order to make an extortionate profit, courts will hesitate to step in.

183. Nevertheless, recently there have been more cases where courts have relied on this concept as a part of the application of Article 90 in particular in order to protect elderly people or some consumers vulnerable to aggressive or oppressive transactions which, in themselves, do not constitute fraud or duress.

III. Unfair Terms under the Consumer Contract Act

184. A contract term is unlikely to be invalidated solely for its substance unless it is so unfair as to violate public policy under Article 90 of the Civil Code. This is due to the traditional idea that a contract should be respected per se, because it is the result of each party's voluntary exchange. But the Consumer Contract Act, taking into consideration the gap in negotiating power between a consumer and a business, permits the following terms of a contract to be unenforceable just because they are unfair in substance.

185. First, an exemption clause is void in a consumer contract if it totally excludes a business from contractual or tort liability for damages, if it partially excludes a business for contractual or tort liability for damages caused with intent or gross negligence of the business or if it totally excludes a business from contractual damages caused by a latent defect in the goods or service of a contract, except in the case where a contract provides that a consumer is entitled to compensation from other businesses, to substitute goods or services or to cure any defect (Article 8). A clause authorising a business to determine its own liability is also void, because it similarly works as an exemption clause.

186. Second, a clause that requires a consumer to abandon the right to terminate a contract in case of its breach is also void in a consumer contract (Article 8-2). A clause authorising a business to determine the consumer's right to cancellation is also void, because it similarly deprives the right of cancellation of consumers.

187. Third, a liquidated damages or penalty clause is void too in a consumer contract to the extent that it requires a consumer to pay more than the average amount of damages by termination of the same kind of contract, or that it requires a consumer to pay more than an interest rate of 14.6% for overdue money (Article 9). For example, if a clause in an admission contract of a private university provides that the university can refuse to refund tuition fees as well as entrance fees to a successful applicant who has already paid them following university instructions and later declines admission before a class starts, it would be invalidated at least as far as the tuition fees are concerned because the amount of the tuition fees clearly exceeds the average amount of damages to the university.

188. Fourth, a clause that authorises a business to cancel a contract solely for the reason that a consumer is subject to a ruling for the commencement of guardianship, curatorship or assistance is void in a consumer contract (Article 8-3).[196]

189. These four kinds of unfair terms, sometimes referred to collectively as a black list, are void without any further fact than that they are such terms. Other unfair terms, sometimes referred to as a gray list, can be found to be void if the two conditions under Article 10 of the Consumer Contract Act are satisfied: first, a term is one that restricts the rights of a consumer or expands the duties of a consumer as compared to those provided under other laws, including the Civil Code, and second, a term is also one that impairs only the interests of a consumer in accordance with good faith. As an example of such a term, Article 10 enumerates an 'automatic renewal' clause, by which a consumer is deemed to give his or her consent to renewal if remaining silent for a specified period.

§4. Consequences of a Defect of Consent or of a Lack of Substantive Validity

I. Void or Rescinded Contract

190. As has been previously explained, a contract or other juristic act is void on some grounds, but it can be rescinded on other grounds. These are equally legal techniques that invalidate a contract or other juristic act, although sometimes as partial voidance or rescission, only some terms, not all, are invalidated.

191. There are some differences between voidance and rescission. First, a void contract or other juristic act does not come into effect at any time from the outset, as if there was no such contract or juristic act. On the other, a rescindable contract or other juristic act is valid until it is actually rescinded and only after that, is it deemed void. Thus, a contract or other juristic act remains valid if it is not rescinded.

192. Second, a rescindable contract or other juristic act may be ratified after a ground for rescission disappears and, once ratified, it cannot be rescinded anymore. A void contract or other juristic act cannot be ratified because it does not exist from the beginning, although it can be deemed to take effect as a new contract or other juristic act from the time a party ratifies it, as long as it fulfils the conditions for it to be valid.

196. This is also one of the amendments of the Consumer Contract Act in 2018.

193. Third, any person is allowed to claim that a contract or other juristic act be void without any limitation of time, whereas a particular person may only claim that it be rescinded within a certain limit of time. According to Article 120, a party who himself or herself gives consent in question, his or her representative or successor in either a case of rescission for defect of consent or for limited capacity and, in the latter case, a person who has authority to give an approval to his or her act as well may rescind that consent, thus invalidating a contract or other juristic act. Article 126 provides that consent to a contract or other juristic act can be claimed to be rescinded under the Civil Code within five years after it becomes possible to ratify it, while under the Consumer Contract Act (Article 7) it needs to be claimed within one year from the same point of time, but no later than five years after it is made.

II. Retroactive Effect

194. When a contract or other juristic act is either void or rescinded, any party to it needs to make restitution of everything he or she has received in order to restore the other party to the original position as if no contract or juristic act had been made (Civil Code, Article 121(2)).

195. But the Civil Code requires a person without or with limited capacity only to make this restitution to the extent that he or she is actually enriched, because he or she deserves to be specifically protected (the proviso of Article 121). For example, suppose that a sales contract for a car was made and was later claimed to be void or rescinded by a buyer after he or she had the car destroyed in an accident. The buyer will need to reimburse the value of the car in money to the seller if the contract is rescinded for the reason of mistake, but he or she will not need to return anything to the buyer if the contract is rescinded for the reason of his or her being a minor. This limitation of the scope of restitution to current actual enrichment is also permitted for a consumer who is entitled to rescind his or her consent to a consumer contract under the Consumer Contract Act, unless he or she knew that his or her consent was rescindable when it was expressed (Article 6-2 of the Act).

196. The effect of the two techniques on a third party can be complicated. Because a contract or other act is treated as void from the beginning when it is either void or rescinded, a transfer of property which it aims to realise has no effect in any case. So even though a third party who is ignorant of the situation and assumes that a contract or other juristic act has legal effect believes that he or she can have legal rights with regard to that property, he or she cannot in fact.

197. However, there are some provisions where voidness or rescission of a contract or other juristic act may not be claimed against an innocent third party so that such a third party can be protected. As has been already mentioned, such provisions comprise Article 93(2), Article 94(2) and Article 96(3) of the Civil Code, as well as Article 4(5) of the Consumer Contract Act, although the latter three aim only to protect an innocent party who enters into a legal relation with regard to that property before the contract or other juristic act is rescinded. Since the retroactive effect of rescission does not unexpectedly give a negative effect on a third party who enters into a legal relation after it is rescinded, those provisions do not contemplate such a third party.

198. In cases not covered by those provisions, a third party may still be protected. Where the property purportedly transferred by a seemingly valid contract or other juristic act is goods, Article 192 enables a third party to have legal rights with regard to the goods if he or she is not at fault in assuming its validity, which has in fact no effect due to its voidness or rescission. Moreover, where a property is immovable an innocent party can have legal rights with regard to that immovable property as a result of the application by analogy of Article 94(2) of the Civil Code in the way explained above.

III. Damages

199. Because no contract or other juristic act exists if is claimed to be void or rescinded, it is possible for a claim to be made in tort for damages caused by the fault of either party. In addition, it is also possible to make a claim for damages on the basis of good faith under the so-called *culpa in contrahendo*, which the Supreme Court has recently found to be of a tort nature too in the endo for the purpose of the extinctive prescription period.[197]

197. Supreme Court, 22 Apr. 2011, Minshu 65-3-1405.

Chapter 3. The Contents of a Contract

§1. Different Clauses

I. Ascertaining and Incorporating Express Terms

200. Before unfair terms are excluded, those terms must be part of a contract. To ascertain contract terms, it is necessary to clarify to which term the contracting parties have consented.

201. Clearly express terms, which are expressly stated and agreed upon by the parties, can constitute a contract. Express terms can be put in writing but can also be orally stated. Although an integration clause is permitted in practice, there is generally no parol evidence rule in Japanese contract law; thus, courts tend not to hesitate to look beyond the writing to ascertain contract terms. Terms can also be incorporated into a contract by referencing the terms of another piece of writing, if such reference is sufficiently clear for the contracting parties to be aware of. For example, when you buy a ticket for a flight, you are bound by the terms listed on the web page, which are referenced on your ticket, even though the terms themselves are not printed on the ticket.

202. In the process of making a contract, many statements are exchanged between the parties, but not all of them become part of the contract. Representations and terms must be distinguished in the sense that the former do not constitute a contract but are simply statements that a party makes to induce the other party to enter into a contract, while the latter form a contract. Statements in advertisements are often considered mere representations, sometimes because they are thought of as puff and sometimes because they are not sufficiently determinate.

203. Terms expressly written in a contract do not always become part of the contract. A case before the Supreme Court disputed the legal effects of a clause in a housing lease by which the lessee was required to assume the cost of repairing normal wear and tear damage that occurred during the lease period such as a hole or a stain on a wallpaper after the contract for housing lease was terminated.[198] Because normal wear and tear to the house was covered by the rent, the Civil Code does not expect that a lessee needs to pay any such costs more than the rent, although it does provide that each party must restore the house to its original condition after a lease contract expires or is terminated. According to the Supreme Court, a clause such as the one in dispute can be effective as a part of a contract to shift such costs to the lessor, but given the unexpected divergence from the premise of the Civil Code that the lessor should assume such costs, an oral explanation must be given to the lessee so that he or she understands and specifically agrees to it. This is why the Supreme Court found the clause not to be a part of the contract in this case; the clause was

198. Supreme Court, 16 Dec. 2002, Hanji 1921-61.

expressly written in the lease contract but an oral explanation was not provided to the lessee on the formation of the lease contract.

II. Implied Terms

204. A contract does not only consist of express terms but also implied terms that can be assumed to be included in a contract even if they are not expressly stated and agreed upon by the parties. These terms may be implied by law, by custom or by fact in order to supplement the express intentions of the parties to a contract.

205. It is impossible for express terms to address all possible events that could arise under a contract. The Civil Code has many default rules in the event that certain terms of a contract are missing. For example, Article 484 provides that unless otherwise agreed, delivery must be made at the current domicile of the obligee but can be made to the place where the specific thing was located when a claim for delivery occurred. For example, where a sales contract for boxes of apples does not specify a place for delivery, a seller must deliver the apples to the buyer's domicile in accordance with Article 484. Thus, with regard to the place for delivery, the term is implied by law, in this case, Article 484 of the Civil Code.

206. However, the result would be different if there is a custom. According to Article 92, the terms of a contract or other juristic act can be implied by custom, regardless of the fact that there is an applicable default rule in the Civil Code, if the parties intended to abide by custom rather than by the default rules. It has been held that he or she is presumed to have had such intention unless a contrary intention is expressed.[199] In the example discussed above, if there is a custom in the trade by which apples are regularly delivered to some specific place, a seller does not need to deliver to the buyer's domicile, but is permitted to deliver to the customary place.

207. Terms of a contract can also be implied by fact. Sometimes courts will imply a term to effectuate an express intention of the parties in specific circumstances. For example, if apples are sold at an unusually low price out of courtesy, meaning that the seller does not ask for a higher price in exchange for avoiding delivery costs, then it would be against the purpose of the contract to permit the buyer to require the seller to deliver apples to his or her domicile in accordance with Article 484; rather, it is more reasonable to require him or her to collect them from the seller at his or her own expense.

---

199. Great Court of Cassation, 2 Jun. 1921, Minroku 27-1038. It held that a local custom applies prior to Article 533 unless otherwise expressed; thus, the price under a sale does not need to be paid in exchange for delivery of the goods simultaneously.

III. Standard Terms

208. Today, contracts with standard terms are commonly used. In this type of contract, terms are unilaterally set by one of the parties, typically a business, while the other party, typically a consumer, cannot negotiate or change the terms; he or she is simply required to accept them on 'take-it-or-leave-it' basis.

209. Such contracts have been regulated by the courts. According to the courts, a contract with standard terms is formed when a party gives blanket consent to the contract as a whole. Specific consent does not need to be given to each individual terms after a party has read them. A party's failure to read the standard terms does not prevent such a contract from being formed.

210. The Civil Code added provisions relating to contracts with standard terms at the very last stage of revision in 2017 after long discussion, although it governs only a certain type of such an agreement, the so-called standard form transaction agreement. According to the definition in Article 548-2(1) of the Civil Code, a standard form transaction agreement is a contract with standard terms prepared by one party for transactions with a number of unknown customers so that all or some of the contents of each transaction can be reasonably uniform for both parties. Under this definition, there is no room in a standard form transaction agreement for terms of the contract to be modified through the negotiation of the parties.

211. Article 548-2(2) provides that a customer shall be deemed to have given consent to each individual term of a standard form transactions agreement if the party preparing the agreement has in advance showed the customer its intention that the agreement forms the contents of a contract and, if the customer agrees, that the agreement will constitute the contents of a contract. Moreover, Article 548-3(1) requires the party preparing the agreement to disclose the terms to the customer upon that customer's request without delay either before or after reaching an agreement, and Article 548-3(2) states that no contract shall be formed if such disclosure is refused, except in the case of a temporary electronic communication failure or other justifiable circumstances.

212. That said, not all standard terms in the agreement will take effect, even if the requirements of Article 548-2(1) and Article 548-3(3) are met. Article 548-2(2) provides that the customer shall be deemed not to have given consent to any terms of a standard form transactions agreement that restricts his or her rights or aggravates his or her obligations if it is considered to be detrimental solely to his or her interests contrary to good faith as set forth in Article 1(2) of the Civil Code in light of the method and circumstances of the transaction and socially accepted ideas. Because such terms are considered to be outside the scope of the customer's consent, they will not be a part of a contract.

IV. Exemption Clauses

213. Sometimes a contract with standard terms includes an exemption clause, which aims to limit or exempt the contractual or tort liability of one of parties, typically a business. An unfair exemption clause can be excluded by application of Article 548-2(2) of the Civil Code in the case of a standard form transactions agreement or in other cases by Article 90 of the Civil Code and by application of Article 8 of the Consumer Contract Act, as long as it is a consumer contract.

V. Liquidated Damages and Penalty Clauses

214. Courts can determine the amount of damages payable for failure to perform an obligation in accordance with Article 416, but the parties to a contract can fix a certain amount of damages in advance by agreement to avoid the unpredictability of a statutory calculation (Article 420(1)). A term providing for such agreement is called a liquidated damages clause, by which a party must pay a fixed amount to the other party in the case of non-performance. It is necessary and sufficient for a party to pay that amount regardless of the actual amount of damages. Courts may not increase or decrease this amount because the clause itself is a kind of contract, although courts may reduce the amount to the extent it violates Article 90. The clause does not hinder the right to demand performance or the right to terminate a contract (Article 420(2)). *See also* Part I, Chapter 6, §2, VII.

215. Distinguished from, though similar to, a liquidated damages clause is a penalty clause. Both clauses require a debtor to pay a certain amount in the event of his or her failure to perform an obligation; however, a penalty clause permits a creditor to make a demand against a debtor for damages as well as for the fixed amount of money, because the debtor's payment of that amount is simply a penalty and does not mean compensation for damages, unlike a liquidated damages clause. The latter prevents a creditor from making a demand against the debtor for any more than the amount set forth in the contract. Article 420(3) of the Civil Code states that any penalty shall be presumed to be liquidated damages; thus unless the presumption is rebutted, a debtor only needs to pay the amount fixed by the clause.

VI. Arbitration Clauses

216. Arbitration clauses are still rarely incorporated into domestic contracts in Japan, arguably because court litigation costs are lower than in several other comparable economies, combined with the attractiveness of various court- and government-supported mediation schemes. Japanese firms do agree to arbitration clauses in cross-border contracts to gain advantages such as easier enforcement of awards worldwide and more neutral or specialist forums. However, they still tend to agree on arbitration with the seat abroad, originally in the core venues in Europe or the United States and more recently in Asian venues such as Singapore and Hong Kong. Accordingly, the numbers of arbitration cases reportedly filed in the Japan

Commercial Arbitration Centre and other arbitral institutions in Japan remain low. They have not increased much despite the enactment of the Arbitration Act (Act No. 138 of 2003), based on the 1985 UNCITRAL Model Law on International Commercial Arbitration (Model Law) and aiming to make Japan a more attractive seat for arbitration.[200]

A. Form Requirements

217. Article 13(2) of the Arbitration Act requires that an arbitration agreement to be in writing, in the form of a document signed by all the parties, letters or telegrams exchanged between the parties (including those sent by facsimile device or other communication device for physically separated parties which provides the recipient with a written record of the transmitted content), or another written instrument. Article 13(3) and (5) provides that the written form requirement is fulfilled if a written contract refers to a document that contains an arbitration clause and the reference is such as to make that clause part of a contract, or if the arbitration clause is contained in a written statement submitted by one party in the arbitral proceedings and if no objection is raised in a written statement submitted in response by the other party. Those provisions derive from Article 7(2) of the 1985 Model Law.

218. Article 13(4) adds that an arbitration agreement is deemed to be in writing if the arbitration agreement is made by the way of electromagnetic records recording its content, namely prepared by an electronic, magnetic or other method incapable of recognition by human perception and used for data processing by a computer. This provision is based on Option I in Article 7(4) of the Model Law, as amended in 2006, and was drafted in light of deliberations by the UNCITRAL Working Group beginning from 2001. Japan's Arbitration Act of 2003 therefore anticipated and introduced a liberal regime for writing requirements for arbitration agreements.

219. The prior (German-inspired) Japanese law on arbitration did not contain any writing requirements, thereby allowing a purely oral arbitration agreement, as in Option II provided by the amended Model Law. However, the drafters of Japan's Arbitration Act decided to introduce a (liberal) writing requirement regime because this had become the prevailing practice in Japan and writing requirements remain under the 1958 New York Convention on the Recognition and Enforcement of Foreign Arbitral Awards (which Japan ratified and brought into force on 20 June 1961).[201]

---

200. *See* generally Nakamura and Nottage, *supra* n. 95, especially at 223. Most of the following points in the ensuing text are also derived from *Id.*, 223.
201. M. Kondo, T. Goto et al., *Arbitration Law of Japan*, 49 (Shoji Homu Co Ltd 2004).

B. Substantive Validity and Interpretation

220. Following the Model Law, Article 2(1) of the Arbitration Act limits the scope of an arbitration agreement to a dispute arising with regard to a 'defined legal relationship', typically based on or concerning a separate underlying contract between the parties.

221. Under Article 2(1) of the Arbitration Act, the parties can refer existing or future disputes to arbitration. However, under Article 3 of the Supplemental Provisions of the Arbitration Act, a consumer may at any time unilaterally cancel an arbitration agreement entered into with a business to submit arbitration disputes that may arise in the future.[202] Under Article 4, an arbitration agreement is also null and void if its subject matter is future individual labour-related disputes.[203]

222. Under Article 13(1) of the Arbitration Act, unless otherwise provided by law, only civil disputes that may be settled by a compromise between the parties can be resolved by arbitration, but a dispute concerning divorce or separation is specifically excluded. Commentators have adopted narrower or broader views as to what sorts of disputes are intended by the legislature to fall within this category of non-arbitrable disputes.[204] There is still little case law but one court has distinguished between an agreement to arbitrate disputes about patent licence contracts in general (such as interpretation of contractual provisions or the consequences of breach) and the validity or otherwise of the underlying patent (considered to be not arbitrable).[205] More recently, a court held that the parties could not have intended for their arbitration clause (requiring arbitrators to be 'commercial men') to extend jurisdiction for the arbitral tribunal to decide matters arising under the Corporate Reorganisation Act due to the insolvency of the Japanese party. One commentator suggests that such matters anyway should be determined exclusively by national courts.[206]

223. Japanese courts have not followed some counterparts abroad in clearly stating that arbitration agreements should be interpreted liberally or broadly, respecting party autonomy to select a neutral and effective alternative to litigation. However,

---

202. The definitions of consumers and businesses are as set out in Art. 2(1) of the Consumer Contract Act (Act No. 61 of 2000).
203. Individual labour-related disputes are as defined in Article 1 of the Law on Promoting the Resolution of Individual Labor Disputes (Act No. 112 of 2001).
204. Nakamura and Nottage, *supra* n. 95, 234; T. Kojima and T. Inomata, *Chusaiho [Arbitration Law]*, 67 (Nihonhyoronsha 2014).
205. *See* Tokyo High Court, 28 Feb. 2006, Hanrei-Jiho 1926-12; and generally, including comparative law observations, C. Heath and L. Nottage, 'Case No. 71: Arbitration Law – Separability and Arbitrability – Terminated Contract' in *Business Law in Japan: Cases and Comments*, 773 (M. Baelz, M. Dernauer et al. eds., Kluwer 2012).
206. Tokyo District Court, 28 Jan. 2015, Hanrei-Jiho 2258-100. *See* the summary and discussion by T. Nakamura, *The Recent Court Decisions on the Japanese Arbitration Law*, 34 JCAA Newsl. 4, 5–6 and 11–12 (2015).

for example, one quite recent judgment applying Japanese law rejected the argument that an arbitration agreement was invalid because it ambiguously referred disputes to the 'International Commercial Arbitration Court'. The court concluded that the intention must have been to allow a party to commence arbitration in the institution of that name in Russia, Belgium or the Ukraine.[207]

§2. Interpretation

224. Terms of a contract, once ascertained, sometimes need to be interpreted to confirm their meaning. This process is meant to clarify what the parties really agreed to in the contract. This is why it is argued that a contract should first be interpreted, according to the common intention of the parties, although the Civil Code itself does not provide for how to interpret a contract.

225. Suppose that the parties make a sales contract for a ship called the '*Nipponmaru*'. Because the seller owns three ships, '*Nipponmaru I*', '*Nipponmaru II*' and '*Nipponmaru III*', this contract needs some interpretation to determine to which among the three, in fact, refers to '*Nipponmaru*'. If both parties have '*Nipponmaru I*' in mind, '*Nipponmaru*' in the contract is '*Nipponmaru I*' in accordance with their common understanding, regardless of what reasonable parties would consider.

226. The controversy would arise when no common understanding between the parties can be found, for example, if the seller thought that it was referring to '*Nipponmaru I*' while the buyer thought that it was '*Nipponmaru II*'. The traditional approach has interpreted a contract in terms of what reasonable parties would intend, but it can be harmful to strictly follow this approach. For example, it would be undesirable for either party if '*Nipponmaru*' in the contract was understood to be referring to '*Nipponmaru III*', even though reasonable parties would think so, because a sales contract for '*Nipponmaru III*' is not what either party wanted and is meaningless to enforce when the seller has '*Nipponmaru I*' in mind and the buyer has '*Nipponmaru II*' in mind. Thus, a new approach has been suggested and is now widely accepted in which the more justifiable interpretation of the parties' understanding is chosen. In the current case, a court must compare the two interpretations, the seller's (*Nipponmaru I*) and the buyer's (*Nipponmaru II*), and select the more justifiable interpretation by reference to the purpose of the contract, the course of dealing, trade usage, common expressions in society and so on.

227. In the process of interpreting a contract, courts bring normative considerations from outside of the contract, sometimes going further to modify the terms of a contract. For example, the Supreme Court interpreted a clause in an automobile

207. Tokyo District Court, 23 Aug. 2013, 2013WLJP-CA08238004. *See*, the summary, and critique that a more plausible argument was that the parties had meant the ICC International Court of Arbitration, in Nakamura, *Ibid.* 4–8 (noting also uncertainty remaining as to what law governs the formation and interpretation of arbitration agreements where the parties have not agreed on the law governing the underlying contract).

insurance contract in such a way that was virtually rewritten. In this case, a claim for personal injury was made under an insurance contract over sixty days following the accident. This violated a clause in the contract stating that the insurance company would not pay an insurance claim unless notice of the claim was provided within sixty days of the accident. Nevertheless, the Supreme Court held that an insurance claim may be made even after sixty days, except in a case where the insured does not provide timely notice in an attempt to deceive the insurance company or to prevent a proper investigation of the accident, as long as the company is permitted to deduct from the insurance claim the damages the company actually incurred as a result of receiving notice after the sixty days. According to the Supreme Court, because the aim of the notice clause is to enable an insurance company, because of earlier notice, to provide instruction to the insured or to take steps to minimise the actual insurable damages, it is not necessary to completely deny the insurance claim. Instead, it is sufficient to permit the insurance company to be reimbursed for the damages caused by the late notice, even if notice of the claim is given after the sixty days.[208]

§3. Conditional Contracts

I. Condition

228. Typically, a contract or other juristic act takes effect when it is formed and remains effective until its purpose is achieved. However, a party can use certain techniques to make it effective or ineffective due to a future event. Conditions and time limits are such techniques.

229. A condition is a legal technique to make taking or losing effect of a contract or other juristic act contingent upon an uncertain event in the future. There are two types of conditions: (1) a condition precedent and (2) a condition subsequent. A contract or other juristic act subject to a condition precedent shall become effective upon fulfilment of the condition (Article 127(1)). For example, where a donor promises to make a gift of his or her property to a donee if the donee can pass the bar examination, it is considered a condition precedent. On the other, a contract or other juristic act subject to a condition subsequent shall become ineffective upon fulfilment of the condition (Article 127(2)). For example, where a seller makes a contract to sell his or her land but also agrees that the contract will lose its effect if a buyer cannot obtain proper financing from a bank, it is considered a condition subsequent. Under either condition, the parties can, by agreement, make the effect of the fulfilment of a condition date back to any time prior to the time of the fulfilment (Article 127(3)).

208. Supreme Court, 20 Feb. 1987, Minshu 41-1-159.

230. Additionally, some conditions can be considered void. First, an unlawful condition is considered void, thereby a contract or other juristic act subject to it shall be void because such a conditional contract or juristic act is itself considered to be against public policy (Article 132).

231. Second, an impossible condition is also considered void. Thus, a contract or other juristic act subject to an impossible condition precedent shall be void, while a contract or other juristic act subject to an impossible condition subsequent shall be unconditional (Article 133).

232. Third, a condition is void if it is already fulfilled or is certain not to be fulfilled in the future because, by definition, it must be uncertain whether or not a condition will be fulfilled. Therefore, if a condition is already fulfilled, a contract or other juristic act subject to such a condition precedent shall be unconditional, while if it is subject to such a condition subsequent, it shall be void in its entirety from the beginning (Article 131(1)). Similarly, if a condition is certain to not be fulfilled in the future, a contract or other juristic act subject to such a condition precedent shall be void in its entirety, while being subject to such a condition subsequent shall make a contract or other juristic act unconditional (Article 131(2)).

233. Fourth, a condition precedent is void if it is contingent solely on the will of the obligor, although such a condition subsequent is valid. A contract or other juristic act subject to such a condition precedent is void in its entirety because it is too illusionary to enforce as a contract, for example in a case where a party promises to make a gift when he or she feels like it (Article 134). On the other, it is still somewhat meaningful to enforce a contract or other juristic act subject to such a condition subsequent because it remains effective until the condition is fulfilled.

234. During the pendency of a condition, a party may not infringe upon the right of the other party to expect the fulfilment of a condition. If this right is infringed, a claim for damages can be made in a case where the condition is actually fulfilled (Article 128). If a condition is not fulfilled due to the obstruction of a party who would be disadvantaged by its fulfilment, it may be deemed fulfilled for the party who would benefit from fulfilment (Article 130). For example, where a donor makes a conditional gift of his or her property upon a donee's success on the bar examination, the donee can claim damages for breach of contract if he or she has passed the bar examination but the donor destroyed the property. Alternatively, if the donor stops the donee from taking the bar examination, the gift must be performed as it would be considered unconditional.

235. Article 130 is now, by analogy, also considered to apply to a case where a condition is fulfilled intentionally by the unfair act of a party who will benefit if the condition is not fulfilled. In such a case, a condition shall be deemed not fulfilled for the party who would be disadvantaged by its failure. The Supreme Court held so, in a case where one company entrapped a competing company in the same trade into selling a certain type of product, thereby having to pay a penalty because an agreement between the two companies was violated to the effect that the latter company may not sell this type of the product anymore and otherwise shall pay a penalty to the former company.[209]

II. Time Limit

236. A time limit (or time bar) is also a legal technique by which a contract or other juristic act can take or lose effect in the future. However, it is different from a condition in that the future event upon which the effect is contingent is certain to be either fulfilled or unfulfilled, while the event is uncertain in the case of a condition.

237. There are two types of time limits: (1) a time for the commencement of validity and (2) a time for the expiration of validity. If a commencement time is assigned to a contract or other juristic act, performance may not be demanded prior to the set time (Article 135(1)). On the other, if an expiration time is assigned to a contract or other juristic act, its validity shall expire upon the set time (Article 135(2)). Because a time limit is presumed to be provided for the benefit of the obligor, he or she may waive that benefit if he or she compensates the creditor for damages that are incurred as a result (Article 136). For example, a borrower can repay a loan to a lender before the due date but must compensate the lender for the interests that would have accrued through the due date.

238. A time limit may be definite when a specific date is designated but may be indefinite when it is not designated, even though the time is sure to come at some point, for example, in a case where an umbrella shall be returned upon the next rain.

239. As a matter of fact, it is sometimes difficult in practice to discern whether it is a condition or a time limit, in particular, an indefinite time limit. An example of this issue is a loan contract by which a borrower is required to repay a loan to a creditor after having some success. The former Supreme Court held that it was interpreted as a time limit, not a condition precedent, because it is reasonable to understand that the creditor did not only intend to be repaid when the debtor could afford to repay the debt but also intended to be repaid when the debtor evidently became too unsuccessful to repay it, rather than to recognise that he or she just intended to receive no repayment of the loan if the debtor was unsuccessful.[210]

240. The same reasoning was extended by the Supreme Court to a case where Subcontractor A did not receive payment for his performed work from a prior subcontractor, Subcontractor B, who ordered the work, because of a so-called payment linkage clause by which Subcontractor A could receive payment only after B subcontractor received payment for work from another prior subcontractor, Subcontractor C, in a vertical chain of subcontractors for a construction project. The

209. Supreme Court, 31 May 1994, Minshu 48-4-1029.
210. Great Court of Cassation, 31 Oct. 1910, Minroku 16-739.

Supreme Court admitted A's claim against B for payment even though B did not receive payment from C due to C's bankruptcy, and held that this was simply a time limit, not a condition precedent. Thus, the time limit for B's obligation to pay A comes when B actually receives payment from C or, when it turns out that B is certain that they are not able to receive payment from C. According to the Supreme Court, this is once again because A and B impliedly intended the clause to be an indefinite time limit in the sense above-mentioned.[211]

211. Supreme Court, 14 Oct. 2010, Hanji 2097-34.

Chapter 4. Privity of Contract

§1. Rule of Privity of Contract

I. Third Parties and Contract

241. The common law privity of contract doctrine provides that a contract binds only its parties and does not confer rights or obligations on a third party.[212] Privity as a legal doctrine is foreign to Japanese law, but the basic concept and exceptions to the doctrine are not.

242. For example, the Civil Code starts with the premise that if 'an obligor fails to perform consistent with the purpose of its obligation, the obligee shall be entitled to demand damages arising from such failure' (Article 415). The code speaks only of obligors and obligees, and the code's scholars define obligations as a relative concept (*soutaisei*) between the transacting parties, with no effect on third parties.[213]

243. There are, however, several distinct legal doctrines allowing third parties to assert claims based on a contract they are not a party to, or to be liable for interfering with a contract to which they are not a party. In the following, the following doctrines will be addressed in turn: contracts for the benefit of third parties (II of this chapter, immediately below); third-party interference with contractual relationships (III below); transfer of contractual rights (§2 of this chapter, below); subcontracts and assumption of performance (§3 below); creditor subrogation rights (§4.I. below); creditor rights to rescind fraudulent transfers (§4.II. below); and direct actions and products liability actions (§5 below).[214]

II. Contracts for the Benefit of Third Parties

244. Japan's Civil Code sections covering contracts for the benefit of third parties are an amalgamation of the nineteenth century French and German Civil Codes.[215] Articles 537 through 539 recognise contracts for the benefit of third parties, which give rise to a third party's right to demand performance following an expression of intent by the third party to receive the benefits of the contract (Article

---

212. *See*, e.g., Black's Law Dictionary (9th ed., 2009).
213. H. Nakata, *Saiken Soron [Obligations in General]* 279 (3rd. ed., Iwanami Shoten, 2017).
214. Doctrine relating to 'contracts with protective effects for third parties' is addressed in academic circles, but less so in practice and omitted form the discussion here. For 'third party effects of exemption clauses', *see* para. 316 for some special statutory rules.
215. Y. Chuman and A. Shindo, Arts 537, in *Shinpan Chushaku Minpo [New Edition Commentary on the Civil Code]*, Vol. 13, (T. Taniguchi and K. Igarashi eds., Supplementary edition, Yuhikaku 2006), 692; M. Okino, 'Contracts for the Benefit of Third Parties in Japan', in *Studies in the Contract Law of Asia Vol. II: Formation and Third Party Beneficiaries* 260 (M. Chen-Wishart et al. eds., Oxford University Press 2017).

537(1)). These provisions of the Civil Code do not simply recognise or confer a *de facto* benefit on a third party; rather, they confer a legal right to the third party to enforce the contract.

245. Disputes over contracts for the benefit of third parties started early in the Meiji Era. Litigants disputed donative contracts for the benefit of certain family members that were executed to avoid the default inheritance provisions in the Civil Code.[216] More common examples today are insurance contracts naming a third party as a beneficiary or specific agreements for one party to pay another to provide a service or product to a third party.[217] Other modern examples include cumulative assumption of obligation where the obligee is the beneficiary (Article 470(4); *see* §2.II.B. of this chapter below) and trusts where a third party is the beneficiary (Article 88, Trust Act).[218]

246. Problems arise where the intent to benefit a third party is less clear, e.g. deciding whether a wire transfer constitutes a 'contract for the benefit of a third party'.[219] Determining whether a contract is one for the benefit of a third party traditionally includes an analysis of the contracting parties' expression of intent; the purpose of the contract; and the quid pro quo exchanged by the parties, i.e. whether it was a donative contract or not.[220]

247. The inquiry is fact-specific:[221]

(a) Courts have found an explicit assignment of rights in third-party debt to be a 'contract for the benefit of a third party'.[222] They have held that a contract between a land owner and developer requiring the owner to continue subleases entered into by the developer even if the original lease was terminated to be construed as a 'contract for the benefit of a third party' and the tenants could assert a right against the owner based on the original lease.[223]
(b) Similarly, courts have found agreements between employers and labour unions or labour union officials to be contracts for the benefit of third parties, giving rise to judiciable claims by individual employees for enforcement of the contract or for damages.[224] Courts have found contracts entered into by promoters in the course of incorporating a business, e.g. contracts for the purchase or sale of goods or property, to be contracts for the benefit of a third party.

---

216. Default provisions of the Meiji era Civil Code bequeathed the entire estate to the eldest son. Chuman and Shindo, *supra* n. 215, 702.
217. With regard to the latter, *see* Chuman and Shindo, *supra* n. 215, 699, 701 et seq.
218. Shiomi, *supra* n. 105, 45.
219. Chuman and Shindo, *supra* n. 215, 722.
220. *Ibid.* 778.
221. *See also*, Okino, *supra* n. 215, 266.
222. Chuman and Shindo, *supra* n. 215, 753.
223. *Ibid.* 746, quoting Tokyo High Court, 21 Dec. 1999, Hanta 1023-194.
224. *Ibid.* 758.

(c) Real estate covenants not to build or block sunlight for a period of years have been held to be contracts for the benefit of third parties allowing successor purchasers to assert claims against the developer where the intent to benefit third parties is clear.[225]

248. A finding that an agreement is a contract for the benefit of a third party has consequences for the (a) promisee, the party to the contract seeking to confer a benefit on a third party by contracting with (b) the promisor, who agrees to provide a service or product to (c) the third-party beneficiary, the recipient of the product or service. Each will be addressed in turn.

A. *Rights of Beneficiaries*

249. The rights of the beneficiary have received extensive treatment in the courts. The third party need not be in existence or identified at the time of the contract, only identifiable (Article 537(2)).[226] Japanese courts have held that contracts for the benefit of a third party may name as beneficiaries unborn children, as well as yet to be formed legal entities.[227] The absence of a requirement to name an identified beneficiary now provides a legal basis for settlements in consumer lawsuits creating contractual benefits for the rights of third-party consumers who are not direct parties to the dispute. [228]

250. Third-party rights in the contract traditionally arise at the time the beneficiary expresses to the promisor its intent to enjoy the benefit of the contract (Article

225. *Ibid.* 763. Courts have rejected assertions by citizen groups asserted that pollution prevention agreements between local governments and local businesses, primarily power companies, are contracts for the benefit of third parties entitling individual citizens to sue to enforce the anti-pollution measures found in the agreements. Courts have characterized the agreements as 'gentlemen's agreements' between local government and business, but they have also permitted citizens to sue as third-party beneficiaries of an agreement between a waste management company and the local government providing examination rights of documents relating to the waste disposal process. Courts have imposed sanctions on business entities for failure to comply with orders to produce the documents. Chuman and Shindo, *supra* n. 215, 764. The issue has arisen more recently with cases involving finance leases. Some courts have recognized contracts for the benefit of a third party where the financier–lessor disclaims liability for any defect in the product leased but contractually provides for liability to run directly from the supplier to the end-user lease. Here, courts imply an expression of intent to benefit from the user. *Id.* 773. Citing Osaka Chihan, 5 Aug. 1985 Hanji 1186-84, Osaka Kohan, 27 Apr. 1988, Hanta 685-241.

226. Chuman and Shindo, *supra* n. 215, 780.

227. Supreme Court, 26 Jun. 1962, Minshu 16-7-1397. Article 537(2), added in the 2017 Reform, is a codification of this case law. *See*, MOJ, *supra* n. 104, 379.

228. Ministry of Justice's 'Annotated Interim Issues for Reforming the Civil Code (Law of Obligations) 203 [*Minpo (Saiken Kankei) no Kaisei ni kansuru Chukantekina Rontenseirino Hosokusetsumei*]'(2011).

537(3)).[229] That expression of intent can be implied or take place as part of a demand for performance, and it can be made by an agent.[230] That expression can take place in the context of litigation.[231]

251. While Article 537(3) provides that beneficiary rights arise when the beneficiary 'expresses' her intent to receive the benefits of the contract, courts have regularly found 'implied' expressions of intent. The issue commonly arises with medical malpractice claims involving unborn children. The courts have found that the parents, acting as agents of a child, impliedly expressed the intent to become a beneficiary of the contract between the parents and a medical provider after the child's birth.[232] In one medical malpractice suit following the death of a minor child, parents alleged breach of contract both individually and on behalf of the child as a third-party beneficiary. The court awarded lost profits for the child as damages, as well as solatium (consolation money) damages for the child individually and the parents, finding an 'implicit' expression on the part of the child to receive the benefit of the contract.[233]

252. In cases involving the forced hospitalisation of mentally ill patients, courts have found that patients without capacity express an intent to receive the benefits of the contract, but rights under the contract were generated 'as a matter of course', recognising their right to demand production of medical records.[234]

253. Other cases have found that where the contracting parties agreed to release the third party from a debt or other obligation, there is an implied expression of intent to be released from that debt by the third party.[235] And where employer's life insurance policies named their employees as insured and the employer as primary beneficiary, some courts have affirmed the rights of the survivors to demand payment of the proceeds.[236] In doing so, the courts found an 'implied agreement' that the company would pay a significant portion of the proceeds to the survivors, construing the contract to be a contract for the benefit of a third party.[237]

254. Following an implied or express statement of intent, the third party obtains an independent right to claim performance by or damages from the promisor.[238] The

229. Chuman and Shindo, *supra* n. 215, 780.
230. *Ibid.*, 781–782.
231. *Ibid.*, 781.
232. Tokyo District Court, 24 Apr. 1979, Hanta 388-147; Nagoya District Court, 17 Feb. 1989, Hanta 703-204.
233. Chuman and Shindo, *supra* n. 215, 767, 769.
234. *Ibid.* 768.
235. *Ibid.* 704 quoting Great Court of Cassation, 26 Jun. 1916, Minshu 22-1268, Great Court of Cassation, 30 Sep. 1941, Minshu 20-1233.
236. *Ibid.* 776.
237. Chuman and Shindo, *supra* n. 215, 776. Special laws regulating insurance and civil trusts similarly provide for rights of beneficiaries without an initial expression of intent by the beneficiary. Articles 8, 42, 71 Insurance Act (Act No. 56 of 2008); Art. 88(1) Trust Act (Act No. 108 of 2006).
238. Chuman and Shindo, *supra* n. 215, 787.

third party is not a party to the contract and, therefore, has no right to cancel or void the contract. It can only demand performance or seek damages for non-performance.[239]

B. Rights of the Promisee

255. There are no limits on the types of rights or benefits that a promise may confer on a third party, and the promisee may contractually impose incidental obligations on the third-party beneficiary as a condition to acceptance.[240]

256. There is no Code provision that specifies whether a promisee can sue the promisor to render performance to the beneficiary. Scholarship generally and early case law recognised such a right.[241] However, more recent lower court decisions have found no such right, given the risk of concurrent and conflicting suits by the beneficiary and the promisee against the promisee.[242]

257. Following expression of intent or acceptance by the beneficiary, the Civil Code expressly provides that neither party to the contract – neither the promisee nor the promisor – may modify or extinguish the beneficiary's rights under the contract, absent the consent of the beneficiary (Article 538). As an example, where a party has opened a bank account on behalf of another, courts have found that the third party obtained a right to demand payment at the point at which he or she expressed intent to receive the benefits of that account, and that expression precluded the financial institution from withholding payment.[243]

C. Rights of the Promisor

258. The promisor's rights and obligations generally correspond to those arising under standard two-party contracts. Inquiries regarding good faith, mistake, fraud, coercion and the like are limited to the actions of the parties to the contract.[244] The promisor may assert *vis-à-vis* the beneficiary any defences it may assert against the promisee arising from that contract for the benefit of a third party (Article 539). This includes, for example, the right to demand simultaneous performance, right to cancel the contract for non-performance of the promisee's counter-obligation or right to set off counter-claims for damages or reduction in price paid for non-conforming product.[245]

239. *Ibid.* 785.
240. Chuman and Shindo, *supra* n. 215, 703, 780; Okino, *supra* n. 215, 270.
241. Great Court of Cassation, 14 Feb. 1917, Minroku 23-152.
242. Okino, *supra* n. 215, 272; Kobe District Court, Itami Branch, 17 Feb. 1975, Hanta 332–314.
243. Chuman and Shindo, *supra* n. 215, 717, quoting Kyoto District Court, 19 Apr. 1917, Shinbun 1276-30).
244. *Ibid.* 785.
245. *Ibid.* 791; Okino, *supra* n. 215, 273–274; Shiomi, *supra* n. 105, 47.

III. Third-Party Interference with Contractual Relationships

259. Third-party interference with contractual relationships is another area in which privity issues arise. Japan's early focus on freedom of contract and narrow definition of 'rights' protected under tort law initially limited legal redress.[246] But Japan now recognises both contract and tort law claims for damages for third-party interference with a contract and, in the context of property leases, claims for injunctions to stop or remove the interference.[247]

A. Tortious Interference with a Contract & Claims for Damages

260. The starting point for the tort claim is the basic Civil Code section defining a tort. Article 709 imposes liability where a person has intentionally or negligently 'infringed any right ... or legally protected interest' of another. The Civil Code as promulgated in 1896 did not have the term 'or legally protected interest', which was added in 2004, and thus the original language of Article 709 provided that tort liability arose only where there was an 'infringement of right'.

261. The criteria for finding an 'infringement of right' have waxed and waned since the Civil Code's adoption, with the drafter and initial case law adopting a relatively liberal interpretation of right and infringement. Stricter limitations during the first part of the twentieth century followed with courts limiting recognition of tortious conduct to violations of specifically enumerated legal rights. Starting in the 1930s, courts began adopting doctrines finding tortious conduct based on 'illegality' (*ihousei*), which once again expanded the realm of tort law.[248] Illegality is determined according to the manner of infringement and the type of interest that was infringed, pursuant to the correlationship (*sokankankei*) theory.

262. The Great Court of Cassation first recognised interference with contractual rights as a tort in 1915, but contractual rights, compared to property rights, were characterised as 'weak rights', and the courts required 'strong illegality' before imposing tort liability.[249]

263. In accordance with the correlationship theory, later decisions suggested that the degree of illegality required depended on the type of infringement.[250] Where

246. Kunihiko Yoshida, 'Saiken Shingai to Fuhoukoui [Third-party Infringement of Obligtion and Torts]', in *Minpono Soten [Issues in Civil Law]*, 187 (Takashi Uchida and Atsushi Omura eds., Yuhikaku, 2007).
247. *Ibid.*, 187. *See also*, Kihara, *supra* n. 72, para. 122.
248. Nakata, *supra* n. 213, 280.
249. *Ibid.*, 281.
250. *Ibid.*, 281.

interference resulted in extinguishing a claim or right (e.g., where an apparent obligee received payment and as a consequence of Article 478 the actual obligee lost its right against the obligor), simple negligence on the part of the apparent obligee was held sufficient to establish a tort.[251]

264. By contrast, where a third-party interference rendered performance impossible and if the obligor is not liable for damages for non-performance, such as where a third party illegally detained a singer who had a contract to sing in a concert, opinions split, with the majority requiring either third-party awareness of the right or an intent to interfere before recognising tort liability, and the minority arguing that mere negligence sufficed.[252]

265. Furthermore, where a third party interfered with a right or claim but the obligor is liable vis-à-vis the obligee for non-performance, legal doctrine provided that the obligee could claim contract damages against the obligor, but may also claim damages against the interfering third party if the interference was intentional and the manner of interference has 'strong illegality'. This applies, for example, to intentional inducement of breach of contracts (e.g., purchasing a property that was already sold to another person).[253]

266. In the latter half of the 1970s, scholars began to attack these types of categorisations as overly rigid, limiting tort liability in a manner that no longer reflected the varied contractual relationships and disputes.[254]

267. Recent studies tend to categorise fact patterns, such as inducement of double sales, unfair competition and diminishment of debtor's asset. Another common, modern example of this inquiry into third-party interference with a contractual right and 'illegality' involves competitors poaching key employees. Courts have imposed tort liability in some cases and declined to do so in others.[255] They narrowly define the scope within which courts will uphold covenants not to compete, but continue to allow original employers to challenge subsequent employment contracts.[256]

268. A commonly cited Tokyo District Court decision states that the employee's right to change employment must be 'fully protected', such that simple solicitation by another prospective employer will not give rise to liability for tortious interference with a contract. However, the court will consider the circumstances in their totality, and where a former employee's acts in soliciting other employees to leave

251. *Ibid.*
252. *Ibid.*, 282.
253. *Ibid.*
254. *Ibid.*, 282.
255. Osaka District Court, 5 Dec. 1989, Hanji 1363-104 (declining to impose liability); Tokyo District Court, 17 Apr. 1990, Haji 1369-112 (imposing liability); Kyoto District Court, 25 Aug. 1993, Hanji 1497-86 (declining to impose liability); Tokyo District Court, 25 Feb. 1991, Hanji 1399-69 (imposing liability).
256. Tokyo District Court, 16 Oct. 1995, Hanji 1566-83.

constitute acts of extreme disloyalty and exceed 'societal bounds of reasonableness', the court will award damages for tortious interference with a contract.[257]

B. Demands to Remove Interference with a Contractual Obligation

269. Remedies for tort liability under the Civil Code are limited to money damages (Articles 722 and 417). Claims for injunctions related to third-party interference with a contractual right are treated separately and case law has limited such injunction to cases involving leases of immovable property.[258] The rationale is that these contractual leases create rights akin to property rights and, hence, are afforded rights similar to those provided under property law.[259] The 2017 Reform codified this case law development (Article 605-4).

270. Under the law prior to the 2017 Reform, courts recognised the right of a lessor of an immovable property who has perfected its right to seek an injunction against a competing lower-ranking lessee or a person illegally possessing the property. Courts have ordered injunctions to cease interference with a contractual right and to return possession of the property.[260] The 2017 Reform codified this case law in Article 605-4.[261]

271. The 2017 Reform also clarified that registration of a lease under Article 605 is a perfection not only vis-à-vis a person who subsequently acquires real rights with respect to the immovable property, such as the new owner, but also vis-à-vis any other third persons, such as competing lessors or persons illegally possessing the property. Perfection can also be achieved by methods provided under the Act on Land and Building Leases (ALBL) (Act No. 90 of 1991)[262]: in the case of land lease, by registration of the building that sits on the land (Article 10(1) ALBL), and in the case of building lease, possession of the building (Article 31(1) ALBL).

257. Tokyo District Court, 2 Feb. 1991, 766 Hanta 247.
258. Nakata, *supra* n. 213, 288. While the Great Court of Cassation recognized a right to sue for an injunction regardless of whether based on a property right or a contractual right, the Supreme Court has rejected claims based solely on contractual rights. *See* cases cited in *Ibid.*, 287.
259. *Ibid.* 289.
260. *Ibid.* 289, 291.
261. Nakata, *supra* n. 61, 454.
262. Nakata, *supra* n. 213, 288.

§2. Transfer of Contractual Rights and Obligations

I. Assignment of Claims (*Saiken Joto*)

A. General Principle

272. Contractual rights and obligations can be transferred to third parties under certain conditions. Three types of such transfer must be distinguished: (1) assignment of claims, (2) assumption of obligations and (3) succession of the contract.

273. In principle, parties are free to assign their claims to third parties by agreement (Article 466(1)). This applies not only to claims arising from a contract but also to claims arising from other grounds such as tort or other statutory grounds. The underlying consideration is that since claims are assets, they should be transferable no differently than other types of assets. The Japanese Civil Code places rules on assignment of claims in the part dealing with obligations in general, rather than in the part on specific contracts, because there can be non-contractual assignment of claims. For example, by testament (will), by subrogation or by order of the court in the context of enforcement of other claims (assignment order [*tenpumeirei*]).

274. This principle also applies to claims embodied in negotiable instruments (e.g., promissory notes, bills of exchange, cheques, bills of lading) although they are subject to special rules. The following paragraph relate only to assignment of 'nominative claims' (*shimeisaiken*), i.e., claims where the right holder is specified and is not embodied in negotiable instruments.

275. In order for the assignee to assert [*taiko suru*] its rights against the obligor, or against other parties, certain steps are to be taken. In the following paragraphs, these steps are referred to as 'perfection'. *See* §2 I C., D., and E. of this chapter below.

276. The principle of assignability of claims is subject to several exceptions. First, assignment does not take effect where 'the nature of the claim' does not permit the assignment (Article 466(1)). These are claims where the performance will change its nature if the obligee is different (e.g., claim to paint a portrait of the obligee), or claims where the identity of the obligee is important. In the latter case, assignment is allowed with the consent of the obligor (e.g., employer's right against the employee (Article 625(1)); lessee's claim against the lessor (Article 612). Second, there are also statutory exceptions: e.g., assignment of rights to payment of alimony or a pension.

B. Non-assignment Clause

277. Prior to the 2017 revision of the Civil Code, non-assignment clauses had 'proprietorial effect' against assignees who knew or were grossly negligent in not knowing about the clause. There has been a major overhaul to this rule in the 2017 Civil Code Reform. The following paragraphs are based on the revised provisions.

278. Even when the parties agree to prohibit or restrict assignment of their claims, claims remain assignable (Article 466(2)). Thus, if a claim that is subject to a non-assignment clause is assigned, the assignor/obligee of a claim may be liable to the obligor (who owed the obligation generating the claim) for breach of the clause, but the assignment takes effect notwithstanding the clause; the assignee becomes the new obligee (able to enforce the claim). Likewise, claims subject to non-assignment clauses can be seized by a creditor of the assignor notwithstanding the non-assignment clause (Article 466-4). It must be noted, however, that there is an important exception to this rule regarding bank accounts (*see* paragraph 282 below).

279. Although non-assignment clauses do not have the effect of stopping assignment, they are not without consequences. First of all, if the assignee/attaching creditor had knowledge or was grossly negligent about not knowing about the non-assignment clause, the obligor has a right to refuse performance and may assert any ground for discharge of its obligation (including performance completed for the assignor) as a defence vis-à-vis the assignee (Articles 466(3) & 466-4(2)). In other words, the obligor has the option of rendering performance to either the assignor or assignee/attaching creditor. Second, provided that the claim assigned is a monetary claim, the obligor may deposit the amount in an official depositary (*kyotakusho*) thereby discharging its debt. In this case, the assignee has a right to refund against the official depositary as the new creditor (Article 466-2).

280. Nonetheless, the interests of the assignee who knew or was grossly negligent about the non-assignment clause are also protected to some extent. First, if the obligor refuses to tender performance to the assignee, the assignee is allowed to demand the obligor to tender performance to the assignor within a specified period of time, and if the obligor does not comply, the obligor loses its right to refuse performance and to raise defence of discharge (Article 466(4)). Without this rule, there would be no party that can demand the obligor to perform.

281. The second protection relates to situations where an insolvency proceeding commences against the assignor. The assignee, provided that it can assert its right against the obligor (*see* paragraphs 283 et seq.), and provided that it is an assignee of an entire monetary claim, may demand the obligor to deposit the entire payment in an official depositary (Article 466-3). This allows the assignee to collect the claim from the official depositary outside the insolvency proceeding.

282. There is an important exception to the rules explained above. If the assigned claim is a claim to deposits in bank accounts, assignment does not take effect (i.e., the assignor remains the creditor) if the assignee had knowledge or was grossly negligent about not knowing the non-assignment clause (Article 466-5(1)). Practically speaking, this results in claims to bank deposits becoming non-assignable since it is widely known that banks universally include non-assignment clauses in their deposit-taking transactions. Note, however, that seizure of claims to deposits in bank accounts is not affected by non-assignment clauses (Article 466-5(2)).

C. Perfection (1): Assertion of the Assignment Against the Obligor

283. Assignment of claims cannot be asserted against the obligor unless certain steps are taken to achieve perfection, i.e. effectiveness against third parties, of the assignment. Perfection vis-à-vis the obligor of the assigned claim is to be distinguished from perfection vis-à-vis other third parties.

284. The Civil Code provides that assignment of claims cannot be asserted against the obligor unless the assignor gives notice of assignment to the obligor, or unless the obligor acknowledges that there was assignment (Article 467(1)). There is no form requirement for such notice or acknowledgement as far as the obligor is concerned, but in order to achieve perfection against other third parties, a certain form is required (*see* paragraph 287). The obligor may raise any defence against the assignee which it had vis-à-vis the assignor prior to receiving the notice or giving acknowledgement (Article 468(1)).

285. Besides the Civil Code, the Act on Special Provisions, etc. of the Civil Code Concerning the Perfection Requirements for the Assignment of Movables and Claims (Act No. 104 of 1998) (the 'PRAMC') provides an alternative measure to achieve perfection of assignment of monetary claims. This is explained in Chapter 4, §2.(I)(E) below.

286. Even if perfection is achieved, the obligor is allowed to set-off its obligations with (i) its claims against the assignor which it acquired before receiving the notice or making acknowledgement; (ii) its claims against the assignor arising from grounds that existed before the notice or acknowledgement; or (iii) its claims against the assignor arising from the same contract that gave rise to the assigned claim (Article 469).

D. Perfection (2): Assertion of Assignment Against Third Parties Other Than the Obligor

287. In order to assert the assignment of claims against third parties other than the obligor, such as competing assignees or attaching creditors, the Civil Code requires that notice of assignment to or acknowledgement of assignment by the obligor be made using an instrument bearing a 'fixed date' (*kakuteihizuke*) (Article 467(2)). Article 5 of the 'Act for Enforcement of the Civil Code' (Act No. 11 of 1898) lists six types of instruments that can be an instrument bearing a fixed date. Among those listed, content-certified postal mail (*naiyoshomei yubin*) and notarised instruments (*koseishosho*) are most commonly used in assignment of claims. This method of achieving perfection was designed so that the obligor may serve as an 'information centre' who can answer to inquiries from potential assignees, creditors or other third parties about the identity of the obligee.

288. PRAMC provides an alternative method of achieving third-party effectiveness against third parties (discussed next in Chapter 4, §2.(I)(E)).

E. Perfection under PRAMC

289. Besides the Civil Code, the PRAMC provides an alternative measure of achieving perfection of monetary claims.[263] The purpose of this special legislation is to facilitate receivables financing. Thus, it applies only to assignment of monetary claims (receivables). Another limitation to the scope of PRAMC is that it applies only if the assignor is a registered juridical person, such as a corporation. The latter limitation is due to concern about the difficulty of identifying a natural person as the assignor in the registration. (There is no universal personal identification number system in Japan.)

290. Under the PRAMC, if the assignor has registered such assignment in a 'claim assignment registration file' (*saikenjoto toki fairu*) maintained by the designated Legal Affairs Bureau,[264] it is deemed that perfection by notice of assignment in accordance with Article 447 of the Civil Code vis-à-vis third parties other than the obligor is achieved (Article 4(1) PRAMC). Thus, third-party effectiveness against third parties other than the obligor is achieved by such registration.

291. With respect to perfection against the obligor, if the assignor or the assignee notifies the obligor about the assignment by delivering a 'certificate of registered matters' (*tokijiko shomeisho*) related to the assignment issued by the relevant Legal Affairs Bureau, it is deemed that perfection by notice of assignment in accordance with Article 447 of the Civil Code vis-à-vis the obligor is achieved (Article 4(2) PRAMC). Thus, perfection vis-à-vis the obligor is achieved by notification using the certificate of registered matters. This makes possible 'silent assignments', in which the assignor is not required to disclose the assignment to the obligor until the assignee intends to collect from the obligor.

F. Priority

292. If there are competing assignees or other third parties other than the obligor who have achieved perfection, priority among them are determined according to:

---

263. *See* generally, O. Morita, 'Timid Cousin in the Far East: The Security Right Registration in Japan and the UCC Filing', 8 *U.Tokyo J. L & Pol.* 20 (2011).

264. These Bureaus are part of the Ministry of Justice. Only the Tokyo District Legal Affairs Bureau is currently designated. Registration and searches can be done online.

(i) the time the notice of assignment 'reaches' the obligor provided that a fixed date is attached to the notice;
(ii) the 'fixed date' attached to obligor's acknowledgement of the assignment; or
(iii) the 'date and time' of the registrations under PRAMC, whichever is the earlier.

293. With respect to perfection by notice of assignment, since the fixed date on the instrument is not the time the instrument actually reaches the obligee, the fixed date itself is irrelevant in determining priority; the fixed dates are simply requirements for the notice to be effective as a means for achieving perfection[265]. The rationale is that the controlling time should be the time the obligor becomes aware of the assignment because the obligor is expected to function as an 'information centre' for prospective assignees.

294. If more than one notice reaches the obligor simultaneously, the obligor may treat any of the assignments to which the notice relates as the sole assignment.[266] The rationale is that the obligor should not be burdened with the responsibility of determining priority. Whether the assignee who received performance from the obligor is obligated to share the performance with other assignees is not clearly settled by the Civil Code or by case law. However, if the obligor has deposited its performance in an official depositary, thereby being discharged from its obligation (Article 494), the Supreme Court has held that each assignee with equal priority may demand restitution from the public depositary only in an amount proportional to the amount its claim has against the total amount of claims of the competing third parties.[267]

295. If the order in which the notices reached the obligor is unknown, such notices are treated as if they have arrived simultaneously.[268]

G. Assignment of Future Claims

296. Assignment of future claims is also allowed (Article 466-6). However, the Supreme Court has held in 1999 that there may be situations where assignment of future claims are considered to be against public policy and thus void (Article 90).[269] They are cases when assignment of future claims imposes undue restrictions on the business activities of the assignor, and when an assignment of all future claims gives excessive security interest to the assignee who is a creditor against the assignor.

265. Supreme Court, 7 Mar. 1974, Minshu 29-2-174.
266. Supreme Court, 11 Jan. 1980, Minshu 34-1-42.
267. Supreme Court, 30 Mar. 1993, Minshu 47-4-3334.
268. *Ibid.*
269. Supreme Court, 29 Jan. 1999, Minshu 53-1-151.

297. The Supreme Court has also held that priority of assignment of future claims is determined according to the general rule explained in Chapter 4, §2.(II)(F).[270] This means that the date the future claim arises is irrelevant in determining priority.

H. Pledge of Claims

298. Pledge of claims is treated similarly to assignment of claims as the pledgee has a right to directly collect from the obligor to the extent of the amount of its credit against the pledgor secured by the pledge (Article 367). The provision of the Civil Code on perfection of assignment of claims, i.e., Article 467 also applies to perfection of pledge of claims (Article 364). Furthermore, the PRAMC allows registration of pledge of monetary claims where the pledgor is a registered juridical person, and its provisions on perfection of assignment of claims by registration apply *mutatis mutandis* to pledge of claims (Article 14 PRAMC). *See also* Part II, Chapter 9 below.

II. Assumption of Obligations (*Saimu Hikiuke)*

A. General Principle

299. By contract, a third party may assume an obligation owed by an obligor, thereby becoming a new obligor against the obligee. Such contracts are used in situations when, for example, a family member agrees to pay the debt of another family member, or when a buyer of an immovable asset encumbered with a hypothec agrees to pay the secured debt of the seller. Depending on whether the original obligor is released from its obligation or not, assumption of obligations can be either 'cumulative assumption of obligation' (*heizonteki saimuhikiuke*) in which case the original obligor also remains as obligor and become joint and severally liable against the obligee (Article 470(1)) or 'dischargeable assumption of obligation' (*mensekiteki saimuhikiuke*, befreienden Schuldübernahme) in which case the original obligor is discharged from its obligation and the new obligor becomes the sole obligor (Article 472(1)).

300. Prior to the 2017 Civil Code Reform, there was no provision on assumption of obligations. The rules were developed by case law, which was incorporated into the Code by the 2017 reform.

270. Supreme Court, 22 Nov. 2001, Minshu 55-6-1056.

B. Cumulative Assumption of Obligation

301. Cumulative assumption of obligation can be made by agreement between the obligee and the party assuming the obligation (Article 470(2)). Cumulative assumption of obligation can also be made by agreement between the obligor and the assuming party. In the latter case, the provisions on third-party beneficiaries apply (Article 470(4)), and the assumption takes effect only if the obligee consents to the assumption (Article 470(3)). The assuming party may rely on the defences that were available to the obligor at the time the assumption took effect (Article 471(1)).

302. If the obligor has a right to rescind or terminate the contract vis-à-vis the obligee, the assuming party may not rescind or terminate the contract because it is not party to the contract, but may refuse performance of the obligation to the extent the obligor will be discharged by the exercise of the rescission or termination right (Article 471(2)). If the assumption was made by an agreement between the obligor and the assuming party, the assuming party may resort to any defences it has against the obligor vis-à-vis the obligee who is a third-party beneficiary (Article 539).

C. Dischargeable Assumption of Obligation

303. Dischargeable assumption of obligation may be made by agreement between the obligee and the party assuming the obligation. The discharge takes effect when the obligee notifies the obligor of the assumption of obligation (Article 472(2)). Dischargeable assumption of obligation can also be made by agreement between the obligor and the assuming party, provided that the obligee consents (Article 472(3)). Unlike cumulative assumptions of obligations, this is not a contract for the benefit of third parties.

304. The assuming party may resort to the defences that were available to the obligor at the time the assumption took effect (Article 472-2(1)). If the obligor had a right to rescind or terminate the contract vis-à-vis the obligee, the assuming party may refuse performance of the obligation to the extent the obligor will be discharged by the exercise of the rescission or termination right (Article 472-2(2)). If the assumption was made by agreement between the obligor and the assuming party, the assuming party may not resort to any defences it has against the obligor vis-à-vis the obligee.

305. In the case of dischargeable assumption of obligation, the assuming party who performed the obligation vis-a-vis the obligee does not have a right of recourse against the original obligor, unless otherwise agreed (Article 472-3).

306. If the obligee had a security right to secure the obligation of the original obligor, which was discharged, it may transfer the security right to secure the obligation assumed, subject to consent of the grantor of the security right. However, such consent is not necessary if the assuming party is the grantor (Article 473-4).

III. Transfer of Contract (Transfer of Contractual Position)

307. Whereas assignment of claims or assumption of obligations deals with change of the party to individual claims or obligations, transfer of contract deals with change of party to the contract from which such claims or obligations arise. By transfer of contract, the transferor withdraws from the contract, and the contract continues between the transferee and the other party. In practice, such transfer can be seen in, for example, lease contracts, franchise contracts and license contracts.

308. Prior to the 2017 Civil Code Reform, there was no provision on transfer of contracts. The rules were developed by case law, which was incorporated into the Code by the 2017 reform.

309. According to the revised Civil Code, contracts may be transferred by agreement between one party to a contract who transfers the contract and the transferee. In principle, transfer of a contract does not take effect unless the other party who remains in the contract consents to the transfer (Article 539-2). For example, a franchisee intending to transfer its contract to a third person must obtain consent from the franchisor.

310. However, there are special rules developed for transfer of lease of immovables (Articles 605-2 and 605-3), as discussed in paragraph 716 below.

§3. Subcontract and Assumption of Performance (Erfüllungsgehilfen)

311. In principle, a party to a contract may seek assistance of a third party in performing its contractual obligation or may delegate performance of its contractual obligation to a third party. In other words, the principle is that the obligor is not obligated to perform by itself. For example, a contractor B under a construction contract may enter into a subcontract with an independent subcontractor C, in order to wholly or partially fulfil its obligation under a construction contract with A. The term 'subcontract' (*shitauke*) is usually used in the context of construction contracts.[271] The broader concept of assistance or delegation of performance under Japanese law is usually discussed in terms of engagement of 'person assisting performance' (*rikohojosha*). No contractual relationship arises between A and C, and therefore, no direct contractual action is possible between A and C.

312. However, engaging third parties to perform may be prohibited or restricted by law or by the terms or nature of the contract. For example, employees are prohibited from delegating performance in labour contracts (Article 625(2)). Delegation of performance by mandataries and depositaries in mandates and deposits is allowed only when there is consent of the mandator or depositor, or when there is

271. Under the 'Act against Delay in Payment of Subcontract Proceeds, Etc. to Subcontractors' (Act No. 120 of Jun. 1, 1956), 'subcontract' means manufacturing contracts and repair contracts whether they are concluded to perform one party's contractual obligation owed to a third party.

unavoidable reason to do so (Articles 644-2 and 658). Performance cannot be delegated also when the nature of the obligation requires performance by the obligor itself (e.g., an obligation to for someone to make a painting).

313. Sublease is another form of subcontract where the lessee engages a third party (sub-lessee) to use or to receive profits from the object of lease. It is necessary to obtain consent of the lessor to enter into a sublease (Article 612(1)). When a sublease is duly concluded, the Civil Code provides that the lessor has a direct right against the sub-lessee up to the extent of the lessee's obligation (Article 613(1)), as discussed in paragraphs 373 and 739.

314. The obligor who engaged a third party to perform is liable for non-performance resulting from the third party's action or non-action if that results in non-performance of its own obligation. Prior to the 2017 Civil Code Reform, it was generally understood that the obligor cannot be exempt from damages liability when the non-performance was caused by the fault of the third party. The rule on exemption of damages liability, however, was revised. Under the revised Code, an obligor is exempt from damages liability only when it establishes that the non-performance was not attributable to the obligor, in light of the contract and the generally accepted senses of trade (Article 415(1)). Although it is not clear how this revised provision will be interpreted in practice, it is clear that the focus has shifted from 'fault' of the third party to the interpretation of risks the obligor has assumed in the contract.

315. Since there is no contractual relationship between the obligee and the third party who was engaged to perform, the obligee cannot make any direct contractual claim against that third party. However, it is possible for the obligee to directly seek tort liability of that third party. One question that arises in this context is whether the assisting person may rely on exemption or limitation of liability clauses in the contract between the obligee and the obligor. There is little support in case law that allows such reliance.

316. Special rules regarding contracts for international carriage by sea and by air allow employees of the obligor to rely on the exemption or limitation of liability clauses in the contract for carriage of goods (Article 20-2(2), Act on International Carriage of Goods by Sea (Act No. 172 of 1957); Article 30, Convention for the Unification of Certain Rules for International Carriage by Air (Montreal Convention)).[272] In the Commercial Code Reform of 2018, a similar rule was expanded to non-international carriage of goods by sea (Article 588, Revised Commercial Code). However, subcontractors do not enjoy the benefit of these special rules.

317. A related question is whether a subcontractor (C) in a building contract is bound by a contract clause between the client (A) and the contractor (B) regarding the ownership of the building built under the contract. Under Japanese law, by

272. *See also*, Okino, *supra* n. 215, 274.

default, the ownership of the building belongs to the party who supplies the substantial part of the materials who in most cases is the contractor.[273] *See* Part II, Chapter 5, §3, III. That ownership can be transferred from the contractor to the owner by agreement between them.[274] One Supreme Court case faced the issue of whether a subcontractor (C), who has supplied the substantial part of the materials and partly built the building, can claim ownership of the partly built building when there was a contractual clause in the building contract between the owner (A) and the contractor (B) stipulating that the ownership belongs to A if the building contract is cancelled. In that case, the building contract was cancelled before the building was completed due to B's insolvency. The Supreme Court held that C, even if he has not been paid by B, is not in a position vis-à-vis A to claim a right different than B because the purpose of the subcontract was to assist in performing the obligation of B. The scope of this ruling is debated, but this court held that the C is bound by the contractual clause between A and B.[275]

§4. Oblique Action, Paulian Action and Direct Action

I. Creditor Subrogation Rights

318. The Civil Code provides that a creditor (the 'obligee') in order to preserve a claim may exercise non-personal rights vested in a debtor (the 'obligor') if certain requirements are met (Article 423 (1)). In other words, the Civil Code recognises subrogation of claims and allows a creditor to step in the shoes of the debtor where the debtor is unable or unwilling to exercise the right.[276] This doctrine goes beyond simple recognition of subrogation rights pursuant to contract. The code contemplates a creditor pursuing rights not subrogated by contract and doing so either unilaterally or by filing suit against a third-party debtor.

319. As a general principle, any right held by the debtor may be subject to subrogation. This includes not just contractual obligations but also rights relating to real property, rights to rescind or void transactions, rights of offset and rights to demand registration of specified property.[277] Typical examples include a creditor asserting the credit rights of a debtor against a third-party debtor in order to avoid the running of the extinctive prescription period,[278] or a creditor asserting the running of a extinctive prescription period against a third-party creditor.[279] A party injured in an automobile accident may similarly assert a claim against the insurance company holding the tortfeasor's supplemental insurance policy in order to preserve a claim

273. Great Court of Cassation, 22 Jun. 1904, Minroku 10-861 and numerous other judgments.
274. Great Court of Cassation, 13 Dec. 1916, Minroku 22-2417; Supreme Court, 5 Mar. 1971, Hanji 628.
275. Supreme Court, 10 Oct. 1993, Minshu 47-8-5061.
276. Supreme Court, 14 Dec. 1953, Minshu 7-12-1386.
277. Great Court of Cassation, 8 Feb. 1919, Minroku 25-75; Great Court of Cassation, 30 May 1933, Minshu 12-1381.
278. Great Court of Cassation, 15 Mar. 1940, Minshu 19-586.
279. Supreme Court, 26 Sep. 1968, Minshu 22-9-2002.

for damages.[280] Subrogation rights are, in principle and subject to the exceptions discussed below, exercised for the benefit of all creditors.

320. A debtor has a basic right to dispose of its rights or assets as it sees fit, and, in order to subrogate that right, courts have generally required: (i) a monetary right or obligation held by the creditor and (ii) the 'need to preserve' such a monetary right because of the debtor's insolvency,[281] although those requirements have been eliminated in some circumstances. *See infra* D. Insolvency is defined here as the debtor lacking sufficient financial resources to meet the debt held by the creditor. The creditor can subrogate and assert the rights of a debtor only to the extent of the creditor's debt it holds vis-à-vis the debtor, since it is enough to allow the creditor to exercise its subrogation rights in order to preserve its own rights (Article 423-2).[282]

321. Having discussed the general requirements, the legal positions of a creditor, debtor and third party where a creditor exercises its subrogation rights will be each addressed next in turn.

A. *Creditors' Rights*

322. With regard to the rights held by the creditor, the creditor must possess a valid obligation[283], but it need not vest before the right to subrogation arises.[284] It is sufficient if the obligation exists at the point at which the debtor refuses to exercise a right against a third-party debtor.[285]

323. The creditor may not exercise a subrogated right prior to the third-party debtor's time of performance. Exceptionally, however, creditors are allowed to take, without court approval and in advance of the time specified for performance, actions that are limited to preservation of rights (Article. 423(2) proviso). Examples include registration of property rights, filing notice as a creditor following the third-party debtor's bankruptcy and other acts to maintain the status quo of the debtor's assets.[286]

---

280. Supreme Court, 29 Nov. 1974, Minshu 28-8-1670. The Supreme Court held in this case that the creditor must prove insolvency in order to exercise its subrogation rights in a direct suit against the insurance company. *Id.* 1976 revisions to standard automobile insurance contracts now allow an injured party to bring suit directly against the tortfeasor's insurance company. Nakata, *supra* n. 213, 228.
281. *Ibid.,* 209.
282. This provision is a codification of prior case law: Supreme Court, 24 Jun. 1969, Minshu 23-7-1079; Supreme Court, 14 Jun. 1958, Minshu 12-9-1449.
283. The obligation that the creditor has to the debtor must be executable under the proceeding of compulsory execution (Art. 423 (3)). Thus, for example, the creditor of a mere natural obligation, mentioned above at para. 94, may not subrogate the debtor's rights.
284. Supreme Court, 15 Jul. 1958, Shinbun 111-9.
285. Nakata, *supra* n. 213, 210.
286. Nakata, *supra* n. 213, 211.

324. In any case, where a creditor exercises a subrogation right and acts to enforce an obligation owed by a third-party debtor, the creditor must act with due care and assumes 'a duty to administer the mandated business with the care of a good manager [acting] in compliance with the main purport of the mandate'.[287]

B. Debtor's Rights Subject to Creditor Subrogation Rights

325. Creditors may not exercise undetermined rights personal to the debtor (Article 423(1) proviso). A debtor's offer or acceptance of a contract may not be completed by subrogation, unless the creditor is manifesting intent as a subrogated beneficiary to a contract for the benefit of a third party.[288]

326. A creditor may not exercise claims to undetermined rights to property that may arise out of a divorce proceeding,[289] or a beneficiary's undetermined rights to a division of the deceased's assets.[290] Creditors may not subrogate rights to claims for solatium, or pain and suffering, unless the parties have objectively determined the amount of the damages.[291] Once the assignment of property rights is final these claims may be subject to subrogation.[292]

327. Creditor subrogation rights do not preclude the debtor from claiming his or her own rights (Article 423-5). Such a debtor's claim will be denied only after those rights are officially seized as a part of the proceeding of compulsory execution (Article 143, Civil Execution Act). A creditor exercising subrogated rights is not the same as the seizure of the rights, by which the debtor is prohibited from disposing of his or her rights.

328. Independently of creditors exercising its subrogation rights, the debtor is still allowed to seek payment from the third-party debtor either directly or by filing suit against the third-party debtor. Thus, each of the competing creditors can subrogate the debtor's rights even after one of them subrogates the rights, until those rights extinguish.

329. Courts have held that judgments obtained by a creditor in a subrogation action bind the debtor, since such a creditor can be considered as the third person under Article 115 (1) (ii) of the Code of Civil Procedure, who is allowed to serve lawfully as a litigant in the place of the debtor without her consent. This is why Article 432-6 of the Civil Code requires the creditor to convey notice of the litigation to the debtor (Article 53, Code of Civil Procedure). Then, the debtor can be fairly guaranteed the opportunity to participate in the creditor's judicial proceedings

287. Great Court of Cassation, 15 Mar. 1940, Minshu 19-586.
288. Great Court of Cassation, 30 Sep. 1941, Minshu 20-1233.
289. Supreme Court, 14 Dec. 1953, Minshu 7-1/2-1386.
290. Supreme Court, 22 Nov. 2001, Minshu 55-6-1033.
291. Supreme Court, 6 Oct. 1983, Minshu 37-8-1041.
292. Supreme Court, 11 Aug. 1980, Minshu 34-4-628.

against the third-party debtor as a co-litigant (Article 52, Code of Civil Procedure) or a supporting intervener (Article 43, Code of Civil Procedure) for the third-party debtor in order to make arguments on her own rights, or as an independent party (Article 47, Code of Civil Procedure) in order to deny the creditor's rights to him or her so as to exercise his or her own rights against the third-party debtor.

C. *Third-Party's Defence*

330. The third-party debtor may assert any defences against the claims of the creditor subrogating the debtor's rights that the third party has vis-à-vis the debtor (Article 423-4). If, for example, the third party has a basis to rescind the contract with the debtor because of the debtor's fraud, it can assert that claim vis-à-vis the creditor exercising the debtor's rights on the contract.[293]

D. *Diversion of Subrogation Rights*

331. The courts have recognised an exception to the basic principle that subrogation is limited to monetary rights held by the creditor and debtor by holding that, in certain instances, rights involving real property may be subrogated. When doing so, they have routinely eliminated the requirement that the debtor be insolvent in order for the creditor to act.[294]

332. Most often these claims involve registration of property, where a debtor purchases property from a third-party debtor then sells it to the creditor, without demanding transfer of the property's registration from the initial owner. In this case, the creditor may demand the third-party debtor transfer property registration to the debtor's name (Article 423-7).[295] Article 423-7 is codified as a typical case of the so-called 'diversion' of Article 423, where the requirement of insolvency exceptionally is not needed.

333. The diversion of Article 423 could also arise where a party leases land, which is then illegally occupied by a third party. While the tenant does not have a direct real property claim against the squatter to vacate the property, the tenant, in order to preserve the value of its lease in the property, may – without proof of insolvency on the part of the owner – exercise a subrogated right to possess the property and seek an injunction evicting the squatter.[296] Article 423-7 does not comprise all cases of diversion.

---

293. Great Court of Cassation, 22 Dec. 1943, Minshu 22-1263.
294. Article 59(vii) of the Real Property Registration Act (Act No. 123 of 2004) permits a creditor to apply for the transfer of a property's registration to the name of a debtor without inquiry into the debtor's financial circumstances.
295. Great Court of Cassation, 6 Jul. 1910, Minroku 16-537.
296. Great Court of Cassation, 16 Dec. 1929, Minshu 8-944; Supreme Court, 24 Sep. 1954, Minshu 8-9-1658.

334. Recent decisions have extended subrogation rights to hypothec holders as well. Courts initially held that a hypothec holder had no right to demand a party illegally occupying the encumbered property to vacate it. They found the hypothec to be no more than a contractual obligation, a non-possessory collateralised interest.[297] More recent decisions have changed that holding finding that where the value of the hypothec and rights to repayment are compromised, the hypothec holder can, in order to preserve the value of the asset, exercise the subrogated rights of the landowner to seek an injunction requiring eviction.[298]

E. The Process of Subrogation

335. Subrogation rights may be exercised through the courts or independently by unilateral action of a creditor.[299] A creditor providing notice directly to a third-party debtor in order to toll an extinctive prescription period is an example of the latter. With the former, the creditor files suit as plaintiff naming a third-party debtor as a defendant in the action.[300] The initial debtor need not be made a party to the action.

336. Where the debtor possess monetary rights or rights to goods that can be delivered, the creditor, in place of the initial debtor, may demand the third-party debtor to transfer the cash or goods directly to the creditor, just in case the initial debtor refuses to receive them (Article 423-3)[301], although under Article 423-5, the third-party debtor can choose to transfer them not to the creditor but to the debtor. When the third-party debtor, as requested, transfers the cash or goods to the creditor, the debtor's rights to the third-party debtor are extinguished.

337. However, where the subrogated right involves real property registration, the creditor is limited in its demand to transfer the registration of the real property to the debtor, since the debtor's refusal can never happen.[302]

338. Where the creditor exercises subrogated rights and a third-party debtor transfers possession of assets other than cash to the creditor, the creditor must have the property transferred to the debtor, and then seek to execute a judgment against the debtor. As a general rule, actions by an unsecured creditor to preserve a debtor's assets redound to the benefit of all creditors. When executing a judgment held by

297. Supreme Court, 22 Mar. 1991, Minhsu 45-3-268.
298. Supreme Court, 24 Nov. 1999 Minshu 53-8-1899.
299. Nakata, *supra* n. 213, 215.
300. *Ibid.* 215; Great Court of Cassation, 15 Mar. 1940, Minshu 19-586.
301. Article 423-3 is a codification of prior case law: Great Court of Cassation, 21 Jun. 1932; Great Court of Cassation, 12 Mar. 1935; Supreme Court, 24 Sep. 1954, Minshu 8-9-1658.
302. Nakata, *supra* n. 213, 215.

several creditors, the creditor who has acted to preserve an asset is, except for costs,[303] given no priority in repayment, but repaid the same percentage on the claim as other creditors.[304]

339. However, where the asset transferred is cash, the creditor may offset its own debt to return to the debtor the cash which it has received against its own right to the debtor. In doing so, the creditor can achieve priority repayment of its unsecured debt not otherwise recognised under Japan's system for executing judgments, unless under Article 423-5 the third-party debtor has made repayment to the debtor. Aiming at this priority repayment, the creditor exercises its subrogation rights under Article 423 to obtain direct payment of a debt without having to obtain and enforce a separate judgment against the debtor. While the drafters of the Civil Code intended Article 423 to be used by creditors to 'preserve' assets, i.e., to prevent the dissolution of the assets of insolvent debtors, it has come to be used in fact as a means for creditors to gain preferential repayment of claims.[305]

II. Creditors' Rights to Rescind Fraudulent Acts of the Debtor

340. Article 424 permits a creditor to file suit to set aside fraudulent acts that a debtor completes knowing that the act will prejudice the rights of the creditor, where the other party to the act also knows that the act will prejudice the rights of the creditor. Common examples of such fraudulent acts include gifts of property made by insolvent debtors and sale for less-than-adequate value. The debtor's unilateral acts can be also rescinded as fraudulent, such as waiver of someone's debt owed to it.

341. Prejudice to the rights of the creditor requires insolvency of the debtor. Insolvency here occurs if the debtor completes an act that prevents it from satisfying a debt owed to the creditor, increases the debtor's amount of insolvency or compromises collateral used to secure a debt that cannot otherwise be paid.[306]

342. Insolvency both at the point of the act and at the point the court completes its factual inquiry into the act is required. Courts will not set aside an act as fraudulent if the debtor becomes solvent prior to completion of its factual investigation.[307]

343. This requirement of the debtor's insolvency presupposes that the creditor's right to the debtor needs to have monetary rights to the debtor[308]. Non-monetary

303. A creditor may demand payment of costs from the debtor associated with executing subrogated rights and obtaining performance by a third-party debtor. In doing so, these costs can be treated as costs giving rise to a common benefit and given priority repayment rights (Art. 307(1)).
304. Nakata, *supra* n. 213, 206.
305. Nakata, *supra* n. 213, 206.
306. *Ibid.*, 245.
307. Great Court of Cassation, 13 Nov. 1926, Minshu 5-798.
308. As with the creditor's subrogation rights, the creditor's (monetary) right to the debtor must be executable under compulsory execution proceedings (Art. 424(3)).

rights of the creditor would not become more likely to be satisfied even if the Article 424 prevents the assets of the debtor from being diminished. There is no need for the creditor to preserve its non-monetary right to the debtor by applying Article 424.

344. In sum, the requirements for the application of Article 424, just as for that of Article 423, are (i) a monetary right held by the creditor to the debtor and (ii) the 'need to preserve' such rights because of the debtor's insolvency.

345. As above, the legal positions of the creditor, the debtor and third parties, here the other parties to the acts, will each next be addressed in turn.

A. Creditors' Rights

346. For the creditor to rescind a fraudulent act of the debtor, the creditor's right to the debtor needs to be based on a cause that has occurred prior to the act in question (Article 423 (2))[309], though the time for performance need not have passed.[310] If the creditor has a right based on a cause that occurs after the act, then the creditor only relies on the already diminished assets of the debtor, thus without involving any prejudice to the creditor caused by the act.

347. As explained above, the creditor's right needs to be monetary one, but courts have considered when the creditor must have a monetary right to the debtor. Suppose that the same real property is sold to two buyers. The Supreme Court allowed the first buyer, as the creditor, to rescind the second sale made by the seller who, as the debtor, is obliged to transfer the property right to the first buyer, even if the first buyer, against the seller, does not have yet a right to demand damages in lieu of performance, but has only the right to specific performance at the time of the second sales.[311] In fact, the first buyer can have a right to demand such damages against the seller only when the real property is later registered in the name of the second buyer, since the seller's obligation becomes impossible to perform by such registration. According to the Court, the first buyer's (the creditor's) right to the seller (the debtor) is a non-monetary right (the right to specific performance) at the time of the fraudulent act (the second sales), but it could be considered as a potential monetary right, since in the end it will change into a monetary right (the right to demand damages). For a fraudulent act of the debtor to be rescinded, the creditor must have such a right to the debtor as will become a monetary right at the time of rescission.

309. The right to rescind fraudulent acts can generally be extended only to the corpus of property that was the subject of a creditor's claim arising prior to the fraudulent transfer, but the claims for late payment that continue to accrue after the fraudulent acts are included.
310. Great Court of Cassation, 27 Dec. 1920, Minroku 26-2096.
311. Supreme Court, 21 Feb. 1958, Minshu 12-2-341.

B. Debtors' Fraudulent Acts Subject to Creditors' Right for Rescission

348. As mentioned above, the debtors' acts of the debtor to be rescinded under Article 424 need to be fraudulent, whereby the total assets of the debtor are diminished and thus creditor's right to them is prejudiced, such as gift or sale for less-than-adequate property value made by the debtor.

349. Sales of property for adequate value cannot be rescinded, because the assets of the debtor are not diminished due to adequate cash paid in exchange for the property. However, such sales may be rescinded as fraudulent acts under the following three conditions: (i) the debtor's sale is such as would make it likely for the debtor to hide or donate to someone the cash or other property exchanged for the sold real property because of the change in the kind of property caused, (ii) the debtor, at the time of the act, intended to hide or donate to someone the cash or other property and (iii) the other party to the sales knew of such debtor's intention at the time of the act (Article 424-2).

350. Repayment by the debtor to only the specific creditor among competing creditors is the same as sales of debtor's property for adequate cash in the sense that the total assets of the debtor is not thereby changed on a balance sheet. Therefore, as a general principle, repayment does not constitute a fraudulent act, unless it is made by the debtor in continuous insolvency in her conspiracy with the specific creditor with intent to prejudice the rights of other creditors (Article 424-3(1)).[312] If repayment is not in the kind of the debtor's obligation, such as repayment before due date or payment in substitute, the repayment can also be rescinded as fraudulent if it was conducted within thirty days before the debtor became in continuous insolvency (Article 424-3(2)).

351. An offer of debtor's collateral to specific creditor conferring prioritised rights of repayment to the detriment of other creditors is regulated in the same way as a repayment of the debtor's debt (Article 424-3), since the assets of the debtor is not diminished on the balance sheet but is also distributed in favour of the specific creditor.

352. Where the value of payment in substitute exceeds the amount of the debtor's original debt, the excessive part of the payment can be rescinded in accordance with Article 424, regardless of conditions mentioned above for rescission in case of repayment (Article 424-4).

353. In fact, these conditions discussed here are almost all parallel to the requirements for the bankruptcy trustee to avoid acts prejudicial to bankruptcy creditors (Articles 160–162, Bankruptcy Act), although conspiracy is not necessary in repayment cases under the Bankruptcy Act.[313]

312. Supreme Court, 26 Sep. 1958, Minshu 12-13-3022.

313. Before the 2017 Reform, the relationship between the Civil Code sections dealing with fraudulent acts and bankruptcy has been a concern. The MOJ Advisory Committee has proposed revisions to

354. Creditors' rights to challenge acts that dissipate the debtor's assets are limited to acts that have as their purpose the exchange of property rights (Article 424(2), Civil Code). As a result, such acts as marriage, adoption and divorce, which may impact property rights, are not subject to rescission.[314]

355. However, where a divorcing spouse agrees to make distribution of property to the other spouse in a divorce, the court may rescind any excess portion of distribution if it transfers an unreasonably large portion of property, in light of the circumstances. [315] It is no longer distribution of property in a divorce, but rather mere disposition of property for the divorcing spouse in order to avoid the creditor's execution of that spouse's debt.

356. Inheritance presents a mixed picture. An heir's renunciation of an inheritance is not subject to challenge as a fraudulent transfer, because that act does not affirmatively dissipate assets, though, in effect, it does put assets beyond the reach of creditors.[316] In contrast, an agreed division by co-hires is construed as a legal act seeking to establish property rights and, as such, is subject to challenge.[317] As with divorce, courts will review an agreement by the parties dividing assets.

C. Third-Party Beneficiary's Protection Against Rescission

357. The Civil Code expressly requires the party to the act of the debtor to know that the act would prejudice the rights of the creditor for the courts to rescind it (Articles 424(1) proviso and 424-5). For example, the debtor's sales of property for less-than-adequate value can be rescinded if the recipient of such sales, as well as the debtor, knew that the sales were fraudulent (Article 424(1)), because the knowledgeable recipient does not need to be protected.

358. The same holds true for any successor in interest to the act (Article 424-5). If the recipient of fraudulent sales by the debtor transfers the property to the successor, then both the recipient and the successor, together with the debtor, are all required to have known that the sales between them were fraudulent (Article 424-5(i)). And if the successor transfers further to another successor, then all successors need to have known so (Article 424-5(ii)). In each of these cases, the creditor may exercise the right to rescind the fraudulent act made by the debtor against the recipient or the successors.

359. The Civil Code provides third-party beneficiaries with remedies in the case the fraudulent act of the debtor is rescinded. First, Article 425-2 allows the recipient

---

the Civil Code seeking, in part, to harmonize its requirements for setting aside fraudulent acts with the rights established under Japan's new Bankruptcy Act to void acts prejudicial to bankruptcy creditors. MOJ, *supra* n. 104, 161.

314. Nakata, *supra* n. 213, 243.
315. Supreme Court, 9 Mar. 2000.
316. Supreme Court, 20 Sep. 1974, Minshu 28-6-1202.
317. Supreme Court, 11 Jun. 1999, Minshu 53-5-898.

of the fraudulent transfer to demand restitution of the cash paid or other property exchanged for the property against the debtor. However, if restitution of the property is difficult, the creditor may demand restitution in cash for its value, against the debtor.

360. Second, where the debtor's repayment of debt to only the specific creditor among competing creditors is rescinded, Article 425-3 allows the extinguished debt to revive for the creditor receiving such repayment, when that creditor returns money for repayment to the debtor.

361. Third, the successor is allowed by Article 425-4 to exercise against the debtor the same remedy rights as would be given to the recipient of fraudulent transfer under Article 425-2 or to the specific creditor receiving repayment of the debtor under the Article 425-3. However, there are limits up to the amount of the price the successor paid in order to acquire the property in the former case, or of the amount of the debt owed to the successor was satisfied in the latter case.

D. *The Process of Rescission*

362. In each case the creditor may only exercise her right to rescission by filing suit. The claim(s) must be brought by the creditor in her own name, and cannot be asserted as a defence to another action.[318]

363. Case law prior to the 2017 Reform held that creditors need not name the debtor in a suit seeking rescission of the contract and return of the property in question from the third-party beneficiary.[319] The action was characterised as a combined action to recognise a basis for rescinding a legal act and demand return of wrongfully obtained property. The action itself did not legally affect the debtor insofar as the debtor was not a party to the action and not bound by it. This rule that the creditor need not name the debtor in the suit seeking rescission of the contract was codified in the 2017 Reform (Article 424-7(1)). However, it is now provided that a judgment allowing rescission affects the debtor (Article 425), and that the creditor must give the debtor notice of suit (Article 424-7(2)).

364. The result of a successful action to rescind a fraudulent act is, in principle, the return of the property to the debtor. The right of the creditor to rescission, however, can be coupled with its claim in lieu for compensation of the value of the property (*kagaku baisho*) against the debtor, the recipient or the successors of the property if the return of the property is difficult to perform (Article 424-6). For example, where the property of the creditor was fraudulently transferred to the recipient and later further to the successor, the creditor, by exercising the right to

318. Supreme Court, 12 Jun. 1964, Minshu 18-5-764.
319. Nakata, *supra* n. 213, 272.

rescission, may either require the successor to return the property to the debtor, or demand restitution in cash of its value against the recipient to whom the property no longer belongs.

365. Where the property in question is divisible and the amount claimed by the creditor is less than the total amount of the disputed transaction, courts have permitted partial rescission of the contract (Article 428-8). Where the property is not divisible, e.g. a transaction involving a building, courts generally require return of the property in question to the debtor and allow payment by a third-party beneficiary of an equivalent amount of damages only on a showing of special circumstances.[320]

366. After the property is returned to the debtor as a result of the right to rescission, the creditor must then seek to execute a judgment against the debtor. It may do so without any preferential rights to repayment from assets recovered by rescinding the fraudulent act.[321]

367. With real property, following rescission of the act, title to the property reverts to the debtor and the creditor will have to seek to enforce a judgment against the debtor for the debt. Courts have rejected demands that a third-party beneficiary directly transfer title to real property to the creditor.[322]

368. With contracts for money or movable property, a creditor may demand transfer of money or movable property from the third-party beneficiary directly to the creditor (Article 424-9). This is because the debtor is likely not to accept transfer for the third-party beneficiary. Creditors, in effect, have a right of set-off with rescission of a cash-based contract. The creditor may deduct money owed to it from the money collected before returning the remainder to the debtor, resulting in a *de facto* priority right for the creditor seeking to set aside the fraudulent act.[323] Courts have held other creditors possess no right of action to demand from the creditor a share of the assets obtained in filing the action to rescind the act. [324]

369. With regard to other creditors, rescission, pursuant to the provisions of the Civil Code, 'shall have an effect on the debtor and all obligees' (Article 425). Prior to the 2017 Reform, this provision provided that rescission 'shall have effect for the benefit of all obligees'. The revised Article 425 extends the effect of rescission to the debtor too, because otherwise it would be impossible to explain theoretically why the creditor exercising the right to rescission could execute the property transferred to the debtor, who should not have enjoyed the effect of rescission

320. Supreme Court, 30 Nov. 1934, Minshu 13-2191; Supreme Court, 11 Oct. 1955, Minshu 9-11-1626.
321. Nakata, *supra* n. 213, 264.
322. Supreme Court, 5 Oct. 1978, Minshu 32-7-1332.
323. Nakata, *supra* n. 213, 267–268.
324. Supreme Court, 16 Oct. 1952, Minshu 16-10-2070.

370. The Civil Code establishes time limitations, until the earlier end of which the creditor must file an action to rescind a fraudulent act of the debtor, of two years from the date that the creditor acquired knowledge of a such an act completed by the debtor knowing that it will prejudice the rights of the creditor, and of ten years from the act itself (Article 426).

371. Notably, courts have also held that a creditor's filing suit against a third-party beneficiary seeking rescission of a contract does not toll the extinctive prescription period of the underlying right – the right of the creditor vis-à-vis the initial debtor.[325]

372. Courts have held that actions seeking to set aside fraudulent acts cannot be filed after the debtor files for bankruptcy.[326]

III. Direct Actions & Products Liability

A. General Observation

373. Japanese law recognises a limited number of 'direct actions' (*chokusetsu seikyuken*) permitting a third party who played no role in the formation of the contract to assert rights against the contract. The Civil Code section dealing with subleases includes a direct right of action created by the Civil Code for a third party to sue on the initial lease contract (Article 613), as discussed in paragraph 739. The Automobile Liability Security Act (Act No. 97 of 1955) is an example of a special law creating a third-party right of action on a contract. It expressly provides that a third party injured in an automobile accident may, pursuant to the insured–insurer's contract, demand damages directly from the insured's insurance company.[327] Unlike the French, Japan does not recognise additional direct actions, such as those by subcontractors based on the original contract between the owner and general contractor.[328]

374. Separate from these direct actions permitting third parties to sue on the contract are third-party claims related to the transaction but not necessarily based on contractual rights arising from it. Product liability is the principle example here, and of the different types of direct actions by third parties, both based on contract and otherwise, it is the one that has generated the most controversy. First recognised by courts applying tort as well as contract provisions in the Civil Code and now by Japan's Products Liability Act, the topic as it relates to privity is briefly addressed below.

325. Great Court of Cassation, 23 Jun. 1942, Minshu 21-716; Supreme Court, 12 Oct. 1962, Minshu 16-10-2130; Nakata, *supra* n. 213, 261.
326. Great Court of Cassation, 23 Oct. 1929, Minshu 8-787.
327. Article 16 Automobile Liability Security Act. Article 16(4) also permits the insurance company to demand payment of compensation from the government where the insurance company has paid damages to an injured party resulting from the bad faith actions of the insured.
328. T. Yamaguchi, *Furansu Saiken Ho [The French Law of Obligations]* 265 (1986).

B. The Product Liability Act and Rights of Third-Party Claimants

375. Product liability actions may be brought under the Civil Code Contract law sections, tort law sections or Japan's 1994 Product Liability Act. *See also* Part II, Chapter 4, §5. The issue of privity arises with each, whether it is a question of who can be sued (vertical privity) or who can sue (horizontal privity).

376. As discussed below in Part I, Chapter 6 on Remedies, Articles 415 and 416 of the Civil Code Contract law set out the basic remedies for damages due to breach. These sections award damages to the obligee from the obligor, limiting on its face recovery to the parties to the contract. The courts have, however, declined to impose such limits. As early as 1955, a court declined to impose a vertical privity requirement, without expressly addressing the issue, allowing purchasers of eye drops from a retailer sue the manufacturer – albeit in tort.[329] In the 1970s, courts similarly rejected horizontal privity requirements where family members or guests of the contracting party suffered injury from the product[330] In a frequently cited example of the latter, plaintiffs purchased a building from its original owner and then brought suit against the construction company for defective construction.[331] Given the case law, there is no privity requirement in the context of tort claims.

377. The same holds true for actions brought pursuant to Japan's Product Liability Act (PLA) of 1994. The Act is silent as to privity requirements, but, in terms of who can be sued, it defines the manufacturers as persons who manufactured, processed or imported the product; who represents themselves as the manufacturers; or who hold themselves out as the manufacturers-in-fact of the product (Article 2(3) PLA). In terms of who can sue, it defines liability broadly to include 'liability for damages to life, body, or property caused by a defect in the product', without limitation as to whose life, body or property. The latter contrasts with the 1985 European Product Liability Directive, which limits consequential loss claims to property ordinarily and actually used by consumers (Article 3 PLA). [332]

378. In 2007, the Japanese Supreme Court expressly addressed privity.[333] In reviewing a tort claim for defective construction brought by downstream purchasers of an apartment building against the original architects and construction companies, the Court found that defect (e.g., loose handrails) that resulted in a 'loss of basic safety' so as to pose a threat of injury, loss of life or property could give rise to tort

329. *See* Z. Kitagawa, 'Contract', in *Doing Business in Japan*, 330 (Z. Kitagawa ed., looseleaf, Matthew Bender 1997) (eBook available from: https://www.overdrive.com/creators/296588/professor-zentaro-kitagawa, US only), s. 13.04 citing Tokyo District Court, 14 Jul. 1955, Kaminshu 6-1440.
330. *See*, e.g., Gifu District Court Ogaki Division, 27 Dec. 1973, Hanji 725-19 (extending the duty of care in a salmonella food poisoning case owed by an egg-tofu manufacturer to members and guests of the buyer's family who became sick after consuming the product); Kitagawa, *supra* n. 329, s. 13.04.
331. Supreme Court, 26 Sep. 1968, Minshu 22-9-2002; Kitagawa, *supra* n. 329, s. 13.04.
332. On further parallels and differences among Japan's Product Liability Act and regimes in the EU, US and Australia, *see* Nottage, *supra* n. 36, Ch. 3.
333. Supreme Court, 8 Jul. 2007, Minshu 61-5-1769.

liability. And this liability could arise 'vis-à-vis residents of the building and others who did not stand in a contractual relationship' with those responsible for constructing the building.[334]

379. In short, whether for economic loss or personal injury arising from a defective product, whether based on contract law, tort law or the Product Liability Act, Japanese courts have declined to impose a privity requirement. The strict language of Civil Code Articles 415 and 416 has been tempered by the courts, and the broad language of Article 709 and the Product Liability Act have been interpreted to provide redress for injuries to parties who were not party to the contract.

334. The Court did not require actual injury to state a claim: economic loss resulting from the defective workmanship is sufficient, and the Court remanded for findings as to whether there was a defect resulting in a loss of basic safety.

Chapter 5. Termination of the Contract

380. Contracts can be terminated on several grounds. Cancellation (*kaijo*) due to breach of contract is a question of remedies, and therefore will be dealt with in Chapter 6, Section §4. This chapter will deal in turn with other general grounds of termination: (i) by discharge of contractual obligations, most typically by performance; (ii) with respect to a continuous contract, by expiration of the contractual period or by notice of cancellation; (iii) by agreement of the parties to terminate the contract.

381. There are other statutory grounds for termination that apply to specific contracts. For example, some contracts are automatically terminated by a party's death. This means in practice that the deceased party's contractual rights are not subject to inheritance. This is the case with death of the borrower in a loan for use [*shiyo-taishaku*] (Article 597(3)), which by definition is a gratuitous contract, and death of either party to a contract for mandate (Article 653(1)). It is also generally accepted that an employment contract is terminated by death of an employee.

382. Likewise, some contracts are automatically terminated by commencement of insolvency proceedings or by a court's ruling of commencement of adult guardianship. Both are grounds for automatic termination of contracts of mandate (Article 653(ii) [upon either party's insolvency] and Article 653(iii) [adult guardianship of the mandatary]). Loans for consumption concluded by writing[335] are terminated if insolvency proceedings of the borrower commence before it receives the object the loan (Article 587-2(3)).

§1. Performance and Breach

I. Performance

A. Termination by Discharge of Obligations

383. If the obligations of both parties to a contract are discharged, this results in termination of that contract. An obligation is discharged when it is satisfied by 'performance' (*bensai*), 'set-off' (*sosai*), 'novation' (*kokai*) or 'merger' (*kondo*). Even when the obligation is not satisfied, it can be discharged by events such as a unilateral 'release' (*menjo*) by the obligee.

384. Prior to the 2017 Civil Code Reform, the general principle was that subsequent impossibility due to a cause not attributable to either party was a ground for

335. If the loan is not in writing, the contract does not take effect until the borrower receives the object, and the lender is not obliged to carry out the loan. Thus, the question of termination of contract before the borrower receives the object does not arise.

automatic termination of contracts (Article 536 of the pre-Reform Code). This principle is now abandoned in the revised Civil Code, except for some types of contracts. Lease contracts are automatically terminated proactively in the event of subsequent impossibility (Article 616-2). Employment contracts and contracts for work are automatically terminated proactively in the event of subsequent impossibility due to a cause not attributable to the party ordering work or to the employer (Articles 624-2, 634).

B. Discharge of Obligation by Performance

1. Who May Perform

385. An obligation is discharged by the performance of the obligor [to the obligee] (Article 473). Third parties are also allowed to perform an obligation in lieu of the obligor (Article 474(1)). A refusal by the obligee to accept third-party performance constitutes delay in accepting performance (*juryochitai*) on the part of the obligee. Third-party performance will discharge the obligor vis-à-vis the obligee and will give rise to the third party's right of recourse against the obligor. The third party is also subrogated to the rights of the obligee against the obligor (Articles 499 and 501(1)).[336]

386. Nonetheless, there are several exceptions to the general rule. Third-party performance falling under these exceptions does not discharge the obligation, and the obligee can rightfully refuse acceptance of third-party performance.

387. First, third-party performance is never allowed if it is contrary to the 'nature of the obligation' (Article 474(4)). For example, a third party may not perform in lieu of a singer engaged to sing at a concert.

388. Second, third-party performance is never allowed if it is contrary to the manifestation of intention of the obligor and obligee, made prior to tender by the third party,[337] that third-party performance is prohibited or restricted (Article 474(4)).

389. Third, third-party performance by parties who have no 'legitimate interest'[338] in performing the obligation may not, in principle, perform if it is contrary to the intention of the obligor (Article 474(2)). The drafter of the 1896 Civil Code provides two rationales for this rule which was carried over from the 2017 Reform.

336. This rule is subject to some exceptions in the case of guarantees (Art. 501(2) and (3)).
337. Great Court of Cassation, 10 Aug. 1932, Shimbun 3456-9.
338. Third parties have legitimate interest when performance affects the rights and obligations of the third party. Typical examples include a third-party grantor of a security interest in its asset to secure another person's obligation, or a third-party acquirer of an encumbered asset. A lessee of a building also has legitimate interest in having the rent for the land being paid. However, without more, family members of such lessee have no legitimate interest since their legal rights and obligations are not affected.

First, third-party performance may come with disadvantages to the obligor. Most notably, the third party who obtains a claim for recourse against the obligor may not be a welcome person for the obligor, such as a *yakuza*. The obligor should be allowed to avoid such situation. Second, the obligor may not consider it honourable (or contrary to the *samurai* spirit) to have its obligation performed by a third party.[339]

390. The 2017 Reform added a fourth exception: the obligee may refuse third-party performance by parties who have no 'legitimate interest' (Article 474(3)). In practice, this means that the obligee may not refuse performance by third parties who have legitimate interest.

391. The rule that third parties who have no legitimate interest may not perform against the will of the obligor or the obligee is further restricted. Such third party may still discharge the obligation by performance even if it is against the will of the obligor to do so, if the obligee accepts the performance without knowing that it is against the will of the obligor (Article 474(2)). Similarly, the obligee may not refuse third-party performance if it knew that the third party was designated by the obligor to perform (Article 474(3)).

2. To Whom Performance Should be Made

392. Performance is effective if rendered to a person who has the authority to receive performance: the obligee (Article 473) or a third party authorised by the obligee or by law to receive performance (cf. Article 478). Even when the obligor is ordered by the court to suspend performance due to attachment by a creditor of the obligee, the obligor's performance to the obligee is still effective and discharges its obligation *vis-à-vis* the obligee. However, the attaching creditor is entitled to require the obligor to perform *de novo* to the extent the third-party creditor suffered any loss (Article 481(1)).

393. Apparent obligees. Performance rendered to a person who is not an obligor or is not authorised to receive performance or payment, but who has the appearance of an obligee (apparent obligee), may become effective performance or payment under certain conditions in order to protect the reliance of the obligee and security of trade in general.

394. The main provision in this regard is Article 478. According to that article, performance to a person who, according to the common consensus of society regarding trade (*shakai ippan no torihiki tsunen*), has the appearance of a person authorised to receive performance, discharges the obligation if the obligor acted in good faith (i.e., without knowledge) and without negligence (Article 478).

339. K. Ume, M*inpo Yogi [The Essence of the Civil Code], (Obligations), Vol. 3*, 235 (1912 reprint ed., 1984).

395. The typically contemplated examples are cases where the obligor made payment to the assignee of the claim when the assignment was null, or when a payment is made to a junior assignee who does not have priority. In practice, however, the issue of the apparent obligee typically arises in banking transactions. For example, a withdrawal of bank deposits by a person who presents a stolen or counterfeit 'bank book *(tsucho)*' and a pre-registered 'stamp (*inkan*)', is considered to be an effective performance by the bank or obligor, if they have reasonably checked the authenticity of the bank book and the registered stamp. (Traditional banking practice requires presentation of bank books and a registered stamp.)[340] It does not matter whether the person making the withdrawal holds itself out as the depositor or its agent.[341] Regarding withdrawals at ATMs, where a holder of a stolen or counterfeit bank card enters the correct PIN, the withdrawal is considered to be effective, if the bank has not breached its duty of care in the establishment and maintenance of the ATM system. Special legislation enacted in 2005,[342] however, enhances protection of the depositor: (i) with respect to use of counterfeit bank cards, replacing Article 478 with a stricter rule for the withdrawal to be effective and (ii) with respect to stolen bank cards, giving the depositor a right to recoup from the bank all or part of the withdrawal which occurred within thirty days prior to the date the depositor gives notice to the bank.

396. In order to protect security in trade (i.e., to protect reliance of the party making payment), the application of the rule interpretation of this concept is expanded to acts that strictly speaking do not constitute performance. For example, this provision has been applied by analogy to a banking transaction where the bank extends a loan to an apparent, but not genuine, depositor involving his deposit as security (*yokin tanpo kashitsuke*).

3. What to Perform and Conformity

397. The obligor must perform in accordance with the terms of the obligation [*saimu-no honshi*], which is to be determined by interpreting the parties' intention. Such terms include the goods' or services' description, quality, quantity, due date and place of delivery.

398. The parties may agree to substitute the performance with something other than what was agreed in the contract. The obligation is discharged when the agreed substitute performance is actually performed (Article 482). Substitute performance has been used as a security device.[343]

340. *See*, Part I, Ch. 1 above.
341. Supreme Court, 21 Aug. 1962, Minshu 16-9-1809.
342. Act on Protection, etc. of Depositors and Postal Saving Holders from Unauthorized Automated Withdrawal, etc. Using Counterfeit Cards, etc. and Stolen Cards, etc. (Act No. 94 of 2005).
343. J. O. Haley, 'The Preliminary Contract for Substitute Performance: A Reflection of Japanese Judicial Approach', 7 *Law in Japan* 133 (1974).

399. Description, quality, quantity and risk of loss. If the obligation is to deliver a specified thing, the general principle is that the obligor is required to deliver the specified thing in the condition it is in when delivery is due. If the obligor does not deliver by the delivery date, any loss or damage that occurs after that date is at the expense of the obligor (Article 483). In other words, the risk of loss passes to the obligee when the delivery is due. However, prior to the delivery date, the obligor is under a 'duty of care of a prudent manager' (*zenryonaru kanrisha-no chuigimu*, commonly abbreviated to *zenkanchuigimu*) (Article 400). An obligor in breach of this duty of care is liable for damages (Article 415).

400. Nonetheless, a special rule applies to sales contracts. In sales contracts, the risk of loss passes to the buyer at the time when the seller 'delivers' the object to the buyer, provided that the object is identified in the contract (Article 587(1)). The risk also passes to the buyer if the buyer has delayed acceptance (Article 587(2)).

401. If the obligation is to deliver a *fungible thing*, the obligor is required to deliver a thing that fits the description and quality specified in the contract. In other words, the obligor is obliged to specify and deliver a thing that fits the contract requirements. If the required quality is not determinable from the contract, the obligor must deliver a thing of 'intermediate quality' (Article 401(1)).

402. The parties may agree on the specification (or identification) of the thing subsequent to the conclusion of the contract. Specification of fungible goods may also occur: (i) when the obligor has identified the thing by exercising its right of specification granted by the obligee (Article 401(2)) or (ii) when the obligor has completed the acts necessary to make delivery. When delivery is to be made at the address or place of business of the obligee, the necessary act is not completed until actual tender of delivery takes place.[344] When delivery is to be made at the address or place of the obligor, simply giving oral tender does not complete the act necessary to make delivery;[345] it is generally considered that the goods to be delivered must be separated from others, and that notice to that effect must be given to the obligor.

403. Once a fungible thing is specified, the same rules described above regarding specified things apply (Article 401(2)).

4. When

404. When the contract has a fixed due date, the obligor must perform by that date. Delay will result in breach of its obligation (Article 412(1)). Japanese law does not adopt the (French) rule of *mise en demeure*: no action on the part of the obligee is required to put the obligor in delay. When a due date is not fixed but is determinable from the contract, the obligor must perform when it becomes aware that

344. Great Court of Cassation, 25 Dec. 1919, Minroku 25-2400.
345. Supreme Court, 18 Oct. 1955, Minshu 9-11-11642.

the due date has arrived (Article 412(2)). When there is no due date in the contract, the obligor must perform when demanded by the obligee (Article 412(3)).

405. Notwithstanding the above, in bilateral contracts, parties have a defence of simultaneous performance (*doji riko no koben),* unless different due dates are agreed (Article 533). When this defence is available, the parties may demand performance in exchange for the countervailing performance. They are also not liable for late performance.

5. Where

406. Unless the parties agree otherwise, the general rule is that delivery shall take place at the current address of the obligee (Article 484, Civil Code), or, in case of obligations arising from a commercial act, at the current place of business of the obligee (Article 516(1), Commercial Code). If a change in the obligee's address subsequent to the conclusion of the contract results in increase of the cost of performance, the obligee must account to the obligor for the difference (Article 485).

407. Exceptionally, if the obligation is to deliver a specified thing, most typically an immovable, the delivery is to take place where the thing was at the time of contract (Article 484, Civil Code). Another exception is that payment of price to be paid in exchange of delivery of a thing is to be paid at the place of delivery (Articles 574, 559).

408. From a comparative law perspective, the general rule in the majority of jurisdictions is that performance should take place at the address or place of business of the obligor (*see also* CISG Article 31). As such, the general rule in Japan on this issue is unusual.

6. Special Rules for Monetary Obligations

409. Monetary obligations must be paid in currency that is legal tender at the time of payment.[346] Court decisions have treated payment by bank check as an effective tender,[347] but payment by other (personal) checks are not effective tender unless accompanied by a bank guarantee.[348]

410. Japanese law adheres to the principle of monetary nominalism: although the value of currencies may fluctuate between the time of contract and the time of

346. The obligor has the option to pay in any currency (e.g., via JPY 1,000 bills or 10,000 bills) of its choice, unless the contract specifies the currency of payment (Art. 402(1)). If the currency specified in the contract is no longer in mandatory circulation at the time of payment, payment must be made in other currencies (Art. 402(2)).

347. Supreme Court, 21 Sep. 1962, Minshu 16-9-2041.

348. Supreme Court, 22 Nov. 1960, Minshu 14-13-2927.

performance, monetary obligations are taken at their face value. However, standard terms assuming currency risk fluctuations, if agreed to by the parties, are considered to be valid.

411. When the amount of obligation is specified in a foreign currency (e.g., Euro, US Dollars), the obligor has the choice to pay in Japanese yen converted at the exchange rate prevailing at the place of payment (Article 403) and time of payment.[349] Likewise, the obligee has the choice of converting its claims to Japanese yen.[350]

412. To the extent of the purpose of the obligation in effect prior to the novation, the parties to the novation may convert the pledge or hypothec created as the security of such obligation to the obligation in effect after the novation, provided, however, that, in cases where any third party created such security, the acknowledgment of such third party must be obtained.

C. *Discharge of Obligation by Novation* (Kokai)

413. The parties may agree to discharge an obligation by substituting it with another new obligation. This is known as novation (*kokai*). Substitution can be of the content of performance, obligor or obligee (Article 513). Novation by substitution of the content of performance can be made by an agreement between the obligor and the obligee. Novation by substitution of the obligor can be made by an agreement between the obligee and the new obligor. The original obligation is discharged when the obligee notifies the obligor of the novation (Article 514(1)). The new obligor has no right of recourse to the original obligor (Article 514(2)). Thus, this is different from the situation of third-party performance. Novation by substitution of the obligee can be made by an agreement between the original and the new obligee, but this cannot be asserted against third persons, including the obligor, unless the agreement is made using an instrument bearing a 'fixed date' (*kakuteihizuke*) (Article 515). This rule is similar to the rule on assignment of claims.[351]

414. The obligee has a right to convert the pledge or hypothec that was created to secure the original obligation to the new obligation, provided that this is done by declaration to the other party (or in case of substitution of the obligee, by declaration to the original obligee) before or at the time of novation (Article 518). If the pledge or hypothec was granted by a third party, the approval by that third party is necessary for the conversion to take effect (proviso in Article 518(1)).

349. Supreme Court, 15 Jul. 1975, Minshu 29-6-1029.
350. *Ibid.*
351. For details of this instrument, *see* para. 285.

D. Discharge by Release (Menjo)

415. The obligee may release the obligor from its obligation by making a unilateral declaration to that effect (Article 519). This is different from the majority of jurisdictions where 'release' is a contract between the obligor and obligee, and even more different from traditional common law where mere agreement to modify one party's original performance obligation is generally ineffective due to the 'pre-existing duty rule' as part of the doctrine of consideration.

E. Discharge by Merger (Kondo)

416. If a claim and obligation become vested in the same person, for example by inheritance or assignment of claim, the obligation is discharged by merger (Article 520). However, this does not apply if the claim is the subject matter of the right of a third party (proviso in Article 520). For example, if the claim is attached by a third-party obligee, the obligation is not discharged by merger.

II. Breach or Non-performance

417. Under the 2017 Revision, the Civil Code adopts a unitary concept of non-performance or breach (the term 'breach' of contract and 'non-performance' of contractual obligation is used interchangeably in this monograph). The distinction between delay (*chitai*), impossibility (*funo*) and incomplete performance (*fukanzen riko*) which existed in Japanese law prior to the 2017 revision is abandoned.

418. If the obligor does not perform its contractual obligation, it amounts to non-performance, and this triggers the remedies available to the obligee which will be explained in Chapter 6. Thus, it is essential to determine what performance each parties agreed to perform and what risk each parties agreed to undertake. A party is not liable for non-performance if performance is disturbed by an event the occurrence of which the obligor did not undertake. Thus, 'fault' is not a requirement in determining whether there was non-performance.

§2. Termination of Continuous Contracts

I. General Rule

419. Continuous contracts, such as loans for use, leases, employment contracts, long-term supply contracts and franchises, are contracts that are continuously or repeatedly performed for a period of time.

420. Continuous contracts with a fixed term (duration) are automatically terminated by the expiration of that term (cf. Articles 597, 622). For example, a lease of a book for one month is terminated by the passing of that period, and the borrower will be obligated to return the book at that time. In principle, the parties are free whether or not to agree on renewal of the term. In reality, parties may continue to perform even after the expiration of the term. This signifies that it is often the parties' intention to renew the contract. Thus, for example, lease and employment contracts with fixed terms are presumed to be renewed unless the lessor or employee objects to the renewal (Articles 619 and 629).

421. Continuous contracts with no fixed term may be terminated by notification of termination (*kaiyaku moshi-ire*). In principle, no reason is necessary for such termination by notification. However, in order to ameliorate the harm caused by abrupt terminations, advance notice of a reasonable period is required or termination takes effect only after passing of a reasonable period of time (cf. Article 617 (lease), Article 627 (employment)).

II. Protection of Continuity

422. Often, however, there will be or there will develop an underlying close relationship between the parties, and expectations for continuity will arise and/or relation-specific investment will be made. In light of this character, there are statutory rules or case law developments that protect the continuity of continuous contracts.[352]

423. Lease of land and buildings and employment contracts are the most representative.[353] For lease of land and buildings, the lessee is given a right to renew the lease. Renewal can be refused by the lessor only when there is a 'justifiable reason' to do so (Articles 6 and 28, Act on Land and Building Leases).[354] Even termination for non-performance of land or building leases is subject to the additional requirement that there must be 'broken trust relation'.[355] For employment, termination by notification by the employer (i.e., dismissal) is invalid, if it lacks objectively reasonable grounds and is considered inappropriate in general societal terms (Article 16, Labor Contract Act). This is a codification of case law that developed from the 'abuse of dismissal right' doctrine.[356]

424. There has also been a series of case law developments regarding termination (or cancellation) of long-term distribution contracts and franchise contracts that

352. On the principle of protecting continuity, *see* Takashi Uchida, *Keiyakuno Jidai [The Era of Contract]*, (Tokyo: Iwanami Shoten, 2000). *See also*, generally, Hiroyasu Nakata, *Keizokuteki Baibai no Kaisho [Termination of Long Term Sales]* (Tokyo: Yuhikaku, 1994) and Hiroyasu Nakata, *Keizokuteki Torihiki no Kenkyu [A Study of Continuous Contracts]* (Tokyo: Yuhikaku, 2000).
353. *See*, e.g., Haley, *supra* n. 55, 145.
354. *See* Part II, Ch. 6, §1.
355. *See* Part II, Ch. 6, §5.
356. For example Supreme Court, 25 Apr. 1975, Minshu 29-4-456. *See* Part II, Ch. 5, §2.

require 'unavoidable reason' or 'justifiable reason' for such termination or cancellation. Although not codified in the 2017 Reform, this can be viewed as established case law.[357]

425. There are various interesting cases, such as those involving supply of cosmetics, or franchise for a lunchbox (*bento*) shop.[358] An indicative example is the Hokkaido Tractor Case.[359] This involved an exclusive distributorship for agricultural equipment entered into in 1971. The agreement contained an automatic renewal clause that renewed the contract annually unless notice of non-renewal was given three months in advance of expiration. The distributor successfully cultivated the market and sold machines until 1987 when the manufacturer abruptly attempted to terminate (not renew) the contract. The distributor applied for an injunction to prevent the distributor from distributing its product through a new distributor. The court's finding included that: (i) during that period, the distributor made considerable efforts in keeping in close contact with farmers (because solicitation of purchase of these machines usually requires 1.5 to 3 years); (ii) the distributor possessed a huge stockpile of machines, worth JPY 116 million, which the distributor would not be able to resell if the distributorship was terminated; (iii) the distributor could not switch to becoming a distributor of another manufacturer; (iv) the manufacturer would acquire at no cost all the customers that the distributor had cultivated. The court granted injunctive relief stating that, given the circumstances, the non-renewal clause should understood to allow termination only when continuation is unjust to one of the parties, and where there is an 'unavoidable reason' for terminating the contract.

§3. Impossibility and the Doctrine of Changed Circumstances

426. Prior to the 2017 Civil Code Reform, the general principle was that subsequent impossibility due to a cause not attributable to either party was ground for automatic termination of contracts (Article 536 of the pre-Reform Code). This principle is abandoned in the revised Civil Code, except for some types of contracts. Lease contracts are automatically terminated proactively in the event of subsequent impossibility (Article 616-2). Employment contracts and contracts for work are automatically terminated proactively in the event of subsequent impossibility due to a cause not attributable to the party ordering work or to the employer (Articles 624-2 and 634).

---

357. Uchida, *supra* n. 109, 83.
358. For a fuller account, *see* Taylor, *supra* n. 30; Willem M. Visser t'Hooft, *Japanese Contract and Anti-trust Law: A Sociological and Comparative Study* 21 (Routledge Curzon 2002).
359. Sapporo High Court, 30 Sep. 1987, Hanji 1258-76.

427. Largely similarly to common law (especially American law) and civil law jurisdictions (especially German law),[360] Japanese law has long recognised the possibility of relief in the event of extreme economic dislocation impacting on contract performance.[361]

428. One possibility is the doctrine of impossibility of performance.[362] Here, impossibility has long been interpreted as including not only physical impossibility but also impossibility in the light of 'common sense in society' (*shakai tsunen*). The 2017 Revision clarifies this point by providing that impossibility is to be determined in light of the contract and the general sense of trade (cf. Article 412-2(1)). Thus, if performance of its obligation would incur extremely high labour or other costs (e.g., the seller of a diamond ring drops it in the middle of a lake),[363] the obligor will be excused from specifically performing the obligation (Article 412-2(1))[364]. However, the obligor is still liable for damages unless the impossibility is not attributable to the obligor (Article 415(1)), and the contract is not terminated unless the obligee terminates the contract for breach (Article 542).

429. The other possibility for relief from severe economic dislocation comes from the more recently developed 'doctrine of changed circumstances' (*jijo henko no hori*). It has proven more popular in providing relief where costs of performance have increased dramatically; where the market price of the subject matter of the contract (such as land) has fluctuated widely; and also where the purpose of the contract is frustrated. The doctrine was developed at first by Japanese academics drawing on German legal theory, itself rooted in the wake of hyperinflation after World War I and bolstered by the German Civil Code's express recognition of a generalised duty of good faith. The Japanese doctrine came to be recognised by the courts, at least in theory, toward the end of World War II and during the decade of economic turmoil and reconstruction that followed.

430. The first of four prerequisites for the doctrine is a *substantial change* in circumstances affecting the basis of the contract. A second prerequisite, sometimes

360. For a comparative analysis, on which the following section is generally based, *see* L. Nottage, 'Changing Contract Lenses: Unexpected Supervening Events in English, New Zealand, US, Japanese, and International Sales Law and Practice', 14 *Indiana J. Global Legal Stud.* 385 (2008).

361. For general discussions of the doctrines of impossibility and frustration in Japanese law, *see also* T. Sawada, *Subsequent Conduct and Supervening Events; A Study of Two Selected Problems in Contract Jurisprudence*, 133 (University of Tokyo Press 1968); K. Igarashi and L. V. Rieke, 'Impossibility and Frustration in Sales Contracts', 42 *Washington L. Rev.* 445 (1967); P. Waer, 'Frustration of Contracts in Japanese Law: The Doctrine of Changed Circumstances', 20 *Law in Japan* 187 (1987).

362. As outlined Part I, Ch. 5 §1(I)(A) above.

363. H. Kubo, '*Rikofuno-no Kihontekigainen-ni kansuru Hikakuhoteki Ichikosatsu: Nihonho, Amerikahooyobi Toitsuho* [A Comparative Study of the Basic Concept of Impossibility Under Japanese,American and Uniform Law]', 24 *Sandai Hogaku* 1-32 (1991).

364. Prior to the 2017 Revision, it was considered that subsequent impossibility not attributable to the obligor discharges the obligation. It was also considered that initial impossibility will result in invalidity of the contract. Both of these principles of automatic discharge were abandoned in the 2017 revision. *See* Part I Ch. 5 §1(I)(A) above.

related in the sense that it can involve weighing any resultant disequilibrium in contractual obligations, is that strictly enforcing the promisor's original obligation would be highly *unfair in light of the principle of good faith.* Although mainly in older cases, courts have found these hurdles to have been cleared often enough for claims of relief under the doctrine to continue appearing before Japanese courts, including in cases involving commercial impracticability. However, significant numbers have failed, sometimes because of further hurdles such as the prerequisites that the changed circumstances *not be attributable to the promisor* and that they *not be foreseen or foreseeable.*

431. This leads to the important point that under the law in Japan, as in the United States, a right of adjustment is recognised as a possible consequence of applying the doctrine. Indeed, as originally proposed by academics, this was to be the primary effect, with termination following only if adjustment was not achievable. In fact, in a survey of the sixty-four reported cases (as of 1994) in which the doctrine had been invoked, only thirteen first sought adjustment and otherwise termination; twenty-eight cases simply claimed termination. On the other, contract adjustment alone was claimed in twenty cases. Of these, adjustment was allowed by the courts in nine cases, and, out of the thirteen seeking adjustment and otherwise termination, adjustment was allowed in four cases.[365] This may seem activist, when compared to rare examples in the United States such as *ALCOA*.[366] But it should be noted that court adjustment in Japan has been by the lower courts (never by the Supreme Court), always within the range proposed by one or both parties, and predominantly in earlier cases (arising during or from World War II).[367] Partly in the hope of providing more legitimacy and background for courts adjusting contracts under the doctrine of changed circumstances, as well as permitting more scope for party autonomy during the course of performance, various scholars have recently suggested a duty to renegotiate in good faith.[368] The contours of such a duty remain unclear, however, and these suggestions mostly are made in the context of much broader theoretical debates. Meanwhile, the notion of a duty to renegotiate has not been clearly affirmed even by lower courts.

§4. Termination by Agreement

432. Parties are free to terminate their contract by agreement. This is one form of contract in itself.

---

365. K. Iijima, '*Jijo Henko no Koka to shite no Keiyaku no Tekio to Kaijo,* [Recission and Adjustment of Contracts as Effects of the Doctrine of Changed Circumstances]' 35 *Toritsudai Hogakkai Zasshi* 127 (1994).
366. *Aluminum Co. of Am. v. Essex Group, Inc.*, 499 F. Supp. 53 (W.D. Pa. 1980), discussed in Nottage, *supra* n. 360.
367. *See* generally Nottage, *supra* n. 360, 59.
368. *See*, e.g., K. Yamamoto, *Minpo Kogi IV-1 Keiyaku [Civil Law Lectures, Vol. IV-1, Contracts]*, 109–111 (2005): and H. Ishikawa, *Saikoshogimu no Riron [Theoretical Analysis of the Duty to Renegotiate]* (Yuhikaku 2011).

433. Thus, in principle, the consequences of such termination depends on the agreement. In the absence of an agreement to the contrary, however, it is considered that the parties are bound to make restitution of what they have received prior to termination as performance. This restitution is based on the rules on unjust enrichment (Article 703), not the provision on restitution for termination due to breach (Article 545).[369] This means that interests, fruits or benefit of use of what has been supplied need not be returned, unless otherwise agreed by the parties.[370]

434. In principle, termination by agreement does not have retroactive effect, unless otherwise agreed. Even when the parties have agreed that the termination takes effect retroactively, it does not bind third parties. Thus, third parties are protected without applying Article 545(1). For example, if a contract for the sale of land is terminated by agreement after the seller has resold the land to a third party, that resale is not affected by termination by agreement because it has no retroactive effect.[371]

369. Supreme Court, 24 Dec. 1957, Minshu 11-14-2322.
370. Cf. Great Court of Cassation, 15 Sep. 1919, Minroku 25-1633.
371. Supreme Court, 14 Jun. 1958, Minshu 12-9-1449.

Chapter 6. Remedies

§1. Overview

435. In case of non-performance by the obligor, several remedies are available to the obligee. They are: (i) specific performance, (ii) cancellation, (iii) damages, – in cases of non-conforming performance – (iv) cure of non-conformity and (v) price reduction.[372] Furthermore, obligee's rights to these remedies are subject to (vi) extinctive prescription. This chapter will examine these in turn, after briefly reviewing self-help remedies.

436. In principle, the obligor may choose which remedy to use, but it cannot combine remedies that are inconsistent with each other. For example, the obligee cannot combine its right to specific performance, right to cure or right to price reduction with its right of cancellation. Damages can be combined with any other remedies, but the amount will be adjusted depending on the combination to avoid double compensation. For example, if the seller does not deliver, the buyer may seek specific performance and damages for the delay, or the buyer may cancel the contract and seek damages for the value of performance.

§2. Self-help Remedies

I. Simultaneous Performance and Right of Retention

437. In the case of non-performance by the obligor, there are several self-help remedies the obligee may rely on, without recourse to the court. They are the defence of simultaneous performance (*doji riko no koben*) (Article 533) and the right of retention (*ryuchiken*) (Article 295). These are explained in the context of the protection of the unpaid seller in Part II, Chapter 6.

II. Set-Off

A. Set-Off as Substantive Law Triggered by Notification and Having Retroactive Effect

438. Japanese law follows the European Civil Law tradition's conception of set-off as a matter of substantive law, in contrast to the common law tradition of viewing set-off as a purely or mainly procedural device.[373]

372. *See* generally T. Yoshimasa, 'The Reform of the Law on Remedies for Breach of Contract in Japan' in *Reactive Instruments of Social Governance (*A. Bruns & M. Suzuki eds., *Mohr* forthcoming).
373. R. Zimmermann, *Comparative Foundations of a European Law of Set-off and Prescription*, 23 (Cambridge University Press 2002). However, courts and commentators increasingly view at least equitable set-off under English law as having a more substantive character: *Ibid*. 28.

439. Set-offs must be effected by one party manifesting its intention to another, and this manifestation takes effect retroactively as of the time when the obligations of both parties become due and suitable for set-off (Article 506). Such manifestation can be done not only in court but also extrajudicially, informally and unilaterally. Thus, set-off has a function of simplifying payment/settlement of claims and also to secure a claim that one party has against the other.

B. The Requirement of 'Suitability'

440. Set-off is allowed only when two obligations are 'suitable for set-off' (*sosai tekijo*) (Article 505(1)). This requirement is satisfied when:

(i) two persons mutually owe to the other any obligation;
(ii) the obligations are of the same kind; and
(iii) both obligations are due.

1. The Requirement for Mutuality of Claims Being Asserted for Set-Off

441. The first-mentioned 'mutuality' requirement is satisfied when two persons owe obligations to each other and both claims are validly in existence at the time of set-off. Thus, a person cannot set-off 'if either of the claims has not arisen or is invalid at the relevant time'. Therefore, 'it is not possible for one party (A) to set off a debt owed by A to a second party (B) against a debt owed to A by a third party (C) pursuant to the statutory set-off provisions contained in the Civil Code. [...] For example, a bank may only apply a credit balance in a bank account held by a customer (the Depositor) with itself in or towards satisfaction of a debt owed by a customer (the Borrower) to the bank, if the Depositor and the Borrower are the same person. The bank may not set off the credit balance owed by the bank to any third party for such purposes in the absence of such third party's consent (whether such third party is a subsidiary or related company or otherwise of the Borrower)'.[374]

442. However, the Civil Code relaxes this requirement in certain cases. First, the Civil Code allows a guarantor (C) to use the defence of set-off against the creditor (A), who asserts a claim against C, any claim that the main debtor (B) may have against A (Article 457(2)). Using the defence of set-off in this situation means that C can refuse to perform its obligation, but that B's obligation is not extinguished by C's assertion of the defence (Article 457(3)). Similar protections are extended to parties who have assumed joint and several liability (Article 439) and to a party faced with a claim from an assignee (Article 468(1)).

---

374. A. Wani, K. Takabayashi and M. Nagai, 'Japan', in *Set-off Law and Practice*, Ch. 19 para. 19.03. (W. Johnston and T. Werlen eds., 2nd ed., Oxford University Press 2010).

2. The Requirement that Set-Off Claims are of the Same Kind

443. The second requirement that the obligations subject to set-off are of the 'same kind' has been broadly construed by courts and commentators. For example, 'a set-off of the obligation to pay cash against the obligation to deliver securities is not allowed, unless the latter obligation is converted into a monetary obligation. However, there is no requirement for the obligation to arise out of the same event, to be the same amount, to have the same maturity date, or to be performed in the same place'.[375]

444. The last-mentioned point is expressly set out in Article 507: 'Set-offs may be effected even if the place of performance of both obligations are different'. However, the party asserting set-off in this situation 'shall be liable for any damages suffered by the counterparty as result of such set-off'. Such damages are hardly conceivable where the set-off involves monetary obligations, but they could arise in the case of obligations to make delivery of goods where costs are involved in moving them.[376]

445. The Civil Code does not distinguish between different subcategories of monetary claims. The only express exception concerns some provisions relating to claims involving foreign currency (Articles 402 and 403). There is still some debate in Japan over whether set-offs of claims in different currencies meet the requirement of having 'the same kind of purpose'.[377]

3. Requirement that Both Obligations are 'Due'

446. The third main requirement for set-off under Civil Code Article 505(1) is that both obligations be due and payable. However, the Supreme Court has held that as far as the claim of the party setting off is due, that party may set-off the claim against its own obligation even if it is not due, because it can waive the benefit of time.[378]

C. Prohibition of Set-Off

447. Even when the 'suitability' requirement is satisfied, set-off is prohibited in some cases. First, statutory set-off cannot apply if not permitted by the nature of the obligation (Article 505(1) proviso). For example, obligations to refrain from doing

375. *Ibid.*, para. 19.02, note 4.
376. Uchida, *supra* n. 109, 250.
377. *See*, in particular, the exhaustive study by K. Motonaga, 'Kokusaiteki na Sosai ni kansuru Shomondai [Issues Related to International Set-off: Parts 1-6]' 113(5)-(10) *Hogaku Kyokai Zasshi* (1996).
378. Supreme Court, 19 Jul. 1957, Minshu 11-7-1297.

something (e.g., non-competition) and obligations to do something (e.g., A's obligation to work for B for two days and B's obligation to work for three days)[379] cannot be set off by their nature, because their purpose will not be achieved if they are not specifically performed. Claims that are subject to any defences of the obligor are also excluded, because the obligor will be unilaterally deprived of the benefit of defence.[380] Furthermore, there are statutory prohibitions: for example, an advance loan by an employer to an employee cannot be set off against the employee's wages (Article 17, Labor Standard Act).

448. Second, set-off of a claim can be prohibited by the agreement of the obligor and obligee. However, this agreement cannot be asserted against a third party who did not know and was not grossly negligent in not knowing about the existence of such agreement (Article 505(2)).

449. Third, certain claims arising from tort cannot be set off by the obligor against other claims (Article 509). This is based on a policy consideration to avoid a situation whereby (i) someone (A) has a claim against another (B) under a contract, yet B refuses to pay, so that (ii) B harms A in the hope that A will assert a tort claim for damages against B – whereupon B can set off its original claim under the contract. Prior to the 2017 Reform, this prohibition applied to a tort claim. However, that exception has been widely criticised as too broad.[381] Accordingly, the 2017 Reform limits the application of this prohibition to situations where B commits an intentional tort (Article 509(i)) or where the tort claim concerns infringement of life or limb (Article 509(ii)).

450. The Civil Code prohibits set-off against claims immune from attachment (Article 510), such as three-quarters of a worker's wages (Article 152 Civil Execution Act).

451. Lastly, a third-party obligor who has been enjoined from making payment by attachment may not assert set-off against any after-acquired claim against the relevant attaching obligee (Article 511(1)). However, such a third-party obligor may assert set-off against claims it acquired before attachment (Article 511(1)).[382] In addition, such a third-party obligor may assert set-off even against after-acquired claims if that claim arose from a ground that already existed at the time of attachment, except for situations where the after-acquired claim is a claim assigned from a third party (Article 511(2)). For example, if a guarantor (C) who became a guarantor at the request of the main obligor (B) makes payment of guarantee to the obligee (A) after B's claim against C was attached, it may assert set-off of its subsequently acquired right of recourse against B, regarding B's claim against C.

379. This example is taken from Uchida, *supra* n. 109, 250.
380. Great Court of Cassation, 1 Mar. 1938, Minshu 17-318.
381. Uchida, *supra* n. 109, 252.
382. This part of the provision is derived from Supreme Court (Grand Chamber), 24 Jun. 1970, Minshu 24-6-587.

This is because although C's claim was acquired after attachment, it arose from a request for guarantee that existed before attachment.[383]

§3. Right to Specific Performance

452. Following the Civil Law tradition, the obligee may not only retain what has been performed by the obligor, but may also require the obligee to perform obligations under the contract if it does do not perform voluntarily.[384] There is no explicit provision in the Civil Code that providing for such a substantive right to performance, but that right is considered to be an inherent attribute of the notion of 'obligation'.

453. If the obligor has performed but that performance lacks conformity with the contract, the obligee also has a right to require the obligor to cure (*tsuikan*) the non-conformity by repair, delivery of a substitute or delivery of missing part. Such right to require cure can be considered a subset of the right to performance, but the 2017 Code Reform provides such a right separately that is available in the case of contracts for value, i.e. contracts which entail economic exchange (Articles 559 and 542).

454. However, this right is subject to a limitation: when it is impossible to exercise the right. Impossibility has long been interpreted as including not only physical impossibility but also impossibility in the light of 'common sense in society' (*shakai tsunen*).[385] A typical example of impossibility is an obligation to deliver a ring that one dropped in lake. The 2017 Reform clarifies this point by providing that impossibility is to be determined in light of the contract and common sense in trade (*torihikijono shakai tsunen*) (cf. Article 412-2(1)). Although interpretation of these criteria is to yet to be established, performance that is prohibited by law, or performance where its cost is disproportionately large in relation to its benefit, is likely to be considered impossible. Impossibility is determined according to the criterion (Article 412-2(1)).

455. When the right to performance is limited because of impossibility, but the obligor has acquired, for the same ground that caused the impossibility, a right or interest that substitutes for the object of the obligation, the obligee has a right to demand transfer of the right or reimbursement of the interest. This right to claim substitute value (*daisho seikyuken*) is limited to the extent of loss suffered by the obligee (Article 422-2). A typical example is the right to claim an insurance payment or right of damages against a third party who has destroyed an object.

383. This example is based on the facts of Supreme Court, 28 May 2012, Minshu 66-7-3123, which formed the basis of Art. 511(2) in the 2017 Reform.

384. *See* generally, K. Nakata, 'Performance and Monetary Remedies for Breach of Contract in Japan' in *Studies in the Contract Laws of Asia Vol. I: Remedies for Breach of Contract*, 115 (M. Chen-Wishart et al. eds. Oxford University Press 2016).

385. *See* Part I, Chapter 5, §3 above (impossibility and changed circumstances).

456. The obligor may request the courts to enforce its right to performance, in accordance with the Civil Execution Act (Act No. 4 of 1979) and other procedural laws, by (i) direct compulsory execution (*chokusetsu kyosei*), (ii) execution by substitute (*daitai shikko*) or (iii) indirect compulsory execution (*kansetsu kyosei*) (Article 414). However, execution by the court is not allowed when 'the nature of the obligation does not permit such enforcement' (Article 414 proviso). These are cases where compelling the obligor to specifically perform the obligation infringes on the free will of the obligor (e.g., an obligation to draw a painting or to sing in a concert).

457. Direct execution is used mostly for obligations to deliver immovable, movables or money. The court will attach and hand over the thing or money under the obligor's possession to the obligee. Execution by substitute is used for obligations to do an act or not to do an act if a party other than the obligor can render the performance (e.g., obligation to destroy a building or obligation not to construct a building). In such case, the court will designate the person (which may be the obligee) to carry out the act (e.g., destruction of the building), and then collect the cost from the obligor. Indirect compulsory execution is a procedure similar to *astreinte* under French law. Under this manner of execution, the court seeks to put financial pressure on the obligor to perform by ordering it to keep paying a certain amount of money (compulsory money) until it performs. Compulsory money is distinguished from damages. Therefore, even if the amount of compulsory money the obligee received exceeds the loss caused by non-performance, the obligee is not obligated to return the excess. If the loss caused by non-performance exceeds the amount of compulsory money received, the obligee may claim damages for the difference (Article 172(iv) Civil Execution Act).

§4. Cancellation of the Contract

458. The function of cancelling the contract due to breach is to discharge, *inter alia*, the counter-obligation of the aggrieved party, when the other party is in breach of its obligation. This frees the aggrieved party from the contract and allows it to take alternative actions such as engaging in a substitute transaction where appropriate.

I. Manner of Cancellation

459. Cancellation takes place when the obligee declares its intention to cancel the contract provided that there is a ground for cancellation (Article 540). Such declaration can be made orally. It takes effect when it reaches the addressee (Article 97).

460. Under prior law, there was an exceptional rule for automatic cancellation that did not require any action by the obligee. If an obligation became impossible subsequent to formation of the contract and if the obligor was not at fault for the impossibility, both the impossible obligation and the counter-obligation were automatically discharged (former Article 536). This rule, although known as the rule associated with 'risk of loss' (*kiken futan*)[386] and formally separate from the general rules on cancellation, was abandoned in the 2017 Revision. Thus, under the revised Civil Code, cancellation for breach always takes place only when declaration is given by the obligee.

II. Grounds for Right of Cancellation

461. The rules of cancellation of contract due to breach underwent extensive revision in the 2017 reform. It was heavily influenced by the global convergence of contract law:[387] the rule on cancellation for breach under the 2017 Revised Code, in essence, requires that the breach is of a serious nature. The grounds for the right of cancellation are conveniently provided in two provisions: Articles 541 and 542.

462. First of all, the 2017 Revised Code provides for a *Nachfrist* cancellation (*saikoku kaijo*) (Article 541). In order to cancel a contract under this provision, the aggrieved party must demand that the breaching party performs its obligation, specifying a reasonable period of time for performance. The right to cancel arises only if the breaching party does not perform within that period of time. However, there is a proviso that denies cancellation if the non-performance, after the additional period of time has expired, is considered 'minor' (*keibi*) in light of the aim of the contract and the general sense of trade (*torihikino shakaitsunen*).[388] The burden of proof that the particular non-performance is minor is on the breaching party. It is still not clear what the criteria for determining 'minor' non-performance are, or whether the drafters intended to differentiate the criteria of 'minor' non-performance under Article 541 from the criteria of 'failure of the purpose of the contract' which limits immediate cancellation under Article 542(1)(v). Fault on the part of the breaching party is not a requirement for cancellation.[389]

463. Second, the 2017 Revised Code provides grounds for rights for 'immediate cancellation' (*musaikoku kaijo*), without the need for demanding the obligor to perform within a reasonable period of time (Article 542). The aggrieved party may cancel the contract immediately without giving an additional period of time for performance to the breaching party in the following five situations – where giving the breaching party an additional period of time would be futile.

464. The first situation under Article 542 is when performance of an obligation has become impossible in whole (Article 542(1)(i)). Impossibility is not limited to

386. *Ibid.*
387. However, the rules prior to the 2017 revision were increasingly interpreted in a way that conform to the global trend. *See* H. Sono, 'The Diversity of Favor Contractus: The Impact of the CISG on Japan's Civil Code and its Reform', in *Towards Uniformity*, 169 (Ingeborg Schwenzer and Lisa Spagnolo eds., 2011).
388. Kozuka 2016, *supra* n. 68.
389. Cf. Part I, Ch. 6, §5 (damages) above.

cases where performance is absolutely or physically impossible. It is a broader concept that is determined according to the contract and the general sense of trade (Article 412-2(1)).[390] Although interpretation of these criteria is to yet to be established, performance that is prohibited by law, or performance where its cost is disproportionately large in relation to its benefit, is likely to be considered impossible.

465. It is irrelevant when the impossibility arises. Prior to the 2017 Civil Code Revision, initial impossibility was a ground for invalidity of the contract, and thus, it was not necessary for the obligor to cancel the contract in order to be discharged from its counter-obligation. However, under the 2017 Revision, initial impossibility is no longer a ground for invalidity of the contract (cf. Article 412-2(2)), and thus, the obligee must cancel the contract in order to be discharged from its counter-obligation.

466. Another change in the 2017 Revised Code from prior law is that 'fault' on the part of the obligor is no longer a requirement for cancellation. Under the prior law, if the obligor was not at fault for subsequent impossibility, the rules on risk of loss provided for automatic termination of the contract where the obligee's declaration of intention is not required (former Article 536). Thus, the rules on cancellation by declaration applied only in cases where subsequent impossibility was due to the obligor's fault (former Article 543). This has been changed in the 2017 Reform, and cancellation for impossibility always requires declaration under the revised Code as already explained in paragraph 464 above.

467. The second ground for immediate cancellation is repudiation by the obligor. If the obligor has clearly expressed its intention to repudiate performance in whole, the obligee may cancel the contract (Article 542(1)(ii)). This provision clarifies that anticipatory repudiation of an obligation can be a ground for cancellation.

468. The third ground for immediate cancellation relates to partial impossibility or partial repudiation. In such case, the obligor may partially cancel the contract and discharge its counter-obligation corresponding to the part of obligation that has become impossible or is being repudiated (Article 542(2)). In addition, if the purpose of the contract cannot be achieved by the remaining portion alone, the obligee may immediately cancel the contract in whole (Article 542(1)(iii)).

469. The fourth ground for immediate cancellation relates to obligations where time is of the essence. If, due to the nature of the contract or a manifestation of intention by the parties, the purpose of the contract cannot be achieved unless the performance is carried out at a specific time and date or within a certain period of time, and if the obligor has failed to perform at the time that period lapses, the obligee may immediately cancel the contract (Article 542(1)(iv)).

470. The fifth ground for immediate cancellation is provided in Article 542(1)(v). For cases that do not fall under the four situations explained above

390. *See*, Part I, Ch. 5, §3 above (impossibility and changed circumstances).

(Article 542(1)(i)–(iv)), the obligee may cancel the contract if the obligor has not performed, and if it is clear that there is little prospect of performance will be given that is sufficient to achieve the purpose of the contract – even if the obligee demands performance specifying a reasonable period of time within which the obligor is to perform (Article 542(1)). One will notice that situations under Article 542(1)(i)–(iv) are all where, by definition, it has become clear that the purpose of the contract cannot be achieved any more. Thus, subparagraph (v) is the catch-all provision, and signifies that the criterion for the availability of cancellation is whether the 'purpose of the contract' is achievable or not.

471. It should be noted that foreseeability by the obligor that the purpose of the contract cannot be achieved by non-performance is not a requirement for cancellation. This is different from rules that can be found in some modern contract law.[391] This lack of foreseeability requirement means that the 2017 Revised Code focuses purely on the failure of the purpose of the contract. This broadens the possibility of cancellation compared to rules found in the CISG and the UNIDROIT Principles.

472. Notwithstanding Articles 541 and 542, explained above, if the non-performance was attributable to the obligee, the obligee cannot cancel the contract (Article 543).

III. Effect of Cancellation

473. When a contract is cancelled due to breach, in principle, the contract is retroactively extinguished as if no contract had been formed (direct effect theory)[392]. Consequently, the parties are released from any outstanding obligation. Furthermore, any performance that has actually been supplied or paid becomes subject to restitution (Article 545(1)). In principle, restitution must be made in kind. If restitution in kind is not possible, the monetary value of whatever that was supplied must be returned.[393] When making restitution, any interest, fruit or benefit of use derived from whatever that was supplied or paid under the contract must also be returned (Article 545(2) and (3)). If both parties are bound to make restitution, they must do so simultaneously (Articles 546 and 533).

474. Cancellation due to breach does not deprive the obligee of its right to damages for breach of contract (Article 545(4)). Thus, the obligee may still claim damages to recover performance interests despite the retroactive effect of cancellation.[394]

475. Since cancellation has retroactive effect, this may affect third parties. Thus, the proviso in Article 545(1) expressly states that cancellation cannot prejudice the

391. Cf. Art. 25 CISG, Art. 7.3.1(2)(a) UNIDROIT Principles of Commercial Contracts.
392. Supreme Court, 22 Sep. 1959, Minshu 13-11-1451.
393. *See*, however, para. 478 for extinction of right to cancellation when restitution cannot be made.
394. Great Court of Cassation, 24 Feb. 1919, Minshu 12-251.

rights of third parties. For example, if a sale of land between seller A and buyer B is cancelled after B has resold the land to a third party C, cancellation would retroactively render B a non-owner of the immovable. Thus, in the absence of the proviso, C cannot acquire the ownership of the land since a non-owner cannot transfer property (the *nemo dat* principle). The proviso changes this result by protecting the interest of the third party: C rightfully acquires ownership in the land. Since the purpose of the proviso is to protect third parties from the retroactive effect of cancellation, it follows that third parties protected under the proviso are only those who entered acquired a right prior to the cancellation. However, in order to justify protection, courts have held that, in case of a third party who acquired an immovable, the third party must have registered the transfer of property[395]. In case of movables this issue does not arise since good faith acquirers rightfully acquire ownership in the movable even if they acquired it from a non-owner (Article 192).

476. However, in case of continuous contracts, cancellation only has prospective effect. For example, cancellation of lease (Article 620), employment (Article 630), mandate (Article 652) or partnership (Article 684) does not overturn whatever that has been performed prior to the declaration of cancellation. In addition, when contracts for work are cancelled before the work is completed, the contractor is entitled to payment proportional to the benefit that is given to the other party by partial performance, provided that the performance is divisible (Article 634).

IV. Extinguishment of the Right to Cancel

477. If there is no time limit for exercising the right to cancel, the breaching obligor may request the obligee to clarify, within a reasonable period of time specified by the obligor, whether it will exercise its right to cancel the contract. The right to cancel is extinguished if the obligor does not receive a reply within a reasonable period of time (Article 547).

478. The party who is bound to make restitution loses its right to cancellation if it has intentionally or by fault significantly damaged or become unable to return whatever that has been supplied, or if it has converted the subject matter into any other kind of thing by processing or alteration (main clause of Article 548). However, this rule does not apply if the obligee was not aware that it had a right to cancellation (Article 548 proviso).

§5. Restitution

479. This matter has been dealt with already. *See* above Part I, Chapter 6, §4, IV.

395. Supreme Court, 14 Jun. 1958, Minshu 12-9-1449.

§6. DAMAGES

480. In case of non-performance by the obligor, including impossibility, the obligee may claim damages for loss it suffered by the non-performance (Article 415(1)).[396] The purpose of damages is compensation of the actual loss, so that the obligee will be put in the same economic position as if the obligation been performed. In other words, the obligee can recover 'performance interest' (*riko rieki*), i.e. the interest it was entitled to had the obligation been performed. Damages are to be paid in monetary terms (Article 417: the principle of monetary compensation). Damages in kind are not allowed under Japanese law

481. Breach of the 'duty to protect' may be seen as a type of tort. Japanese law adopts the *cumul* principle under which the obligee may claim either contract damages (Article 415) or tort damages (Article 709).[397]

482. Punitive damages are not allowed. In rejecting recognition of a Californian state court decision that ordered a Japanese corporation to pay punitive damages in tort, the Japanese Supreme Court reasoned that punitive damages are contrary to the compensatory principle in Japanese tort law, and therefore constitute a violation of public policy (cf. current Article 118, Number 3, Code of Civil Procedure).[398] The same reasoning and principle should apply to contract damages generally under the Civil Code.

I. Requirements

483. The obligee must prove (i) the existence of non-performance, (ii) occurrence of loss and (iii) causation between non-performance and the loss. However, causation is merged into the question of scope of damages, and therefore, it is not necessary to be dealt with that here. The following explanation sets out the types of claimable losses. There are several viewpoints to categorise types of losses that are recoverable.

A. *Pecuniary Loss and Non-pecuniary Loss*

484. Pecuniary loss can be further divided into positive loss (*sekkyokuteki songai*), which is a decrease of the obligor's asset base, and negative loss (*shokyokuteki songai*), which is loss of profit.[399] For example, if a customer in a taxi is injured due to the driver's carelessness, the customer should be able to recover the

396. *See* generally, Nakata, *supra* n. 384, 121, primarily dealing with the law prior to the 2017 Reform.
397. *See* Kihara, *supra* n. 72.
398. Supreme Court, 11 Jul. 1997, Minshu 51-6-2573.
399. For an analysis of recovery of lost profit under Japanese law, *see* H. Kojima, 'Calculation of Damages and "Lost Profits" under Japanese Law: A Comparison with German and United States Law', 31 *J. Japan L,* 223 (2011).

medical fees as positive loss, and also lost earnings as negative loss. For pecuniary loss, the economic value of the loss is recoverable.

485. Non-pecuniary loss is also recoverable as contract damages. It will take the form of payment of solace money (or solatium). Usually, however, recovery of pecuniary loss will also compensate for non-pecuniary loss. Non-pecuniary loss is recoverable separately from pecuniary loss only in situations where a 'personality interest' is infringed, for example to life, limb, liberty or honour, or where recovery of pecuniary loss is not sufficient to compensate for the loss (e.g., loss of a pet).[400]

B. Damages for Delay and Damages in Lieu of Performance

486. Another distinction in recoverable loss can be made between (i) loss caused by delay in performance (damages for delay, *chien baisho*) and (ii) loss caused by performance not being made (damages in lieu of performance, *tenpo baisho*). Damages for delay in the case of non-performance of monetary obligation are measured by interests that accrue from the time the obligor is in delay (Article 419). For this special rule, *see* Part I, Chapter 6, §1, IV. Damages in lieu of performance may be sought if the obligation cannot be performed because of impossibility, or if the obligor has equivocally refused to perform, or if the contract has been cancelled or a cancellation right has arisen (Article 415(2)). The value of performance can be recovered. In addition to the above two situations, (iii) if the obligor was under a 'duty to protect' the life, body or property of the obligee, then death, personal injury or property damage caused by the breach of that duty is also recoverable.

II. Exemption

487. The obligor is exempt from damages liability if it establishes that the non-performance was caused by an event that is not attributable to the obligor, in light of the contract and common sense in trade (*torihikino shakai tsunen*: Article 415(1) proviso). Prior to the 2017 Reform, the Civil Code provided simply that the obligor is not liable for damages if the non-performance was not attributable to the obligor. Traditionally, this was interpreted to mean that the obligor is exempt when it was not at 'fault' in the sense of not being 'negligent' (*kashitsu*). Under this understanding, the determination of fault was detached from the contract. However, this view came under criticism in the 1990s: it was argued that the grounds for contract damages, as distinguished from tort damages, should lie in the fact that the obligor did not perform what it agreed to perform.[401] The 2017 reform emphasises that the determination is to be made in light of the contract. However, the relationship

400. Z. Kitagawa and Y. Shiomi, 'Article 416', in *Shinpan Chushaku Minpo [Commentary of the Civil Code]*, Vol. 10(II), 295 (M. Okuda ed., Yuhikaku 2011).

401. *See*, e.g., H. Morita, *Keiyakusekinin-no Kiseki Kozo [The Structure of Contract Liability]* (Yuhikaku 2002); Shiomi, *Saimufuriko-no Kyusaihori [Remedies for Non-Performance of Obligations]*, (Shinzansha 2010).

between the two elements of exemption, namely the '(aim of the) contract' and 'the general sense of trade' is not set out or defined clearly. There are conflicting views on this. One view considers that the 'general sense of trade' is a subfactor in determining the aim of the contract (because contractual obligation is determined not only in accordance with the subjective intent of the parties, but also to the nature, purpose and history of the contract), and thus 'contract' is the controlling element.[402] Another view considers that the two are independent factors, one that focuses on the aim the contract, while the other focuses on extra-contractual reasonableness.[403]

488. If impossibility of performance occurs due to causes not attributable to either party while the obligor is in delay, that impossibility is deemed to be attributable to the obligor (Article 413-2(1)). Thus, the obligor is not exempt from damages liability when such impossibility occurs.

489. Prior to the 2017 reform, fault of a third party engaged by the obligor to assist in performing the obligation (*rikohojosha*) was considered to be equivalent to the fault of the obligor (more precisely: it was considered to be against the good faith principle for the obligor to claim otherwise). Thus, the obligor was not exempt from damages liability when non-performance was caused by the fault of such third party. However, under the 2017 Reform, such reasoning no longer stands because the focus in determining whether non-performance was attributable to the obligor has shifted from 'fault' to 'contract and the general sense of trade'. Although the treatment of such third parties under the 2017 Reform is not yet established, it is generally agreed that the treatment depends on factors such as (i) whether using such a third party was prohibited by the contract, (ii) whether the contract guaranteed a result, (iii) whether the third party's act constitutes non-performance by the obligor or (iv) whether the obligor exercised due care in appointing, directing and supervising the third party.[404]

III. Scope of Damages

490. The scope of damages is determined in accordance with Article 416, which was drafted based on English case law,[405] although there are some deviations.[406] As such, this is a provision that was drafted under heavy influence of the common law.

402. *See*, e.g., K. Yamamoto, Keiyakusekininho-no kaisei [Reform of Laws of Contract Liability], 68 *Hoso Jiho*, 1232 (2016); Shiomi, *supra* n. 108, 379.
403. *See*, e.g., H. Nakata, 'Saikenho ni okeru go-i no igi [The Role and Significance of Agreement in the Law of Obligations]' *Hokkaido J. New Global L. and Pol'y*, Vol. 8 (2010) 20; H. Morita, *Saikenhokaiseiwo Fukameru [Deepening the Obligations Law Reform]*, 31 (Yuhikaku 2013).
404. *Hadley v. Baxendale* (1854), in turn influenced by French law: *see* Z. Kitagawa, 'Damages in Contracts for the Sale of Goods', 3 *Law in Japan* 43 (1969); and Shiomi, *supra* n. 108, 405 et seq.
405. Y. Hirai, *Songaibaishohono Riron [The Theory of the Law of Damages]*, (Tokyodaigaku Shuppankai 1971).
406. *See* generally, Nakata, *supra* n. 384, 131.

However, after the era of 'theory reception' of German law,[407] the term 'adequate causation (*soto inga kankei*)' was often used to describe the rule in Article 416. However, since the term is used differently than it is used in German law, there is growing consensus that it is most sensible to stick to the language of Article 416 to avoid confusion.[408]

491. Article 416 provides for recovery of 'ordinary loss' and 'special loss'. This distinction is important because for special loss, the obligee must prove 'foreseeability', while that is not necessary for ordinary loss. However, the distinction can be blurry, and it is advisable for the obligee seeking damages to always prove foreseeability.

492. 'Ordinary loss' (*tsujo songai*) is loss that will categorically occur by non-performance of an obligation (Article 416(1)). Typical examples are the lost benefit of using the goods due to delay in delivery, the economic value of goods which will not be delivered or interest accruing in the case of non-performance of monetary obligation are typical. In the case of sale between a wholesaler and a retailer, lost profit of the retailer caused by non-delivery by the wholesaler is also an example of ordinary loss.

493. 'Special loss' (*tokubetsu songai*) is loss that do not ordinarily occur, but that occurred due to special circumstances. Special loss is recoverable only when the 'special circumstances' (not the loss itself) were foreseeable to the obligor. For example, if a buyer had already entered into a contract with a sub-purchaser who agreed to pay more than the market price, and if due to seller's non-delivery the buyer failed to make that profit, the lost profit that exceeds the difference between the contract price and the market price (i.e., the usual lost profit) is a 'special loss'. Such special loss is recoverable only if the seller should have foreseen the special circumstances (i.e., the existence of the favourable resale contract). Likewise, if due to contamination of a food product, several buyers who consumed the product suffered diarrhoea but one of them died because of an idiosyncrasy, the seller is liable for the death only if it should have foreseen the idiosyncrasy.[409]

494. The relevant time for 'foreseeability' of the special circumstances is not explicitly provided in Article 416. Courts have consistently interpreted that the relevant time is the 'time of non-performance', and not the time of contract formation.[410] On the other, there is considerable support among scholars for using the time of contract formation as the relevant time.[411] That is a rule that favours predictability of the contract, and one which is adopted in the common law and the CISG. Nonetheless, the 2017 reform maintained the formulation of Article 416, which

407. *See* above Introduction to the Law of Contracts §1.
408. Hirai, *supra* n. 405, 88; Uchida, *supra* n. 109, 159.
409. These examples are taken from Uchida, *supra* n. 109, 160.
410. T. Uchida, *Saikenho no Shinjidai [The New Era of Obligations Law]*, 31 (Shojihomu 2009); Uchida, *supra* n. 109, 161. *See* also Sono, *supra* n. 387, 177.
411. *See*, e.g., Hirai, *supra* n. 405, 153.

means that the existing court practice will continue.[412] The rationale for using the 'time of non-performance' is that since the obligor has undertaken to provide the obligee with a certain interest by way of performance, the obligor should not simply sit back and leave the obligee to incur loss that was foreseeable by the obligor at the time of non-performance.[413] This is perhaps a unique characteristic of Japanese law.

IV. Special Rule Regarding Monetary Obligation

495. Damages for non-performance of monetary obligation is subject to a special rule. First of all, obligors of monetary obligations are never exempt from damages liability. Even force majeure is not an excuse (Article 419(3)).[414]

496. Second, it is not necessary for the obligee to prove that loss was caused by non-performance of a monetary obligation (Article 419(2)). The amount of damages for non-performance of monetary obligations will automatically be calculated by the statutory interest rate effective at the time the obligor becomes liable for non-performance, or according to a contractual interest rate if the parties have agreed on such a rate (Article 419(1)). The rules on statutory interest rate prior to the 2017 Reform adopted a fixed rate of 5% per annum for civil claims (former Article 404) and 6% per annum for commercial claims (former Article 514 Commercial Code). The 2017 reform adopted a fluctuating rate, which will be re-examined every three years (Article 404). When the reform comes into effect, the initial rate will be 3% per annum for both civil and commercial claims.

497. On the other, even if the obligee proves that there was loss that exceeds the interest, the obligee is not allowed to recover such loss.[415] For example, the obligor cannot recover the cost of collection, or the profit it lost for not being able to make an investment for lack of funds.

V. Attorney Fees

498. Attorney fees are not recoverable as damages because it is not compulsory to use attorneys in filing lawsuits under Japanese law. However, exception is made for damages claims brought under tort.[416] Likewise, if a damages claim is brought

412. Rather, there was an attempt in an early draft to explicitly provide that the relevant time is the time of non-performance. *See*, *Minpo (Saikenkankei) no Kaiseini kansuru Chukanshian [Intermediate Draft for the Civil Code (Law of Obligations) Reform]*, Item 6, para. 10. That draft included a rule stating that the obligor is not liable for such special loss even if the special circumstance was foreseeable at the time of non-performance, if it had taken reasonable steps to avoid such loss. These proposals were abandoned altogether, leaving the solution to the courts.
413. Sono, *supra* n. 387, 177.
414. *See*, Part I, Ch. 5, §3 above (impossibility and changed circumstances).
415. Supreme Court, 11 Oct. 1973, Hanji 723-44.
416. Supreme Court, 27 Feb. 1969, Minshu 23-2-441.

as a contractual claim, but if the non-performance also amounts to tort, the claimant may recover attorney fees as damages.[417] With respect to the amount that is recoverable when the case falls under those exceptions, courts tend to limit the recovery of attorney fees to 10% of the amount of other recoverable damages, rather than allowing recovery of the actual amount paid to attorneys. If the 10% of the recoverable damages is unreasonably high, the court will make necessary adjustments.[418] 'Court fees' must be distinguished. They are borne by the losing party (Article 61, Code of Civil Procedure).

VI. Adjustment of Damages Amounts

A. Deduction of Interim Interest

499. If damages include compensation for future loss, interest that would have accrued on the future loss is to be deducted, because the obligor will receive compensation for futurc loss in advance. The amount of deduction will be calculated according to the statutory rate that is effective at the time the damages claim arose (Article 417-2).

B. Comparative Negligence

500. In determining the amount of damages, courts will take into account the contribution of the obligee to the non-performance, occurrence of loss or aggravation of loss (Article 418).[419] In effect, this results in reduction of the amount of damages. Courts use numerical terms in describing the contribution of the obligee to the occurrence or aggravation of harm, and reduce the amount of damages proportionally according to the proportion of negligence on the part of the obligee as compared to that of the obligor. This is a widely used provision to achieve just compensation.

501. Although the provision uses the term 'negligence' (*kashitsu*), it is generally agreed that it does not mean breach of duty of care in the sense used in tort law. It is used more loosely in the sense of whether the obligee has taken reasonable steps in light of the contract and the general sense of trade.[420]

417. Supreme Court, 24 Feb. 2012, Hanrei-Jiho 2144-89.
418. S. Okamoto, *Songaibaisho-no han-i I Soron/baibai [The Scope of Damage I General & Sales]*, 261 et seq (Ichiryusha 1999).
419. *See* generally, Nakata, *supra* n. 384, 135.
420. Hirai, *supra* n. 405, 107–108; Uchida, *supra* n. 109, 169.

502. The 2017 Reform clarified that this rule applies not only when the obligor contributed to the non-performance but also when the obligor contributed to the occurrence or aggravation of the loss. This clarification may be seen as codification of a duty to mitigate loss.[421]

C. *Adjustment for Profit and Loss* (Son-eki Sosai)

503. Although there is no explicit provision, if the obligee received profits from non-performance of the obligor, that amount will be deducted from the amount of damages. For example, if a construction contract is cancelled due to the owner's non-performance, the contractor may claim damages for the price it was entitled to, but the cost for the materials that the contractor avoided using for the project will be deducted.[422]

VII. Liquidated Damages

504. Parties are free to agree on liquidated damages, which is an agreement for a sum due upon non-performance (*songaibaishogakuno yotei*) (Article 420(1)).[423] Payment based on such agreement replaces damages based on the Civil Code, but does not replace the right to performance or a right of cancellation (Article 420(2)). Fixed 'penalties' (*iyakukin*) that are to be paid in addition to damages can also be agreed, but such penalty clauses are presumed to be an agreement of liquidated damages replacing damages based on the Civil Code (Article 420(3)). *See also* Part I, Chapter 3, §1, V.

505. Courts do not have the power to increase or decrease the agreed sum. However, if the agreed sum is against public policy (Article 90), courts may hold that the agreement is partially or wholly void.

506. The Consumer Contract Act regulates liquidated damages and penalty clauses in consumer contracts. Clauses stipulating an amount of liquidated damages or fixed penalty in the event of cancellation by the consumer are void to the extent the amount exceeds the 'average loss' (*heikintekina songai*) that would be caused to the other party (the business operator) by such cancellation (Article 9 (i), Consumer Contract Act). Likewise, clauses stipulating an amount of liquidated damages or fixed penalty in the event of default (non-payment) by the consumer are void to the extent the amount exceeds the amount calculated by the amount of default multiplied by 14.6% per annum (Article 9 (ii)). The rate of 14.6% per annum was chosen

421. Shiomi 2017, *supra* n. 402, 503.
422. Uchida, *supra* n. 109, 171.
423. *See* generally, Nakata, *supra* n. 384, 137.

as a customary rate for the upper limit of damages for non-payment. Thus, the basic idea here is also to limit liquidated damages or penalty to the extent of 'average loss'.[424]

VIII. Subrogation by Payment of Damages (*Baishosha Daii*)

507. If the obligee receives the whole value of the thing or right as damages, the obligor is automatically subrogated to the obligor's right for the thing or right (Article 422). For example, if a deposited good is damaged by a third party, and if the depositary pays damages to the depositor for whole value of the damaged goods, the depositary is subrogated to the depositor's ownership of the goods and right to claim damages against the third party.

§7. Cure and Price Reduction

508. In contracts for value (*yusho keiyaku*),[425] there are special remedies in case the obligor's performance does not conform to the contract. In addition to damages and the right of cancellation, the obligee has a right to demand cure (*tsuikan*) or, if the obligor does not cure, to reduce the price (or counter obligation). In order to resort to these remedies, the obligee must give notice of non-conformity to the obligee, within one year from the time it becomes aware of the non-conformity, unless the obligor knew or was grossly negligent in not knowing the non-conformity. The provisions on these remedies are placed within the provisions of sales contracts (Articles 562–564, 566), which are applied *mutatis mutandis* to other types of contract for value (Article 559). For these remedies, *see* below Part II, Chapter 6.

509. There are further special rules regarding right to demand cure and right of price reduction tailored to the peculiarities of contracts for work. Under the special rules, the owner cannot resort to remedies for non-conformity of the work if the non-conformity was caused by the material supplied by owner, or if the non-conformity was caused by instructions given by the owner, unless the contractor was aware that the material or instruction was inappropriate (Article 636). These remedies are subject to the same one-year notice requirement as in sales and other contracts for value (Article 637(1)). However, the notice requirement does not apply if the contractor knew or was grossly negligent in not knowing about the non-conformity at the time of delivery of the work or in cases where delivery of work is not necessary (e.g., contract to give a lecture), at the time the work was finished (Article 637(2)). For these remedies, *see* below Part II, Chapter 5.

---

424. *Chikujo Kaisetsu Shohisha Keiyakuho [Article-by-Article Commentary of the Consumer Contract Act]*, 224 (Shohishacho Shishaseidoka [Consumer Affairs Agency, Consumer Institutions Division] ed., 3rd ed., Shojihomu 2018).

425. *See* Part I, Introduction to the Law of Contracts § 3 above (classifications of contract).

§8. Extinctive Prescription

510. With respect to time limitations for exercise of rights, Japanese law adopts the civil law tradition's approach of extinctive prescription (*shometsu jiko*) periods that consider that claims are extinguished, as a matter of substantive law, as the result of expiration of a certain period of time. It does not adopt the common law's approach (typically now found in statutes of limitations), which considers that bringing claims to courts is time-barred as a matter of procedural law.

511. The rules on extinctive prescription underwent major streamlining in the 2017 Civil Code Reform. In particular, it considerably shortened the time that claims may possibly be extinguished by prescription, from ten years to five years. Commencement periods are different, and therefore more careful analysis is necessary (as will be done in the following paragraphs). However, in essence the 2017 Reform is in line with the comparative trend of adopting a shorter limitation period,[426] which promotes the exercise of rights.

I. Duration and Commencement of Extinctive Prescription Period

512. The 2017 Reform adopts a dual prescription period for contractual claims. The length and commencement of the general prescription period are:

(i) Five years from the time the obligee became aware that it can exercise the claim (Article 166(1)(i)); or
(ii) Ten years from the time the claim can be exercised (Article 166(1)(ii)).

513. The claim is extinguished by the expiration of whichever period expires earlier. The ten-year prescription period is the same rule under the Civil Code prior to the 2017 Reform. The 5-year period was added in the 2017 Reform. The 2017 Reform deletes the prescription period for commercial claims that was provided in the Commercial Code (five years from when the claim can be exercised), and therefore, there is no distinction between civil and commercial claims with respect to prescription periods.

514. Since the commencement of the first prescription period depends on the awareness of the obligor (a subjective commencement time), it may never commence. The second prescription period places a cap on the duration by adopting an objective commencement time of 'when the right can be exercised': i.e., when there are no legal obstacles to the exercise of the right. For example, for claims which have due dates, the period commences on the day following the due date (Article 140 provides that the first day of the period is not included in the calculation). For claims which do not have due dates, the period commences from the time the obligation arises (e.g., for claims for damages for non-performance, prescription period

426. R. Zimmerman, *Comparative Foundations of a European Law of Set-Off and Prescription* 86 (Cambridge University Press 2010).

commences at the time of non-performance). However, courts have sometimes adopted a less rigid approach. For example, in a case involving a claim for life insurance that was made after three years of the death of the insured (three years being the prescription period in this case under an old Commercial Code provision and the insurance policy), because the insured was missing for three years until his body was discovered, the court held that the prescription does not run from the time of death; instead, the court held that 'where, in light of the objective circumstances, there is special reason that makes it unrealistic to exercise the right at the time the claim arises, the prescription period does not commence to run form that time'.[427]

515. Attention should be given to prescription periods for the right to cancel a contract due to non-performance. This is a right categorised as a 'formative right' (*keiesiken*) because their unilateral exercise has the power of forming legal rights and duties (e.g., right to restitution). Nonetheless, the same prescription period applies to rights to cancel the contract due breach.[428] Another example of formative rights is the right to rescind the contract (due to incapacity, mistake, fraud or duress). They are subjcct to a special prescription period of five years from the time the rescindable act can be ratified, or twenty years from the time of the rescindable act (Article 126). The right that arises as a consequence of exercise of these formative rights is subject to an independent prescription. Therefore, if a right to restitution arises by exercise of a right of cancellation, the prescription period for the right to restitution commences from the time the contract was cancelled.[429]

516. There are several special rules regarding the duration of prescription periods. First, claims based on torts are subject to a different prescription period. Here, again a dual prescription period is adopted:

(i) Three years from the time the victim becomes aware of the loss and the tortfeasor (subjective commencement time) (Article 724(i)); or
(ii) Twenty years from the time of tort (objective commencement time).

517. Second, for damages claims for infringement of life or limb, the ten-year prescription period under Article 166(1)(ii) is extended to twenty years (Article 167) from the time when the right can be exercised, to give greater protection to the victims of bodily harm.

518. Third, for rights that give rise to periodic payments (e.g., right to a pension and not the right to an individual pension payment), a dual prescription period is adopted:

(i) Ten years from the time the obligee becomes aware of its right to the individual payment (subjective commencement time); or

427. Supreme Court, 11 Dec. 2003, Minshu 57-11-2196.
428. *See*, e.g., T. Sakuma, *Minpono Kiso [The Foundation of Civil Law]*, Vol. 1, 408 (4th ed., Yuhikaku 2018).
429. *Ibid.*, 231.

(ii) Twenty years from the time the right to individual payments can be exercised (objective commencement period).

519. Lastly, the prescription period for judgment claims and claims that have the effect equivalent to judgment claims is ten years from the time the claim becomes binding (i.e., the time when the judgment becomes unappealable) (Article 169(1)). Claims that have equivalent effect as judgment claims include, for example, rights established in a court-annexed settlement or conciliation (Articles 267 and 275(5) Code of Civil Procedure), demand for payment by the court (Article 396 Code of Civil Procedure) and arbitral awards (Article 45(1) Arbitration Act).

520. Traditionally, it has been considered that extension of the prescription period by agreement is not allowed, as that will be tantamount to an agreement to waive the benefit of prescription (*see* paragraphs 536 et seq. *infra*), and this tends to harm obligors in a weaker position. On the other, it was considered that an agreement to shorten the prescription period is allowed. However, such a view has been increasingly questioned, and currently it is not established whether the prescription period can be modified by agreement or not.[430] The 2017 Reform did not take any position on this issue.

II. Suspension and Renewal of Prescription Period

521. Once the prescription period commences to run, but before it expires, it can be suspended (*kansei yuuyo*) so that the period will not expire, or it can be renewed (*koshin*). The following paragraphs explain the grounds for suspension of expiration or renewal of the prescription. Suspension and renewal are effective solely among the parties with respect to whom the ground of such suspension or renewal arose, and their respective successors (Article 153: the 'relative effect' of suspension and renewal).

522. First of all, if the obligor acknowledges its obligation, the prescription is renewed and runs anew from the time of such acknowledgement (Article 152).

523. Second, the expiration of prescription period is suspended by commencement of certain proceedings. The running of the period is not suspended; it is only the expiration that is suspended. Suspension will last until the end of the proceedings. However, if the proceedings are terminated before the judgment or its equivalent becomes binding (becoming unappealable) or if the filing withdrawn, the suspension ceases after the expiration of 6 months from the time of termination or withdrawal of the proceedings. In other words, the obligee is given a six-month grace period to take the next step.

430. On the debate, *see* N. Kano, 'Jikoto Go-I [Prescription and Agreement]', in *Shometsujikohono Genjoto Kaiseiteigen [The State of Extinctive Prescription and Reform Proposals]*, 52 (N. Kanayama ed., Shojihomu 2008).

524. Such proceedings include:

(i) filing of an action, filing of demand procedures,[431] filing for settlement procedures prior to filing of an action,[432] filing for conciliation in court in accordance with the Civil Conciliation Act or the Domestic Relations Case Procedure Act, or participation in insolvency proceedings (Article 147(1));
(ii) compulsory execution, enforcement of a security rights, judicial auction to enforce security rights,[433] property disclosure procedure[434] (Article 148(1));
(iii) filing of an arbitration proceeding (Article 29(2) Arbitration Act (Act No. 138 of 2003));
(iv) making a request for conciliation or mediation to a certified disputed resolution provider, provided that the certified dispute resolution provider, after attempting to arrange a settlement, has terminated the procedure on the grounds that it is impossible to arrange a settlement, and the party who made the request for certified dispute resolution brings a suit within one month from the date of being notified of the termination (Article 25(1) Act on Promotion of Use of Alternative Dispute Resolution (Act No. 151 of 2004)).

525. If, according to these proceedings, the rights are fixed by judgment or its equivalent, or if the execution proceedings are finished, the prescription period is renewed (runs anew) from that time (Articles 147(2) and 148(2)).

526. If, the proceedings are commenced, but not against the party who enjoys the benefit of extinctive prescription, suspension or renewal does not take effect until the party who enjoys the benefit of extinctive prescription is notified (Article 154). For example, if a security right granted by a third party is enforced, suspension or renewal of the prescription period regarding the secured obligation does not take effect until the obligor is so notified.

527. If, due to any natural disaster or other unavoidable contingency, measures of suspension by commencement of proceedings listed under Articles 147(1) or Article 148(1), explained above, cannot be taken, the expiration of the prescription period is suspended until after three months from the time such impediment has ceased to exist (Article 161). Thus, the parties are given three months grace period to commence proceedings listed above.

528. Third, provisional seizure and provisional disposition suspend the expiration of the prescription period until after six months from the time the provisional measures are terminated (Article 149).

---

431. For demand procedures, *see* Arts 382 et seq. of the Code of Civil Procedure.
432. For settlement procedures prior to filing of an action, *see* Art. 275(1) of the Code of Civil Procedure.
433. For judicial auction to enforce security rights, *see* Art. 195 Civil Execution Act.
434. For property disclosure procedure, *see* Art. 196 Civil Execution Act.

529. Fourth, out-of-court demand for performance suspends the expiration of the prescription period for six months from the time of the demand (Article 150(1)). Thus, the party making the demand must take the next step such as filing an action within the six-month grace period. The obligor cannot extend the six-month period by repeating the demand (Article 150(2)).

530. Fifth, agreement to negotiate over the claim also suspends the expiration of prescription periods (Article 151). This is a new rule that was introduced in the 2017 Reform. Its purpose is to avoid the expiration of the prescription period while negotiation over the claim is underway. However, the application of this rule is limited to agreements to negotiation made in writing (Article 151(1)), including writings in electronic form (Article 151(3)). If such agreement is made, Article 151(1) provides that expiration of the prescription period is suspended until the earlier of:

(i) one year from the time of that agreement;
(ii) if the negotiation provides for a period of negotiation under one year, the time of expiration of that period; or
(iii) if one party has notified the other party in writing that it refuses to continue negotiation, six months from the time of that notification.

531. The parties may extend the suspension of expiration by repeatedly entering into an agreement to negotiate while the expiration of the prescription period is suspended, but the maximum length of suspension cannot exceed five years (Article 151(2)). The parties cannot extend the suspension of expiration by resorting to the suspension by demand under Article 150 while the expiration is suspended by an agreement to negotiate. Nor can the parties extend the suspension of expiration by resorting to suspension by agreement while expiration is suspended by a demand under Article 150 (Article 151(3)).

532. Lastly, there are also rules on suspension of expiration that cover situations where rights cannot be exercised due to incapacity (Article 158 – six months from the time exercise becomes possible); where the dispute is between spouses (Article 159 – six months from the time of dissolution of the marriage); or where the dispute relates to inherited property (Article 160 – six months from the time the heir is identified, the administrator is appointed or the commencement of insolvency proceedings).

III. Effect of Expiration of the Prescription Period

A. *Invocation*

533. Courts will not rely on the expiration of the prescription period in making its judgment unless it is invoked by a party which has a legitimate interest in the extinction of the right (Article 145). It is left to the consideration of the parties whether they wish to benefit from extinctive prescription or not. Article 145 as revised in 2017 explicitly provides that parties who have legitimate interest in the extinguishment of the right includes guarantor, third-party grantor of security right, third-party acquirers of an encumbered asset. This is an incorporation of the case law development. Case law prior to the 2017 Reform depended on the criterion that a party must be a party who 'directly' benefits from extinctive prescription. Courts have held that unsecured competing creditors[435] and lower-ranking secured creditors (with respect to extinction of a higher-ranking secured creditor's claim)[436] do not directly benefit from extinctive prescription of the obligor's obligation.

534. The effect of invocation of the expiration of the prescription period only affects the rights of the invoking party and party against whom it is invoked. Thus, invocation by a guarantor does not affect the right against the main obligor. On the other, if an obligor whose obligation is secured by a guarantor invokes the expiration of the prescription period, the obligation of the guarantor is also extinguished. However, this is a result of a rule that guarantee obligations are discharged when the main obligation is extinguished.[437]

B. Retroactive Effect

535. When the expiration of the prescription period is invoked, it has retroactive effect (Article 144). Namely, the claim will be considered extinct from the time of commencement of the prescription period. Thus, for example, the obligor is not obligated to pay interest on its monetary obligation that is extinguished by the prescription period.

536. However, if a claim which is extinguished by prescription had been suitable for set-off prior to such extinguishment, it is still possible to use that claim for the purpose of set-off (Article 508) – introduced generally above.

C. Waiver of the Benefits of Prescription

537. The benefit of the prescription may not be waived before the time of expiration (Article 146). On the other, waiver after the expiration is allowed. If the benefit is waived, a new prescription period commences to run.[438]

538. There may be situations where, after the expiration of the prescription period, the obligor acknowledges its obligation (including request for deferment, or making partial payment) without being aware of the expiration. This cannot be a post-expiration waiver if the obligor did not know of the expiration. The Supreme Court, overturning earlier decisions to the contrary, held in 1966 that post-expiration acknowledgment cannot be presumed to be a waiver. However, the

435. Grand Court of Cassation, 30 Jun. 1937, Minshu 16-1037.
436. Supreme Court, 21 Oct. 1999, Minshu 53-7-1190.
437. Sakuma, *supra* n. 428, 438.
438. Supreme Court, 21 May 1970, Minshu 24-5-393.

Supreme Court further held that the party who made the post-expiration acknowledgement may be barred by good faith from invoking the expiration.[439]

439. Supreme Court (Grand Bench), 20 Apr. 1966, Minshu 20-4-702.

Part II. Specific Contracts

Chapter 1. Agency

539. The law structuring principal–agent relationships is found in Civil Code Articles 99 to 118. The Code starts with the basic principle that a manifestation of intent to a third party by an agent, acting within the scope of authority and representing that she acts on behalf of a principal, binds the principal (Article 99(1)). The agent then assumes no rights and incurs no obligations vis-à-vis the third party. The transaction affects the principal alone.

§1. Types of Agency

540. Japanese law recognises two categories of agency: (1) 'agency established by law' (*houtei dairi*) and (2) 'voluntary agency' (*nin'i dairi*).[440] Examples of agency relationships established by law include parent–child agency relationships (Articles 818 and 819), guardianship (Article 839) and administrators of assets or estates (Articles 25). Voluntary agency relationships include agreements between a principal and an agent, employers and employees, partnerships and owner–contractor relationships.[441]

541. Agency established by law may be recognised as a matter of course, as with parent–child agency relationships, or by court order, as with bankruptcy trustees and estate administrators. Voluntary agency relationships are generally created by written delegations of authority, with the principal affixing his or her seal to a mandate (*ininjou*), or power of attorney, and providing the mandate to the agent.[442] Notarisation is not required.

§2. Authority of Agent

542. In most situations, the principal defines the scope of the agent's authority. For example, a corporation will execute a mandate specifically requesting that a

440. K. Shinomiya & Y. Nomi, *Minpo Sosoku [General Provisions of the Civil Code]* 346 (9th ed., Kobundo, 2018).
441. *Ibid.*, 347.
442. *Ibid.*, 349.

judicial scrivener (*shihou shoshi*)[443] complete corporate filings on its behalf, or a principal will execute a mandate specifically requesting that an agent complete and file the principal's tax returns.

543. When mandates are executed without specifying the scope of authority, the Civil Code states that agents have the authority to engage only in 'acts of preservation' and acts that use or improve the property or right but do not change its nature (Article 103).

544. In practice, Japanese law recognises both specific mandates and 'blank' mandates (*hakushi ininjou*), with special laws restricting some parties, such as lenders, from demanding the latter (Article 20 Money Lending Industry Regulation Act). A 'blank' mandate is not necessarily a blanket grant of authority, or a general power of attorney. Mandates are generally provided to an agent for a specific purpose, often apparent from the mandate itself, resulting in limitations not based on an express grant of authority but rather the type of the mandate. A blank mandate to a tax agent, for example, will not confer on the tax agent a general authority to conduct the principal's business.

545. Courts have also recognised oral or implicit grants of authority made to agents residing with, or family members working for, the principal.[444]

546. Whether the grant of authority is explicit or implied or the agency is created voluntarily or by law, Japanese law envisages three different legal relationships: (1) agent and principal; (2) agent and third party; (3) principal and third party. Each relationship will be addressed in turn.

I. Agent and Principal

547. An agent owes a duty of care to the principal. That duty of care is defined by the Civil Code sections on mandate,[445] discussed *supra*, as an obligation to exercise the 'care of a good manager in compliance with the main purport of the mandate'. (Article 644)

548. In contrast to Japan's Company Act, which imposes a general duty of loyalty on corporate directors (Article 355, Company Act),[446] the Civil Code contains no general duty of loyalty for agents. Instead, the code specifically prohibits an agent, absent consent, from self-dealing or representing both parties in a transaction (Article 108, Civil Code). The courts, in turn, have interpreted this provision more

---

443. On these and other 'quasi-lawyers', *see* generally Abe & Nottage, *supra* n. 1, 474.
444. Great Court of Cassation, 4 Feb. 1941, Shimbun 4674-8; Great Court of Cassation, 10 Oct. 1935, Hanketsu Zenshu 1-23-4.
445. In general, a civil law mandate is simply 'a written command or commission given by a principal to an agent': *Black's Law Dictionary*, 1047 (9th ed., 2009).
446. *See* generally Hideki Kanda and Curtis Milhaupt, 'Re-examining Legal Transplants: The Director's Fiduciary Duty in Japanese Corporate Law', 51 *Am. J. Comparative L.* 887 (2003).

generally to preclude conflicts of interest between the agent and principal, but they analyse such conflicts in terms of unauthorised agency rather than a general breach of a duty of loyalty.[447] Absent ratification, a conflicted transaction, has no legal effect on the principal.[448]

549. Sometimes the agent acts within the scope of authority on behalf of the principal, but in fact not for the benefit of the principal. Consider, for example, a case where an employee–agent executed a sales agreement within the scope of authority, but with the intent to divert the proceeds of the sale.[449] Such an act of the agent is generally binding on the principal, because otherwise it would be to the detriment to the third party, with whom the agent has a transaction, reasonably believing that the act binds the principal. Article 107, however, provides that it is deemed to be an act without authority if the third party knew or should have known of the agent's intent.[450]The third party with knowledge of the agent's intent no longer needs to be protected, so the act is not considered to be binding on the principle.

550. Given the duties owed by agents to their principals, agents may employ assistants in the performance of their duties. However, absent authorisation by the principal or 'unavoidable reasons,' agents may not appoint subagents to complete the agent's obligations in voluntary agency (Article 104), whereas agents may appoint subagents at any time on their own responsibility in agency established by law (Article 105). There is more necessity for subagents to be appointed in agency established by law than in voluntary agency because the agents established by law may not resign at will while on the other they assume broad liability to protect the principal. This is why subagents can be more easily appointed in agency established by law.

551. If a subagent is appointed, he or she acts with the same rights and obligations as the agent vis-à-vis the principal and third parties (Article 106(2)), though he or she may discharge obligations owed to the principal by providing goods or services to the original agent.[451] In other words, the subagent owes obligations to the principal as well as to the original agent, and thus may discharge his or her obligation by performance offered either to the original agent or the principal.

447. Great Court of Cassation, 6 Jun. 1932, Minshu 11-1115; Supreme Court, 4 Apr. 1972, Minshu 26-3-373. The MOJ advisory committee has proposed codifying this case law. MOJ, *supra* n. 104, 39.
448. Acts in violation of this section are generally considered void, but may be ratified by the principal. *Ibid*. at 116; Great Court of Cassation, 24 May 1923, Minshu 2-323; Shinomiya & Nomi, *supra* n. 440; Supreme Court, 4 Apr. 1972, Minshu 26-3-373.
449. Supreme Court, 20 Apr. 1967. Minshu 21-3-697.
450. Therefore, the act of the agent can be ratified by the principal. By contrast, it could not be ratified before the 2017 Reform, since it used to be considered void, according to the courts applying by analogy the proviso of the former Art. 93 (now the revised Art. 93(1)) in the sense that the manifested intention of the agent looks like one expressed for the benefit of the principal, but in fact is not. (The case mentioned at *supra* note 449 used to be the leading one).
451. Supreme Court, 9 Apr. 1976, Minshu 30-3-208.

552. In agency established by law, the agent is responsible for any act by the subagent, although the agent remains only responsible for the selection and supervision of the subagent in the case of appointment of subagents for unavoidable reasons (Article 105). By contrast, in voluntary agency, according to the general rule of non-performance caused by the third party engaging in performing the obligor's obligations,[452] it depends on the purport of an agency contract between the principal and the agent what responsibility the agent would assume to the principal regarding the acts of the subagent.

II. The Agent and Third Parties

553. The Civil Code requires that the agent represent to the third party that the agent is acting on behalf of the principal. In practice, this can be done by the agent expressly executing documents as an agent, or demonstrating a principal–agent relationship by signing documents and adding a title and company name or affixing a company seal after signing.[453]

554. Absent such a manifestation of intent to act on behalf of another, the Civil Code deems the act to have been made on the agent's own behalf, unless the third party knew or should have known it was on behalf of a principal (Article 100). With business entities, the Commercial Code reverses the presumption and deems an act to have been made on the principal's behalf even without a declaration of intent by the agent, unless the third party was unaware that the agent was acting on behalf of the principal, in which case the third party may demand performance by the agent (Article 504, Commercial Code).[454]

555. Absent ratification by the principal, the unauthorised agent is liable for performance of the contract or for damages to a third party who did not know, and had no basis for knowing, that the purported agent was acting without authority (Article 117, Civil Code).

556. The courts have interpreted Article 117 to impose strict liability on the agent.[455] However, the agent need to only prove negligence on the part of the third party, i.e. that the third party should have known about the lack of authority, to avoid liability.[456] Assuming no knowledge and no negligence, the courts recognise claims

452. *See supra*, para. 489.
453. Shinomiya & Nomi, *supra* n. 440, 365; Great Court of Cassation, 27 Mar. 1907, Minroku 13-359. Executing contracts in Japan is discussed above in Ch. 1, §2.
454. In comparison, the common law's undisclosed principal doctrine provides that an agent acting in his or her own name may be held liable, along with the undisclosed principal, because the principal authorized the conclusion of the contract. *See*, e.g., H. Verhagen & L. Macgregor, 'Agency and Representation', in *Elgar Encyclopedia of Comparative Law*, 55 (J. Smits ed., 2nd ed., Edward Elgar 2012).
455. Supreme Court, 7 Jul. 1987, Minshu 41-5-113.
456. *Ibid.*

for expectation damages or for performance if the nature of the contract is such that not only the principal but also the agent can perform it.[457]

557. With regard to the agent's manifestation of intention expressed to the third party, it is the agents having no intention, being in mistake, under fraud or duress, and knowing or being negligently ignorant of certain circumstance that bear on its effect. (Article 101(1). For example, the principal may rescind the agent's manifestation of intention if such manifestation is expressed under fraud by the third party. Note, for your reference, that fraud or duress by the agent enables the third party to rescind the contract with that agent, regardless of whether or not the principal knows of the circumstance, since the principal should be liable for the agent's act. This is outside of the scope of Article 101(1)).

558. On the other, with regard to the third party's manifestation of intention expressed to the agent, it is also the agent's knowing or being negligently ignorant of certain circumstance that bears its effect (Article 101(2). For example, the principal may argue that the third party's manifestation of intention based on concealment of true intention is valid as long as the agent does not know of the circumstance, even if the principal knows of it).

559. Where the principal entrusts the agent to act specifically, the Civil Code does not allow the principal to claim that the agent does not know of the circumstance if the principle knows it, nor claim that the agent is innocently ignorant of it if the principal is negligently ignorant of it (Article 101(3)).

560. With voluntary agency, the act of the agent with limited legal capacity may not be rescinded for such capacity (Article 102), since it binds only the principal, not the agent. For example, a minor may act on behalf of and bind a principal. At the same time, the appointment of a guardian for the agent or the agent's bankruptcy will terminate agency authority (Article 111(1)(i)).

561. With agency relationships created by law, however, the act of the agent with limited legal capacity may be rescinded for the purpose of protecting the principal (Article 102, proviso), although at times, appointment of such an agent will be prohibited (Articles 847 and 876-2).[458]

III. The Principal and Third Parties

562. Absent actual authority, the basic principle is that the act of a purported agent without authority does not bind the principal (Article 113(1)).

457. Supreme Court, 5 Dec. 1957, Shimbun 83-84-16. The common law similarly imposes liability on the agent for a breach of warranty of authority, unless the other party 'knows that the agent is not so authorized'. *See,* e.g., Restatement (Second) Agency §330 (1958). This inquiry into the other party's knowledge regarding the unauthorized act is, in part, an attempt to establish causation, 'reliance' on the misrepresentation. *Id.* at § 331.

458. Great Court of Cassation, 2 Apr. 1906, Minshu 12-553, Shinomiya & Nomi, *supra* n. 440, 371.

563. The exceptions to this are common to both common and civil law traditions. A principal, with legal capacity to act, may ratify the unauthorised act of an agent validating an otherwise non-binding contract (Articles 113(1) and 116).[459] A third party may demand ratification by the principal within a 'reasonable period' and, if there is no response, the principal is deemed to have refused to ratify (Article 114). The third party, unless she should have known about the lack of authority, may also rescind the contract prior to ratification by the principal (Article 115). The courts have held that ratification may be expressed or implied.[460] Absent agreement otherwise or prejudice to a third party, with ratification the contract in question is given retroactive effect back to the date the agent executed it (Article 116).

§3. Apparent Agency

564. Japanese law also recognises the basic principles of apparent agency. The Civil Code distinguishes three types of apparent agency: (1) apparent agency based on a manifestation of a grant of authority (Article 109(1)); (2) apparent agency exceeding that grant of authority (Article 110); and (3) apparent agency following termination of the agent's authority (Article 112(1)).[461]

I. Apparent Agency and Manifested Authority

565. First, conduct by a principal suggestive to a third party that authority to act has been granted to an agent is liable for acts within the scope of the manifested authority, unless the third party knew or reasonably should have known that the person did not in fact have authority to act as the principal's agent (Article 109(1)).[462] For example, proof that the agent possessed the principal's registered seal, a blank commission of authority (*hakushi ininjou*) and proof of completed property registration is considered a reasonable basis for the third party to believe the agent had authority to transfer the property.[463]

566. Issues relating to this type of apparent agency arise frequently in Japan with the blank mandates (*hakushi ininjou*) discussed at paragraph 544 above as well as

459. *See also* Great Court of Cassation, 7 Aug. 1936, Minshu 15-1630 (holding that the unauthorized acts of a guardian may be ratified by a minor after achieving the age of majority; Great Court of Cassation, 9 Sep. 1934, Minshu 13-1777 (unauthorized acts taken during a principal's incapacity may be ratified by the principal after regaining mental capacity); Supreme Court, 21 Jan. 1993, Minshu 47-1-265 (joint beneficiaries of a decedent, if unanimous, may ratify unauthorized acts completed prior to the passing of the decedent).

460. Great Court of Cassation, 6 Mar. 1931, Shimbun 3252-10.

461. In each case of those (1)˜(3), there is (i) an appearance of authority when there is none, (ii) the principals involvement in creating such appearance and (iii) the good faith reliance, i.e. no knowledge and no negligence, by the third party. Japanese scholars characterize this as an application of the '*Rechtsschein* principle'.

462. Supreme Court, 22 Apr. 1961, Minshu 20-4-752 (holding that a principal proving bad faith or negligence by the third party avoids liability for acts completed by an agent with apparent authority).

463. Shinomiya & Nomi, *supra* n. 440, 391.

'name lending' (*meigi gashi*), where one party permits another to do business or complete transactions in his or her name. With a business entity, the Commercial Code imposes joint liability on both the borrower of the trade name and the lender (Article 14, Commercial Code).

II. Apparent Agency and Exceeding the Grant of Authority

567. The same principles hold true for apparent authority and actions that, in fact, exceed the authority granted. The courts will protect third parties having reasonable grounds for believing that authority exists (Article 110, Civil Code).

568. In this case, however, the courts have held that the initial grant of authority must be to complete a private act. For example, courts have held that loaning a registered seal in order for an agent to file a report of death does not constitute a basic grant of authority to the agent sufficient to give rise to apparent agency.[464]

569. With claims based on apparent authority exceeding actual authority given, courts have also held that the third party bears the burden of proving a 'reasonable basis' for its belief that the agent had authority to complete the transaction.[465]

570. In order to protect the good faith, reasonable expectation of third parties, apparent agency based on manifestation of authority shall be recognised even if it also involves apparent agency exceeding the grant authority (Article 109(2)).[466]And courts have further applied the Article 110 by analogy where there is no apparent agency, but instead the agent purports to be the principal and acts beyond his or her authority. The courts will protect the third party where there is 'a reasonable basis' for believing that the act was an act of the principal.[467]

III. Apparent Agency Following Termination of Authority

571. Finally, with regard to apparent authority after termination of the agency relationship, liability of a principal for the acts of a former agent arises with the principal's failure to remove the vestiges of the former agent's authority (Article 112 (1)). The third party must have acted without knowledge nor negligently being ignorant of the circumstance in order to enforce claims against the principal. This

464. Great Court of Cassation, 25 Nov. 1932, Shimbun 3499-8. Compare Supreme Court, 3 Jun. 1971, Minshu 25-4-455.
465. Shinomiya & Nomi, *supra* n. 440, 391.
466. Before the 2017 Reform, this had been already settled as case law: Supreme Court, 28 Jul. 1970, Minshu 24-7-1203 (applying the former Arts 109 and 110 where the apparent agent possessed registered seal certificate, a blank mandate and other indices of authority).
467. Supreme Court, 19 Dec. 1969, Minshu 23-12-2539.

includes liability based on apparent authority for transactions completed by the former agent that exceeded the original scope of the agent's authority (Article 112 (2)).[468]

572. The issue arises most frequently with former officers, directors and employees of a business entity. In this context, the courts have held that registration with the Ministry of Justice's Civil Affairs Division of the resignation or an officer or director provides definitive notice of removal of agency authority.[469]

573. Even beyond the corporate context, with Japan's use of seals to execute documents (*see* above Part I, Chapter 1, §2), problems with apparent authority arise frequently. Courts have struggled to protect the interests of third parties and purported principals acting in good faith. In some cases, courts have imposed liability on the principal where she has provided the apparent agent with his or her registered seal or registered seal certificate. In other cases, particularly where a family member is acting with apparent authority, courts have declined to impose liability on the alleged principal because of the ease with which a family member can remove a registered seal and Certificate of Seal Registration from the home.[470]

§4. Termination of the Agency Agreement

574. The authority of an agent also terminates with the principal's death (Article 111(1)(i)), unless the principal agrees in advance for the agent to continue in some capacity.[471] Where the agent's authority is based on a mandate, the authority also terminates with the termination of the mandate (Article 111(2)). In fact, termination of the agency relationship may only be asserted against third parties with knowledge of the termination or where a third party should have known of the same (Article 112).

575. While not required by the Civil Code, courts have also found that the principal's commencement of bankruptcy proceedings terminates an agent's authority, because the principal has lost, and the bankruptcy trustee has gained, the capacity

468. Before the 2017 Reform, this had been already settled case law: Great Court of Cassation, 22 Dec. 1944, Minshu 23-626, applying the former Arts 110 and 112 (substantively the same as the current Art. 112(1)). A former agent continued to possess the principal's registered seal and executed additional unauthorized loan guarantees).

469. Supreme Court, 19 Apr. 1994, Minshu 48-3-922. *See* Japan's Company Act and the Commercial Business Registration Act for the general registration requirements for business entities and their officers and directors. A general discussion about setting up a business in Japan can be found at JETRO, 'Laws & Regulations on Setting up a Business in Japan', available at https://www.jetro.go.jp/en/invest/qa/setting_up/pdf/settingup_201210.pdf (accessed 21 Jun. 2018).

470. Compare Supreme Court, 28 Jul. 1970, Minshu 24-7-1203, Great Court of Cassation, 22 Dec. 1944, Minshu 23-626 with Supreme Court, 25 Jun. 1976, Minshu 30-6-25 (rejecting reliance on agent's purported authority to enter into a contract naming the principal as a guarantee for debt held by the agent, because the contract clearly provided no benefit to the principal).

471. Supreme Court, 23 Apr. 1953, Minshu 7-4-396.

to manage the principal's assets.[472]The death of the agent or commencement of bankruptcy or guardian proceedings against the agent similarly terminates the agency relationship (Article 111(1)(ii)).

§5. Other Forms of Indirect Representations

576. In addition to the agency relationships defined in the Civil Code, Japanese law allows other forms of indirect representation. The Commercial Code recognises 'indirect agency' relationships, allowing a party to act as a commission agent for a principal (Articles 551 to 558, Commercial Code).[473] In this case, the commission agent legally acts in her own name rather than the principal's name, with the economic effects and rights of possession residing with the principal. At the same time, since the commission agent, not the principal, becomes a party to the contract with the third party, the contractual rights and obligations vis-à-vis the third party reside with the agent. [474]

577. Separately, special laws provide for the formation of trusts, either pursuant to the general trust act (Article 2(1), Trust Act), or specific laws regulating the formation of Maintenance Trusts for Special Disabilities, Securities Investment Trusts, Pension Trusts, Loan Trusts and Public Interest Trusts.[475] In each case, as with standard common law trusts, a settlor provides assets to a trustee to administer on behalf of a beneficiary.[476]

§6. Mandates

578. Mandates have their origins in Roman law, which provided for gratuitous contracts allowing one party – commonly a cleric, a teacher, a doctor or lawyer – to act in the name of another.[477] Later Civil Codes, including the French, specifically addressed representative agency. Japan's Civil Code, modelled on the French Civil Code, does as well.[478]

---

472. The courts invoke Civil Code, Art. 653 (on mandates) as a basis for doing so. Shinomiya & Nomi, *supra* n. 440, 361.
473. *See* Shinomiya & Nomi, *supra* n. 440, 344.
474. *See*, Supreme Court, 11 Jul. 1968, Minshu 22-7-1462 (holding that a party may demand transfer of an object obtained by the broker on the party's behalf following the broker's bankruptcy).
475. *See* generally, Shinomiya & Nomi, *supra* n. 440, 345–346. For a general overview of trust law in Japan, *see* H. Dogauchi, 'Overview of Trust Law in Japan' at http://www.law.tohoku.ac.jp/kokusaiB2C/link/dogauchi.html (accessed 21 Jun. 2018); and Makoto Arai, 'Trust Law in Japan: Inspiring Changes in Asia, 1922 and 2006', in *Trust Law in Asian Civil Law Jurisdictions: A Comparative Analysis*, 27 (Cambridge University Press 2013).
476. *Ibid. See* generally Introduction to the Law of Contracts, §6.
477. Shiomi, *supra* n. 105, 257.
478. *Ibid.* 257.

579. While Japan's Civil Code provides as a default that services performed pursuant to a mandate are gratuitous, the Code expressly permits parties to agree otherwise (Article 648(1)). Contracts of mandate with remuneration are everyday occurrence. Examples include requests: to a broker to sell property or purchase stocks; to a bank to wire funds; to a judicial scrivener (*shihou shoshi*); to complete and file registration documents for a company or parcel of land; or to a person to serve on the board of directors of a company.[479]

580. In each instance, a mandator requests a mandatary to perform a specific service. Substituting the language of the common law, a principal expressly contracts with an agent to act vis-à-vis a third party in the principal's name. The contract (an *ininjou*) operates similarly to a limited power of attorney, with the principal specifying the service to be performed by the agent or attorney in fact.

I. Legal and Factual Acts

581. A mandate, or commission to act, becomes effective when one party 'mandates the other perform a juristic act'.(Article 643) The Civil Code divides the law of mandate into actions involving juristic or legal acts (*houritsu koui*) (Article 643) and actions involving factual or material acts (*jijitsu koui*) (Article 656). The former are actions that require an expression of intent by parties to the transaction, e.g., the mandatary, or agent, expresses an intent to contract with a third party on behalf of the mandator, or principal. These acts affect the rights and obligations of the mandator. The latter, 'factual acts', require no such expression of intent, and the actions themselves have no legal affect. For example, one party may provide a basic service like cleaning pursuant to a mandate.[480] The law of mandate applies directly to 'legal acts' and by analogy to 'factual acts'. (Article. 646) Substantively, the law is the same.

II. Duties of the Mandatary

582. A mandatary assumes 'a duty to administer the mandated business with the care of a good manager in compliance with the main purport of the mandate'.(Article 644) The 'duty of care' is an objective one, requiring the mandatary to exercise the care taken by a reasonable person in a similar profession.[481] The rights and obligations assumed by the mandatary remain the same, regardless of whether the services are provided for compensation or not.[482]

1. The Civil Code does not expressly impose a duty of loyalty on the mandatary. However, commentators interpret the original intent of the drafters of the Civil Code to include duties of loyalty in the basic requirement that

479. *Ibid.* 255.
480. MOJ, *supra* n. 104, 501.
481. Shiomi, *supra* n. 105, 258.
482. *Ibid.* 257.

the mandatary act with the 'care of a good manager'.[483] Special laws including, *inter alia*, the Attorney Act, Trust Act, Financial Instruments and Exchange Act and Japan's Company Act separately and specifically impose a duty of loyalty on mandataries operating pursuant to those acts.[484]

583. A mandatary specifically assumes a duty to follow the directions, if any, of the mandator.[485] The mandatary, absent consent otherwise, also assumes a duty to perform the service personally, i.e., to refrain from subcontracting the work.[486] The mandatary further assumes a duty to provide a full report regarding the work when requested or on completion (Article 645).

584. The Civil Code expressly requires that a mandatary deliver money or other property received on behalf of the mandator, and to transfer rights to any property obtained in the mandatary's name on behalf of the mandator (Article 646). Commentators have interpreted these provisions along with the Civil Code's general duty of care to require segregation of assets, i.e., to prohibit commingling the assets of the mandator and the mandatary.[487]

585. Beyond these basic obligations, special laws regulating the various types of mandataries impose additional obligations, including confidentiality requirements, disclosure obligations and duties to explain important terms of a transaction or to maintain records.[488]

586. The Civil Code expressly requires a mandatary, if she has diverted any funds to personal use, to repay the mandator with interest starting at the point of diversion (Article 647). The mandatary also remains liable for any additional damages arising from the act.[489] She is similarly liable for any damages proximately caused by a breach of her duty of good care or other enumerated duties.

587. Absent agreement otherwise, where the mandatary has agreed to act for a fee on behalf of the mandator, payment for such services is due after completion of the work (Article 648(2)). Usually remuneration is to be paid for the mandatary's works even without any outcome, but the mandatary and the mandator can make an agreement that it only needs to be paid for a certain outcome as a result of the mandatary's work, such as a lawyer's contingency fees. In this case, remuneration is to be paid in exchange for the delivery of a product as a work outcome, if its delivery is a part of the mandatary's obligation (Article 648-2(1)).

---

483. *Ibid.* 259.
484. *See*, e.g., Art. 1(2) Attorney Act (Act No. 205 of 1949); Art. 30 Trust Act (Act No. 108 of 2006); Art. 36, Financial Instruments and Exchange Act (Act No. 25 of 1948); Art. 355 Company Act (Act No. 86 of 2005).
485. Shiomi, *supra* n. 105, 260.
486. *Ibid.*
487. Shiomi, *supra* n. 105, 262.
488. *Ibid.* 263.
489. *Ibid.*

588. Partial remuneration shall be paid to the mandatary to the extent that the mandatary's work already has been rendered (a) if the mandate ends, either by cancelation or any applicable reason, before its completion or (b) if the work becomes no longer possible due to any impediment not attributable to the mandatary (Article 648(2)). In the case of remuneration to be paid for a work outcome, partial remuneration shall be awarded according to Article 634, which is provided for a contract for work (Article 648-2(2)), as discussed in paragraph 703 below. When the mandatary cannot continue his or her work due to the mandator, the mandatory must pay the whole amount of remuneration even if the work has been not completed (Article 536 II).

589. A mandatary may demand advance payment of costs necessary for the performance of the mandate (Article 649) and may demand reimbursement plus interest for reasonable costs incurred without advance payment (Article 650(1)).

590. Where the mandatary has incurred an obligation or debt on behalf of the mandator, the mandatary may demand payment by the mandator, or reasonable collateral to secure payment not yet due (Article 650(2)).

591. The Civil Code provides as a default that where the mandatary incurs damages, through no fault of his/her own and while acting in the course of the mandate, the mandatary may seek compensation for the damages from the mandator (Article 650(3)). The theory is that, but for the representation the mandator, not the mandatary, would have suffered the damage and should compensate the mandatary as a result.[490]

III. Termination of the Mandate

592. Given the personal nature of the contract, Article 651, paragraph 1 provides that either the mandator or the mandatary may cancel the contract, at any time.

593. In order to cancel the contract, either party needs to pay the other party for damages caused by the cancelation if the cancelation is made at 'a point that is detrimental to the other party' or if the mandate is for the benefit of not only mandator but also of mandatary, e.g. where a creditor mandatary seeks to collect on a debt owed to it as well as the mandator[491] (Article 651(2)).

594. Courts have found that where a mandatary's interest is solely in remuneration for services performed, e.g., a tax consultant's interest in regularly occurring consulting fees, that interest is not protected, by holding that such mandate is not considered to be one for the benefit of mandatary.[492] Thus, courts will not require the mandator to pay the mandatary damages just because the mandator cancels a

490. MOJ, *supra* n. 104, 490.
491. Great Court of Cassation, 24 Apr. 1920, Minroku 26-562.
492. Supreme Court, 16 Dec. 1965, Minshu 81-651; Supreme Court, 20 Sep. 1968, Hanji 536-51.

contract specifying the fees; however, as explained in paragraph 588 above, partial remuneration could be awarded to the mandatary in certain situations.

595. Payment of damages involved by the cancelation, however, is not needed in any case if the cancelation is based on 'unavoidable grounds' (Article 652(2) proviso). Unavoidable grounds here include no longer needing the services of the mandatary, or illness on the part of the mandatary, or a breach of trust by one of the parties.[493]

596. The Civil Code provides, as a default, that a mandate is terminated on the death or bankruptcy of the mandator, or the death, bankruptcy or a determination of incapacity of the mandatary (Article 653).[494] With regard to a bankruptcy filing by the mandator, courts have held that mandates unrelated the bankruptcy administrator's right to dispose of bankruptcy assets remain valid.[495] In other words, courts limit the Civil Code sections on termination following a bankruptcy filing to those mandates involving action on bankruptcy assets.

597. The Civil Code imposes a duty to act on the mandatary even after termination if there are 'pressing circumstances' for the mandatary to take 'necessary measures' to protect the interests of the mandator until the mandator, an heir or a legally designated representative can assume administrative control of the rights and assets initially subject to the mandate (Article 654).

598. The Civil Code expressly states that termination of a mandate may not be asserted against a third party 'unless the other party was notified or knew of the same'.(Article 655) In other words, the Civil Code protects third parties acting in good faith where an appearance of mandate remains.

---

493. Supreme Court, 19 Jan. 1981, Minshu 35-1-1; Shiomi, *supra* n. 105, 270.
494. The mandatory and the mandatary, however, may make a contract by which a mandate can continue after the mandator's death: Supreme Court, 22 Sep. 1992, Kinho 1358-55.
495. Supreme Court, 10 Jun. 2004, Minshu 58-5-1178.

Chapter 2. Deposit

§1. General Introduction

599. Deposit (*kitaku*) is a contract under which one party (the 'depositary') receives a tangible from another party (the 'depositor') and agrees to keep it for the depositor (Article 657, Civil Code). Examples include luggage checked at an airport. Modern-day use of deposits predominantly take the form of warehouse business and is mostly governed by the Commercial Code (Articles 593–628), rather than the Civil Code. Deposit contracts are to be distinguished from a lease of a storage space, such as contracts for the use of pay lockers, safe deposit boxes in banks or trunk rooms. The criterion is whether the party taking possession of the tangible is agreeing to confer 'services' or not. The distinction between deposit and quasi-mandates is also often blurry (e.g., keeping a pet dog for a week). However, some provisions on rights and obligations of the mandatary in quasi-mandates are applied *mutatis mutandis* to deposits (Article 665).

600. Deposit of funds in a bank account is also to be distinguished, because whereas a regular depositary is not permitted to use or exploit the tangible it keeps, and must return the specific goods that it received from the depositor, a bank is permitted to use the deposited funds (note that money is tangible), and to return to the depositor the same amount (and if interests if agreed). This type of deposit is denominated 'deposits for consumption'. Although the Civil Code provisions on deposits apply *mutatis mutandis* to deposits for consumption (Article 666 JCC), the private law rules governing bank deposits are mostly found in standard form contracts.

601. Depositary may charge fees for its service if the parties so agree, or if the depositary is a merchant in the business of taking deposits, for example a warehouse (*see* Article 512, Commercial Code (merchant's right to claim fees)). However, the default rule under the Civil Code is that deposits are gratuitous. This means that some of the obligations of the depositary set forth in the provisions on deposits are not readily suitable when fee is charged by the depositary. For example, the level of duty of care the depositary must exercise in holding the object is one 'identical to that he or she exercises for his or her own property', rather than the more demanding 'due care of a prudent manager' (or *bonus pater familias*) (cf. Article 400, Civil Code).

602. Since the depositary does not obtain the ownership of the tangible, he is subject to return the goods to the owner based on property right even in the absence of a contract. One difference that a deposit contract makes is that it imposes contractual obligations described below. On the other, even when the contractual rights are extinguished due to the running of the prescription period, rights based on ownership, e.g. return of the tangible, may still be claimed.[496]

496. Great Court of Cassation, 21 Aug. 1922, Minshu 1-493.

§2. FORMATION

603. Prior to the 2017 Reform, a deposit contract was formed when goods were actually received by, i.e. handed over to, the depositary. This was changed in the 2017 Reform, which provides that deposit contracts are consensual (Article 657). However, except for cases where the deposit contract is in writing or if it is for fee, the depositary has a right to cancel the contract before it receives the item (Article. 657-2(2)). The depositor can cancel the contract at any time (Articles 657-2(1) and 662(1)). This is in line with the regulation of other gratuitous contracts such as gifts (Article 550) and loan for use (Article 593-2). *See* Part II, Chapter 10, §2 for loan for use. However, with respect to cancellation by the depositor, the depositor is liable for damages for loss caused to the depositary due to the cancellation (Articles 657-2(1) and 662(2)).

§3. OBLIGATION OF THE DEPOSITARY

604. The main contractual obligation of the depositary is to provide service of keeping the tangible for the depositor and to return it to the depositor upon termination.

I. Returning the Goods

605. The depositary must return the specific tangible that is deposited, unless otherwise agreed. Examples of agreement to the contrary include 'deposits for consumption' (*see* paragraph 600), and 'commingled deposits'. Commingled deposits are those where the depositary receives multiple tangibles of the same kind and quality from multiple depositors, and agrees to return to individual depositors the same quantity of the tangible, instead of the specific tangible that it had received (Article 665-2 (commingled deposit)).

606. The depositary must also return the fruit of the tangible, both legal and natural, that the depositary acquired in the course of the deposit (Articles 665 and 646).

607. The depositor may demand return of the goods at any time (Article 662). This is because the depositary has no interest in keeping the goods. This applies even when there was agreement as to the time of return. In that case, the depositor must pay in addition to the fee in proportion to the period agreed (Articles 665 and 648(3)). However, if the agreement of the time includes a stipulation that the depositor will not seek return of the tangible before that time, a demand for return prior to that time is a breach.

608. The depositary may also return the goods at any time if there was no agreement as to the time of return. On the other, if there was agreement as to the time of return, the depositary may not return the goods to the depositor prior to that time, unless there were unavoidable grounds (Article 663).

609. The tangible must be returned at the place where they were to be kept according to the contract or, if the place of keeping the goods were changed due to justifiable reasons, where the tangibles were actually kept (Article 664).

610. The depositary must exercise duty of care when keeping the goods for the depositor. If the deposit is gratuitous, the depositary must exercise care 'identical to that he or she exercises for his or her own property' (Article 659). If the deposit is for a fee, the more demanding 'due care of a prudent manager' (cf. Article 400, Civil Code). However, if the depositary is a merchant in the business of deposits, he must exercise due care of a prudent manager irrespective of whether the deposit is gratuitous or not (Article 593, Commercial Code). Moreover, when deposits occur in the context of establishments for gatherings of customers (e.g., hotels, restaurants, bathhouses), the proprietor of the establishment is not released of liability by proving that it exercised due care. In order to be exempt from liability, such proprietor must prove that the loss or damage was due to *force majeure* (Article 594(1), Commercial Code (*receptum cauponum*)).

611. The depositary may not use [or exploit] the goods, or make a third party keep the goods, without permission of the depositor (Article 658(1)). Fruit of the tangible, both legal and natural fruit, that the depositary acquired in the course of the deposit must also be returned to the depositor (Articles 665 and 646).

II. Sub-depositary

612. If the depositary uses a sub-depositary by permission of the depositor, the depositary is liable for loss or damage to the goods, only if it failed to exercise reasonable care in the appointment and supervision of the sub-depositary (Article 658(2); Article 105). Further, if the sub-depositary was designated by the depositor, the depositary is liable only if it was aware that the sub-depositary is unsuitable or untrustworthy, and failed to notify the depositor thereof or failed to terminate the sub-deposit. The sub-depositary, in turn, will have the same rights and obligations towards the depositor (Article 658(2); Article 107(2)).

§4. Obligation of the depositor

613. The depositor must pay the cost of keeping the tangible. The depositary may claim this amount in advance (Articles 665 and 649), or claim reimbursement later (Article 665 and 650(1)). If the deposit is for fee, the fee becomes payable after the service is rendered (Article 665 and Article 648(2)). The defence of simultaneous performance (Article. 533) is available for the return of the deposit and payment of the fee.[497]

614. The depositor is strictly liable to pay damages to the depositary for loss caused by the nature or defect of the deposited tangible. For example, if a deposited battery causes fire and causes loss to depositary's property, the depositary will be liable to pay damages for the loss. However, the depositor is exempt from liability if he proves that he was not at fault in not knowing the nature or defect, or if the depositary was aware of the nature or defect (Article 661). In effect, the depositor is held liable unless he informs the depositary of the nature or defect of the tangible that he knew or should have known.

§5. Remedies

615. The usual contractual remedies are available for breach of deposit contracts.

497. Great Court of Cassation, 31 Oct. 1903, Minroku 9-1204.

Chapter 3. Aleatory Contracts

§1. Gambling (Gaming and Betting)

616. In general, gambling is considered to be against 'public policy and good morals' due to its 'extraordinarily aleatory nature' or because it constitutes a crime (cf. Articles 185–187 Criminal Code). Accordingly, gaming and wagering contracts ('gambling' contracts) are null and void (Article 90, Civil Code).

617. Some publicly controlled gambling, however, are legalised under special legislations to promote certain industries or for fiscal reasons. These include horse racing (*keiba*) [promotion of stock farming], motorboat racing (*kyotei*) [promotion of shipping industry], bicycle racing (*keirin*) and football (*totocalcio*). Lotteries are also regulated under the Act against Unjustifiable Premiums and Misleading Representations (Act No. 134 of 15 May 1962). Legislation enacted in July 2018 allows casinos in certain specified areas.[498]

618. Some contracts that are aleatory in nature, but not extraordinarily so, are considered to be valid. These include insurance (cf. Insurance Act) and life annuity contracts (cf. Articles 689–694, Civil Code). Insurance should require little explanation to the readers of this book. Life annuity contracts (*shushin teikikin keiyaku*) are contracts where one party (obligor) promises to deliver to another person money or other property periodically (e.g., monthly) until the death of himself, the other party or a third person. In some cases, the obligor receives principal funds for the annuity; in other cases, the obligor receives nothing in exchange. In either case, the total amount of annuity varies depending on when the death of the relevant person arrives. Thus, life annuity contracts are aleatory in nature. However, life annuity contracts are valid under the Civil Code (*see* Articles 689–694). In practice, life annuity contracts are rarely used as various pension schemes regulated by special legislation substitute for life annuity contracts.

619. Courts refuse to enforce [the loser's] debt incurred by gambling. Moreover, once payment of a gambling debt is made, restitution on the basis that the gambling contract was null and void is refused under the principle of 'performance for illegal cause' (Article 708, Civil Code). In effect, courts refuse any judicial assistance to gambling contracts.

620. These refusals of protection extend beyond enforcement or restitution of gambling debts. Loans of funds for gambling or for repaying gambling debts are also against public policy [if the lender knew at the time of lending that the fund will be used for gambling].[499] Likewise, settlement contracts (compromise) regarding gambling debts are against public policy.[500] Moreover, when a receivable [monetary claim] arising from gambling is transferred, the debtor retains its defence

498. Act on the Development of Specified Integrated Resort Areas (Act No. 80 of 2018).
499. E.g., Supreme Court, 25 Apr. 1972, Hanji 669-60; Supreme Court, 4 Sep. 1986, Hanji 1215-47.
500. Supreme Court, 9 Apr. 1971, Minshu 25-3-264.

against the transferee that the receivable is null and void. This is despite the general rule under Article 468 that the debtor loses all the defence it had against the transferor if the debtor acknowledged the transfer without raising any objection.[501]

§2. LIFE ANNUITY CONTRACT

621. Life annuity contracts (*shushin teikikin keiyaku*) are contracts where one party (obligor) promises to deliver to another person, including a third-party beneficiary, money or other property periodically (*e.g.*, monthly) until the death of himself, the other party or a third person. The total amount of annuity varies depending on when the death of the relevant person arrives. The typical use of life annuity contract is for maintenance of the party receiving the annuity. Despite the aleatory nature of life annuity contracts, they are valid under the Civil Code (*see* Articles 689–694).

622. In principle, life annuity contracts are gratuitous in nature, and thus the provisions on gift contracts (Articles 522-5, Civil Code) apply cumulatively. However, payment of life annuity may also be agreed in exchange for value. An example is where a buyer of an immovable agrees to paying life annuity instead of paying a fixed sum. Life annuity contracts are consensual and no form is required.

623. The obligor is obliged to make periodical payment of the annuity in accordance with the contract. At the end of the contract, calculation of the amount of annuity is to be made on a daily basis (Article 690, Civil Code).

624. If the obligor fails to perform, the obligee is entitled to the general remedy of specific performance and damages. In addition, if the obligee had conferred a principal sum to the obligor, the obligor is also entitled to immediate termination of the contract. Upon termination, the obligor is entitled to restitution of the *entire* principal funds. At the same time, however, the terminating obligor must make restitution of the annuity it has already received, less than the statutory interest on the principal funds (Article 691(1)). This special rule on termination simplifies the general rule under which (a) an additional period of time of performance must be granted (Article 541, Civil Code) and (b) each party must make restitution of the sum they had received plus interest on the sum (cf. Article 545(2), Civil Code).

625. If the death of the relevant person is attributable to the obligor, its obligation may not be discharged. Upon the request of the obligee or heirs, court will declare that the life annuity contract continues for a reasonable period of time (Article 693).

626. In practice, however, life annuity contracts are rarely used. The purpose of maintenance is substituted by various pension arrangements which are regulated by public law (social security law). In addition, adoption of an adult whereby duty of

501. Supreme Court, 11 Nov. 1997, Minshu 51-10-4077.

maintenance arises (Articles 727, 877, Civil Code) often functions as a substitute. In some cases, the obligor receives principal funds for the annuity; in other cases, the obligor receives nothing in exchange.

Chapter 4. Sale of Goods

§1. Delivery

627. The seller is obligated to transfer ownership and possession of the goods to the buyer. In principle, the seller must actually (i.e., physically) transfer the possession of the goods to the buyer (cf. Article 182(1)). However, the parties may agree on other modes of transfer. These include, 'summary delivery' [*kan-i no hikiwatashi*] which takes place by manifestation of the seller's intention if the buyer is already in possession of the goods (Article 182(2)); 'constructive transfer of possession' [*sen-yu kaitei*] which takes place by the seller's manifestation of intention to transfer, while the goods will remain in the seller's possession (Article 183); 'transfer of possession by instruction' which takes place by the seller's instruction to a third party in possession of the goods to possess the goods on behalf of the buyer and by the buyer's consent (Article 184).

628. On the other, the buyer, being an obligee with respect to the obligation to deliver, is not obligated to take delivery although he is obligated to pay the price. Therefore, the seller is without remedies when the buyer refuses to take delivery as far as the buyer pays. However, courts have traditionally held that there are exceptional situations where the principle of good faith obligates the buyer to take over the goods.[502]

I. Time

629. In the absence of an agreement to the contrary, the seller must deliver the goods immediately when the buyer demands delivery (Article 412(3)). The seller is not liable for delay until that time.

II. Place and Manner

630. For actual transfer of possession, the seller is obligated to deliver the goods at the address of the buyer in the absence of an agreement to the contrary (Article 484(1)). One exception is the case where the goods are already identified at the time of contract. In that case, the seller must deliver the goods at the place where the goods were located at the time of contract (Article 484(1)).

631. Even if the buyer does not take delivery, the seller is released from his liability for delay, by tender of delivery of the good (Article 492). For that purpose, the seller must actually tender the goods at the place of delivery (Article 493). 'Actual tender' is done by placing the goods at the buyer's disposal. If the agreed

502. For example, Supreme Court, 16 Dec. 1971, Minshu 25-9-1472 (buyer held liable for damages for rejecting delivery of ore in an output contract in which the buyer agreed to purchase the whole amount produced by the seller.).

place of delivery is a place other than the buyer's address, actual tender of the goods consists of making the goods available to the buyer at that place. In that case, no notice that delivery is ready is required unless the time of delivery is not determined or determinable by the contract. However, if the buyer rejects taking delivery in advance, or if delivery requires the buyer's cooperation, it is sufficient for the seller to make an 'oral tender' of the goods. Oral tender consists of a notice to the buyer that delivery is ready and a request to take delivery (proviso of Article 493).

III. Cost

632. The cost of delivery is to be borne by the seller, provided that any increase in the cost of delivery caused by the buyer, including change of address, must be borne by the buyer (Article 485).

§2. Transfer of Ownership and Risk

I. Ownership

633. The seller is obligated to transfer ownership of the goods to the buyer. In principle, transfer of ownership occurs by the manifestation of intentions by the parties (Article 176). Unless the parties agree to further delay the transfer of ownership, it is considered that ownership is transferred at the time of contract (in case of sale of specified goods)[503] or when the goods are identified to the contract (in case of sale of unidentified goods)[504]. In practice, many contracts provide that transfer of ownership occurs at the time of payment.

634. In addition, the seller is obligated to allow the buyer to obtain perfection (or 'opposability') of the ownership against third parties (Article 560). This is necessary for the buyer to duly assert ownership against persons other than the seller and his or her comprehensive successors (e.g., heirs) who have a justifiable interest in asserting lack of opposability. For ownership of goods, there are several ways to achieve perfection. First, perfection can be achieved by transfer of possession (Article 178). In this case, nothing special is required other than the seller performing their general obligation to transfer ownership and possession. Second, perfection can be achieved by registration of the transfer (assignment) of the goods in the movables registration file (Article 3, Act on Special Provisions, etc. of the Civil Code Concerning the Perfection Requirements for the Assignment of Movables and Claims). This method of achieving perfection is available only when the seller is an incorporated entity. In this case, the seller is obligated to cooperate with the buyer to register the transfer in order to achieve perfection (Article 7(2), Act on Special Provisions, etc. of the Civil Code Concerning the Perfection Requirements for the

503. Supreme Court, 20 Jun. 1958, Minshu 12-10-1586 (although dealing with sale of immovables).
504. Supreme Court, 24 Jun. 1960, Minshu 14-8-1528.

Assignment of Movables and Claims). Third, for registrable goods such as automobiles, perfection can be achieved by registration (cf. Article 5, Road Transport Vehicle Act).

635. In principle, the fruit of the goods belongs to the owner (Articles 206). However, in the context of a sale, Article 575 provides that the fruit of goods not delivered yet vests in the seller, while the buyer does not have to pay interest on the price until delivery. The purpose of this rule is to allow a summary settlement of the fruit and interest. Thus, this rule does not apply if the seller is in delay while the buyer has already paid.[505]

II. Passing of Risk

636. Prior to the reform of the Civil Code in 2017, the language of the Civil Code adopted the principle of *res perit domino*. However, this position has come under criticism as being unfair particularly when the loss occurs while the goods are still in the sphere of seller's control, and the buyer is still forced to pay the full price of the goods. This resulted in a reinterpretation that depended more on the idea that the party in a better position to control the goods should bear the loss. The current Civil Code revised in 2017 adopts the latter approach for sales, and the passing of risk is severed from the transfer of ownership of the goods.

637. More concretely, Article 567(1) of the Civil Code provides that if loss of or damage to the goods which are not attributable to either party occurred after delivery of the goods, (i) the buyer is without remedies available for seller's non-performance and (ii) the buyer must pay the price. One significant requirement under that provision is that the goods must be identified to the contract. 'Delivery' in this context is considered to refer only to actual transfer of possession. The reverse interpretation of this provision results in a rule that, if such loss occurred before delivery by the seller, the risk of loss remains with the seller, and the seller is held liable for non-performance. In that case, the buyer may resort to remedies for the seller's breach including two rules allowing the buyer not to pay the price (Article 536 on the right to refuse to pay price and Articles 541 and 542 on termination).

638. In addition, Article 567(2) provides that the same rule applies if the loss occurred after the buyer refused to or cannot take delivery of the goods notwithstanding the seller's conforming tender of the goods.

639. Identification of the goods can be done either by (i) agreement of the parties, (ii) the seller exercising his right of designation granted by the buyer or (iii) the seller completing the action necessary for providing the goods (Article 401(2)). Examples of 'completion of the action necessary for providing the goods' include the following. If the place of delivery is the buyer's address, the action necessary

505. Great Court of Cassation (Combined Chambers), 24 Sep. 1924, Minshu 3-440.

for performance is completed by actual tender.[506] However, in a case involving a sales contract in which the place of delivery is the seller's address, the Supreme Court held that oral tender without separating the goods from others of the same kind does not constitute completion of such action.[507] It is generally accepted that 'separation' of the goods from others of the same kind is necessary for completion of such action, but there is debate as to whether 'notice' of separation is also necessary.

III. The Option of Repurchase

640. In practice, the seller might wish to obtain the option of repurchase or redemption (*kaimodoshi*) in order to secure payment or compliance with a condition of use (or the buyer may wish to have that option if ownership is transferred to the seller for security purposes). However, this cannot be used for sale of goods. Under the Civil Code, this kind of security right is allowed only for the sale of immovables, and the option must be obtained at the time of contract and must be registered for it to have priority over third parties such as sub-purchasers, secured creditors, lessees (Article 581). The parties are free to agree on an option (*yoyaku kanketsu-ken*) to enter into a contract of repurchase (*saibaibai no yoyaku*). This is not governed by Article 581 and is more flexible, but is of little use for sale of goods. This is because the option must be still registered (as a provisional registration of ownership), while ownership of movables is not registrable.

IV. Party Autonomy and Retention of Title Clause

641. The parties are free to agree to delay the transfer of ownership, even after possession is transferred to the buyer. The purpose of such a clause is to secure payment of the price by the seller retaining ownership until the buyer has paid the price. This is done by inserting a 'retention-of-title clause' in the contract. Under the Installment Sales Act, a seller in instalment sales (under which payment is deferred over a period of more than two months and is divided into more than three payments) of a durable goods, as specified by Cabinet Order, is presumed to have retained ownership of the goods (Article 7, Installment Sales Act).

642. In retention-of-title sales, the seller remains the owner of the goods. The retention-of-title seller may assert its ownership in compulsory execution proceedings filed against the buyer by a third party (Article 38, Civil Execution Act)[508] and

506. Great Court of Cassation, 25 Dec. 1919, Minroku 25-2400.
507. Supreme Court, 18 Oct. 1955, Minshu 9-11-1642.
508. Supreme Court, 18 Jul. 1974, Minshu 28-5-743.

insolvency proceedings of the buyer.[509] However, there may be situations where the assertion of ownership may amount to an abuse of rights (cf. Article 1(3)).[510]

643. The retention-of-title buyer is usually allowed to use the goods, but as a non-owner, the buyer cannot transfer ownership of the goods to third parties. However, good faith purchasers of the goods may acquire ownership under the rules on immediate acquisition (Article 192). Therefore, in practice, the retention-of-title seller usually makes it externally apparent that possession of goods is transferred on a retention-of-title basis (e.g., by posting a nameplate to that effect on the encumbered asset), thereby precluding third party's assertion of good faith. For automobiles and other movables that are registrable, registration of ownership plays the same function.

644. There is no general consensus on the question of passing of risk when ownership is retained by the seller. However, since the passing of risk is severed from the transfer of ownership, it is likely that the normal rules on the passing of risk should apply.

§3. Seller's Warranty of Quality and Title

I. Sale by a Non-owner

645. Under Japanese law, a sales contract to sell goods that do not belong to the seller is valid. The non-owner seller is obligated to acquire the ownership of the goods from the owner and to transfer it to the buyer (Article 561).

646. If the seller does not perform, the general remedies for non-performance (i.e., right to performance, termination and damages) are available to the buyer. The right to performance is unavailable if it is impossible for the seller to acquire and transfer the ownership (Article 412-2(1)). Impossibility is determined according to the contract and general senses of trade. Courts have held, for example, that the seller's obligation is impossible if the right holder definitely refuses to transfer ownership,[511] or if the right holder transfers the ownership of goods to a third party and that transfer is perfected against third parties.[512]

647. When part (either physical portion or equity) of the goods belongs to a third-party right holder, the buyer has the right to cure (Articles 562 and 565) and price reduction (Articles 563 and 565), in addition to the general remedies for non-performance. With respect to termination, two points should be noted. First, partial

509. Supreme Court, 4 Jun. 2010, Minshu 64-4-1107 (rehabilitation proceeding).
510. Supreme Court, 28 Feb. 1975, Minshu 29-2-193 (holding that an automobile dealer's assertion of retention of title against a user who purchased the automobile from a sub-dealer is an abuse of rights when the dealer terminated the sales contract with the sub-dealer due to non-payment by the latter. The dealer in this case was involved in the sale between the sub-dealer and the user).
511. Supreme Court, 26 Oct. 1950, Minshu 4-10-497.
512. Great Court of Cassation, 22 Nov. 1921, Minroku 27-1978.

termination of the contract is allowed (Article 542(2)). Second, if the purpose of the contract cannot be achieved by the remaining parts, the buyer may terminate the entire contract (Article 542(1)(3)).

648. In addition to the above, the buyer has a right to refuse payment of the price if there is a likelihood of losing ownership, in whole or in part, because there is a third person asserting his right in the goods, unless the seller provides adequate security (Article 576). The seller may request the buyer to deposit the price in a public depositary (Article 578).

II. Warranty for Conformity of Rights

649. The Civil Code prior to the 2017 revision had special rules on warranty for eviction, in addition to remedies for non-performance. This dual remedy scheme was revamped in the revision of 2017. The revised rule adopts a unitary remedial scheme for non-performance of the duty of conformity of 'rights' (Article 565).

650. Delivering goods which only partially belong to the seller is considered to be a breach of this duty (*see* paragraph 647 above). Other situations where the seller is in breach of this duty is (i) when the buyer cannot use the goods because it is subject to a third party's proprietary right of retention or pledge or (ii) when the buyer loses the right because of the enforcement of a third party's security right attached to the goods. It is irrelevant whether the buyer knew or did not know of the non-conformity at the time of contract.

651. If the seller breaches this duty of conformity, the buyer has the right to cure (Articles 562 and 565) and price reduction (Articles 563 and 565), in addition to the general remedies for non-performance.

652. In the case of auction, including compulsory judicial sales, the purchaser has all the rights for non-conformity of rights described above, except for the right to cure (Article 568(1)).

653. In addition to the above, the buyer has a right to refuse payment of price if there is a likelihood of losing the ownership, in whole or in part, because there is a third person asserting his right in the goods, unless the seller provides adequate security (Article 576). The seller may demand that the buyer deposit the price in a public depositary (Article 578). The buyer's failure to act accordingly will result in his losing his right of refusal under Article 576.[513]

513. Great Court of Cassation, 15 Apr. 1939, Minshu 18-429.

III. Warranty for Conformity of Description, Quality and Quantity

654. The Civil Code prior to the 2017 revision had special rules on warranty for hidden defects (*kashitanposekinin*), in addition to remedies for non-performance. This dual remedy scheme was revamped in the revision of 2017. The revised rule adopts a unitary remedial scheme for non-performance of duty of conformity of 'description, quality and quantity' (Articles 562–564 and 566). It has also been clarified that the rules on warranty apply to sales of unspecified goods, an issue which had been subject to extensive and long debate. Furthermore, under the revised rules, the non-conformity or defect need not be 'hidden'.

655. Under the revised rules, the seller is obligated to deliver goods that conform with to the contract in terms of description, quality and quantity. The contract is the criterion for determining whether there is lack of conformity in the goods delivered. For example, even if goods do not match current quality standards, that does not render the goods non-conforming, if the parties did not contemplate such quality standards at the time of contract.[514]

656. In the absence of the parties' agreement as to quality of the goods, the seller of unspecified goods is obligated to deliver goods of average quality (Article 401(2)). Non-conformity of quality includes non-compliance with statutory restrictions (e.g., regulations on food safety).

657. The goods must conform to the contract at the time of delivery. Article 567(1) makes this point clear regarding non-conformity resulting from damages to goods that occur before delivery. The same should apply to non-conformity resulting from reasons other than damage to the goods (e.g., change of regulation or overgrowing of plants).

658. Damages and termination. When the seller's goods delivered do not conform to the contract, the buyer can exercise his general remedial rights of damages and termination for non-performance (Article 564). In addition to these two rights, the buyer is granted two other remedies that are only relevant in the case of non-conformity. They are the right to cure and the right of price reduction.

659. Right to cure. The buyer has a right to cure (Article 562). Under this right, the buyer may require the seller to repair the goods or to deliver substitute goods, or to deliver missing quantity, unless the non-conformity was caused by the buyer. The seller may resort to a method of cure different than that requested by the buyer, if the change does not place undue burden on the buyer.

660. Right of price reduction. If the seller does not cure within a reasonable period designated by the buyer, the buyer may resort to a right of price reduction (Article 563(1)). If there is little prospect of a cure (including cases when a cure is impossible; when the seller equivocally repudiates; when time is of essence to

514. Cf. Supreme Court, 1 Jun. 2010, Minshu 64-4-953 (applying prior law).

achieve the purpose of the contract), the buyer may immediately reduce the price without granting any reasonable period of cure (Article 563(2)). However, if the non-conformity was caused by the buyer, price reduction is not available to the buyer (Article 564(3)). The amount of price reduction is to be calculated proportionally.

661. However, note that when non-conformity is caused by the buyer, the buyer may not resort to right to termination (Article 543), right to cure (Article 542(2)) or right of price reduction (Article 543(3)). Damages are available, but the amount of damages will be determined after taking into account the buyer's contribution to non-performance or enlargement of the loss (Article 418).

662. Buyer's duty of notice. In order for the buyer to resort to any of the remedies for non-conformity (i.e., cure, price reduction, termination and damages), the buyer must give the seller notice of non-conformity within one year from the time he became aware of the non-conformity (Article 566). The buyer loses his right to all remedies if he fails to give this notice. The purpose of this rule is to protect the seller's reliance that he has completed performance, and to allow him to collect relevant evidence.[515] This rule does not apply if the seller knew or was grossly negligent in not knowing the non-conformity (Article 566 proviso).

663. In case of a sale between merchants, the Commercial Code provides a rule stricter to the buyer. Under that rule, the buyer must examine the goods 'without delay' after taking delivery (Article 526(1), Commercial Code), and must give the seller notice of non-conformity of description, quality or quantity, 'immediately' after becoming aware of such non-conformity (Article 526(2), sentence 1, Commercial Code). There is also an ultimate cut-off period of six months from the time of taking delivery for giving notice (Article 526(2), sentence 2, Commercial Code). This rule does not apply if the seller knew or was negligent in not knowing the non-conformity (Article 526(3), Commercial Code).

664. In the case of auction, including compulsory judicial sales, the purchaser does not have the right to any of the remedies for non-conformity of description, quality and quantity of the goods (Article 568(4)).

665. Exemption clause. The parties are free to exempt or limit the seller's liability for non-conformity by including an exemption clause or limitation of liability clause in the contract. However, the seller cannot be released from liability for non-conformity which he knew but did not disclose to the buyer (Article 572). This is a mandatory rule.

515. This is a rule that has been changed in the 2017 Reform. *See supra* n. 33, for an account of the rules prior to the 2017 Reform.

§4. Remedies of the Unpaid Seller

666. The unpaid seller has the ordinary right to performance of the buyer's obligation to pay, right to damages and right of termination. In addition, there are other statutory remedies that allow the seller to refuse delivery. They are the (i) defence of simultaneous performance, (ii) proprietary right of retention and (iii) statutory lien (or privilege). The following paragraphs deal with these statutory schemes. However, once the seller parts with ownership, protection is limited. Thus, the seller may wish to include a retention-of-title (ownership) clause in the contract. For retention-of-title sales, *see* paragraphs 640 et seq.

I. Defence of Simultaneous Performance and Right of Retention

667. The seller may refuse to deliver the goods until the buyer tenders payment of price, if the buyer's payment obligation is already due (Article 533). This is known as the 'defence of simultaneous performance' (*dojirikono koben*). This defence is usually available unless the seller agrees to extend credit to the buyer, because it is presumed that the time for payment is the same as the time for delivery of the goods (Article 573).

668. The seller may also refuse to transfer possession, even if the ownership has already passed to the buyer, if he has a claim arising with respect to the goods, for example, the claim for payment of the price, provided that the claim is already due (Article 295). This is known as the 'right of retention' (*ryuchiken*). Furthermore, between a merchant seller and merchant buyer, the seller has the right to retain any asset of the buyer to secure payment of his claim against the buyer (Article 521 Commercial Code). This is known as the 'merchant's right of retention'.

669. Both allow the seller to put pressure on the buyer to pay. However, one major difference between the two stems from their different nature. The defence of simultaneous performance is only available between parties to bilateral contracts, while the right of retention is a statutory proprietary right that may be invoked against third parties. Therefore, if the buyer, who has ownership because in principle ownership passes when the goods are specified, resells the goods to a sub-purchaser, and if the sub-purchaser demands transfer of possession based on his ownership, the seller may no longer rely on the defence of simultaneous performance. However, the right of retention can be invoked against the sub-purchaser.

670. The right of retention under the Civil Code ceases to be effective in insolvency proceedings (Article 66(3) Bankruptcy Act), while the merchant's right of retention will be relegated to a junior statutory lien.

II. Seller's Statutory Lien

671. The seller of goods has a statutory lien or privilege (*sakidori tokken*) in the goods if ownership has already passed to the buyer (Article 311(v) and Article 321). The seller is entitled to preferential recovery from the proceeds of the goods in judicial sale (Article 303). That lien ranks lower than the lien for lessees of immovables, innkeepers and for the preservation of movables (Article 330).

672. However, this statutory lien is lost once the goods are delivered to third parties because of, for example, resale or lease (Article 333). But the seller is entitled to preferential recovery from the buyer's 'claim' for benefits the buyer receives as a result of sale, lease or loss of or damage to the goods, provided that the seller attaches the claim before its payment is made (Article 304).

III. Seller's Right of Termination

673. If the buyer does not pay by the due date, the seller may terminate the contract in accordance with the procedure set forth in Article 541. Under that provision, termination is allowed after demanding the buyer pay within a specified reasonable period of time, and if the buyer does not tender payment within that period of time. Article 542 dealing with termination in situations when demanding performance is futile has little relevance for non-performance of monetary obligations.

674. It is understood that termination results in the retroactive extinction of the contract. If the seller has already delivered the goods, the seller may require restitution of the goods delivered (Article 545(1)). However, the seller cannot assert the consequences of termination against a third party (proviso of Article 545(1)). For example, if the buyer has already transferred ownership to a sub-purchaser, the seller has no recourse against the sub-purchaser.

§5. Products Liability

675. Buyers who suffer loss due to defects in the goods can claim damages against the seller, if the defect constitutes non-conformity with the contract (Article 415). However, the buyer has no contractual claim against a remote manufacturer of the goods. This is because the remote manufacturer and the buyer are not in a contractual relationship. The buyer may bring tort claims against the manufacturer, who in many occasions have a deeper pocket than the seller, under the general tort liability provision, Article 709. However, that claim requires the buyer (plaintiff) to prove, among other requirements, 'negligence' of the manufacturer (defendant), which can be an obstacle that does not exist for Article 415.

676. Thus, the Product Liability Act (Act No. 85 of 1994) (PL Act) was enacted to allow purchasers of defective products to pursue liability of the manufacturer by proving 'defect', without recourse to Article 709 of the Civil Code. Part I, Chapter 4, §4, III.B. Article 3 of the Product Liability Act provides that the manufacturer is 'liable for damages arising from the infringement of life, body or property of others which is caused by the defect in the delivered product [...]'. For the purpose of the Product Liability Act, 'defect' is defined as 'a lack of safety that the product ordinarily should provide, taking into account the nature of the product, the ordinarily foreseeable manner of use of the product, the time when the manufacturer, etc. delivered the product, and other circumstances concerning the product'. (Article 2(2)). The existence of defect is to be determined as of the time the product was 'delivered', i.e. when it was put into distribution.

677. Product liability arises only with respect to defective movables which are manufactured or processed (Article 2(1)). It does not arise with respect to unprocessed movables (e.g., such as fish caught in the sea, but not farm-raised fish) or immovables (e.g., building).

678. The person liable for product liability is not limited to the 'manufacturer' in the strict sense. It also includes 'importers' (Article 2(3)(i)), any person who represents himself on the product as the manufacturer or who provides a representation on the product that misleads others that he is the manufacturer (Article 2(3)(ii)), and any person who otherwise makes a representation on the product that, in the circumstances, amounts to holding himself out as its substantial manufacturer (Article 2(3)(iii)). Wholesalers and retailers who do not meet the criteria above are not liable under the Product Liability Act.[516]

679. Any person who has suffered loss to life, body or property, not just the buyer, may bring a claim under the Products Liability Act.

680. Damage recoverable is determined by the general rules of tort liability. Any damage, including damage to life, body or property, which has adequate causation with the defect, is recoverable (Article 6, Product Liability Act and Article 709). However, if the damage occurs only to the product itself, the manufacturer is not liable under this Act (Article 3). That is a loss that should be settled within the contractual relationship between the seller and the buyer.

681. Even when the requirements under Article 3 are satisfied, two grounds of exemption are available to the manufacturers. The first exemption is known as the 'defence of development risk', if the manufacturer proves that the particular defect could not have been discovered given the state of scientific or technical knowledge at the time the manufacturer delivered the product (Article 4(i)). The second exemption concerns a defence available to manufacturers of components or raw materials used in the product, if such a manufacturer of components or raw materials proves that the defect was caused primarily because of following the instructions on design

516. *Chikujokaisetsu Seizobutsusekininho [Commentary on Product Liability Act]*, 87 (Keizaikikakucho Kokuminseikatsukyoku Shohishagyosei Daiikka [Economic Planning Agency, Quality of Life Bureau, Consumer Affairs Section 1] ed., 1994).

given by the manufacturer of the product, and that he is not negligent with respect to the occurrence of such defect (Article 4(ii)).

682. The Product Liability Act provides a dual limitation period (extinctive prescription period) with different commencement times and duration. The first is a three-year limitation period which runs from the time the victim or his legal representative becomes aware of the loss and the party liable for the damages (Article 5(1)(i)). However, if the loss is to life or body, the duration of this period will be five years instead of three years (Article 5(2)). The second is a ten-year limitation period which runs from the time the product was delivered by the manufacturer (Article 5(1)(ii)). However, where such damages are caused by substances which become harmful to human health only after accumulating in the body, or where the damage is of which the symptom appears after a certain latent period, the ten-year period runs from the time such damage occurs (Article 5(3)).

§6. The Sale on Instalment

683. The Installment Sales Act (Act No. 159 of 1961) applies to five types of credit sales: (i) instalment sales, (ii) loan-backed sale, (iii) intermediation of comprehensive credit purchases, (iv) intermediation of individual credit purchase and (v) specified prepaid transaction. Types (ii) to (iv) involve third parties who extend credit ((iii) is better understood as 'credit card transactions'). The following paragraphs focuses on (i).

684. For the purpose of the Act, 'instalment sales' is defined as the sale of goods, rights or services for which the payment is to be made in three or more instalments over a period of two or more months (Article 2(1)(i)) or to be made in a revolving payment basis (Article 2(1)(ii)). The Act applies only to the sale of goods, rights or services designated by a Cabinet Order as being befitting to sell under standardised terms and conditions (Article 2(1)(v)).

685. The Act provides the following regulations for instalment sales:

(a) Requirement to disclose to the buyer certain contract terms (price, payment, interest, etc.) (Article 3(1)).
(b) Requirement to deliver to the buyer documents indicating certain contract terms (Articles 4 to 4-3).
(c) Buyer's 'cooling-off' period of 8 days if contract was concluded in a place other than the seller's place of business (Article 4-4).
(d) Substantive regulation of termination clauses and acceleration clauses which require notice in writing more than twenty days before termination or acceleration to take effect (Article 5).

(e) Substantive regulation of liquidated damages and penalty clauses limiting the maximum amount of damages to a minimal amount[517] plus interest (Article 6).
(f) Presumption of retention of title until payment is completed (Article 7).

517. In summary, the maximum amount set forth in Article 6(1) is as follows: (i) if the goods are returned, the amount of ordinary fee to use the goods or the amount of the instalment price of the goods less than the market value of the goods at the time of their return, whichever is larger; (ii) if the goods are not returned, the instalment price of the goods; (iii) if the goods are not yet delivered, the amount of costs normally required for concluding and performing such contract.

Chapter 5. Building Contracts, Hire of Work and Skills

§1. Distinguishing Between Employment Contracts, Contracts for Work and Mandate Contracts

686. For a building contract, and hire of work and skills, the Civil Code provides for an employment contract and a contract for work, as well as a mandate contract. These three contracts are commonly known as services contracts, under which one party must provide a particular service to the other party, but they can be distinguished from each other in two respects. The first is whether the service provider will receive direction and supervision from the other party in relation to the performance of his or her obligation. The service provider in an employment contract (the employee) does not have any discretion in performing work, whereas the service provider in a contract for work or a mandate contract (a contractor or a mandatary) has discretion.

687. The second distinguishing feature is whether the service provider is obliged not only to work but also to produce a specific work outcome. The obligation of the service provider in an employment contract (an employee) or a mandate contract (a mandatary) is simply to work, whereas in a contract for work, the provider (a contractor) is obliged to produce a specified work outcome. This is why an employee or a mandatary will not be liable even if his or her work does not result in a specific outcome as long as he or she has worked in accordance with the contract, whereas a contractor will be liable if he or she does not provide the promised results of the work. For example, a house-cleaning service usually qualifies as a contract for work, but it can be considered an employment contact in cases where the provider agrees only to work at cleaning and does not promise how clean the house is made.

688. A mandate contract is explained above in Part II, Chapter 2, §5, so here only an employment contract and a contract for work are reviewed.

§2. Employment Contract

I. Importance of Labour Law Statutes

689. An employment contract is a contract under which an employee agrees to work for an employer in exchange for remuneration. An employment contract is regulated in the Civil Code, but the rules of the Civil Code are mostly overridden by special labour law legislation, such as the Labor Standards Act and the Labor Contracts Act.[518]

518. The Labor Standards Act (Act No. 49 of 1947) is to protect an employee by providing for minimum standards of working conditions and punishing an employer on the public law if the standards are violated. In 2007, the Labor Contracts Act (No. 128 of 2007) was enacted to regulate an individual labour contract, as is considered substantially the same as an employment contract under

690. However, there are the two exceptions where the rules of the Civil Code apply. First, its rules for an employment contract still apply to an employment contract between relatives living together. Second, as explained below, the rules of the Civil Code apply to any employment contract with regard to its termination or an offer to terminate it made by an employee. Neither of these is governed by the Labor Standards Act or the Labor Contract Act.

II. Effect

A. Duties of the Employee

691. An employee is obliged to work as promised for an employer (Civil Code Article 623). While working, the employee needs to obey the rules of employment, which sometimes include the duty not to compete and so on.

B. Duties of the Employer

692. For its part, the employer is obliged to pay remuneration to the employee for his or her work (Article 623). Remuneration is to be paid after the employee's work has been completed (Article 624), but partial remuneration shall be made to the employee for that part of his or her work already rendered (a) if the employment ends, either by cancellation, an offer to terminate, or any applicable reason, before the term of the contract expires or (b) if the work becomes no longer possible due to any impediment not attributable to the employer (Article 624-2). When the employee cannot continue his or her work due to the employer, such as when the employer has left the workplace in a dangerous condition, the employer must pay the whole amount of remuneration even if the work has been not completed (Article 536 II). The employer also needs to ensure that the working environment is safe for the employee.

III. Termination

693. An employment contract sometimes has a fixed term and sometimes has an indefinite term. A fixed-term employment contract ends once the term has expired.[519] If an employer knows that an employee is still working after the end of

---

the Civil Code, made within the Labor Standards Act. For practical management of labour contracts in Japan, *see* JETRO, 'Section 4. Human Resource Management 4.3 Labor contracts' in *How to Set Up Business in Japan* at https://www.jetro.go.jp/en/invest/setting_up/section4/page3.html (accessed 21 Jun. 2018).

519. In order to protect the employee's reasonable expectation on continuing the indefinite-term contracts, under the revised Article 18 of the Labor Contract Act (Act No. 128 of 2007), which is in force from 1 Apr. 2018, an employer shall be deemed to accept the employee's offer to convert a current fixed-term labour contract into an indefinite-term labour contract if the total contract term of two or more fixed-term labour contracts that he or she has concluded with the same employer

the contract and does not intervene to prevent this, the contract shall be considered to have been renewed with the same content as the original contract, but with an indefinite term (Article 629). After five years from the start of employment, either party may cancel the contract at will, at any time before the fixed term expires, with three months' notice in the case of cancellation by an employer or with two weeks' notice in the case of cancellation by an employee (Article 626). The employee can also cancel an employment contract without waiting for the expiration of the fixed term if there is an unavoidable reason of any kind, such as the inability of the employee to continue working due to an injury, although the employee will be liable to an employer for damages (Article 628). Furthermore, the employee can offer to terminate an employment contract before the fixed term expires if the employer is subject to a ruling for the commencement of bankruptcy procedures (Article 631).

694. In an indefinite-term employment contract, either party may offer to terminate the contract at any time, but this requires two weeks' notice whether the offer is made by the employer or the employee under the Civil Code (Article 627). However, as a matter of fact, Article 20 of the Labor Standards Act requires thirty days' notice in the case of an employer's offer to terminate a contract, so two weeks' notice as required by the Civil Code is enough only in the case of an employee's offer to terminate a contract.

695. Furthermore, an employer's offer to terminate the contract has been severely restricted by the courts under the established doctrine of Abusive Dismissal, according to which the employer's exercising of the right of dismissal will be void as an abuse if it lacks any objectively reasonable ground and thus it cannot be considered appropriate in a socially accepted sense.[520] The doctrine has been developed as a kind of an abuse of right under the Civil Code,[521] and it is now expressly provided as the Article 16 of the Labor Contract Act.

696. In application of this doctrine, the courts generally specify that the following four requirements should be satisfied before employees can be collectively dismissed (or made redundant) due to the employer's economic circumstances: (1) the objective economic necessity of the dismissal, (2) the employer's efforts to avoid

exceeds five years. The Act on Special Measures Concerning Fixed-term Employees with Expert Knowledge and Skills (Act No. 137 of 2014) permits the two exceptions. One of the exceptions is that a fixed-term employee who continues to work after retirement does not have such a right of contract conversion during the period of the current contract term. Another one is that a fixed-term employee for the project ending after the specified period of more than five years with expert knowledge and skills has the right of contract conversion only after the period, but not exceeding ten years, from the start of their first employment with that employer.

520. Supreme Court, 24 Apr. 1970, Minshu 29-4-456. For abusive dismissals, *see* generally, K. Sugeno & K. Yamakoshi, 'Dismissal in Japan – Part One: How Strict is Japanese Law on Dismissal?' 11 *Japan Lab. Rev.* 83 et seq. (2014), also available athttp://www.jil.go.jp/english/JLR/documents/2014/JLR42_sugeno_yamakoshi.pdf (accessed 21 Jun. 2018). *See also* D. H. Foote, 'Judicial Creation of Norms in Japanese Labor Law: Activism in the Service of – Stability?' 43 *UCLA L. Rev.* 635 (1996).

521. See *supra* n. 356 and the accompanying text.

dismissal, (3) reasonable criteria for selecting which employees should be dismissed and (4) a reasonable process for dismissing an employee.

§3. Contract for Work

I. Building Contract as a Typical Example

697. A contract for work is found when a contractor promises to accomplish a certain work product for a client in exchange for remuneration. Although there are many situations when contracts for work are used, a typical example is a building or construction contract. In practice, a standard form of building contract is commonly used in the industry to amend or supplement the Civil Code's rules for a contract for work.

II. Effect

A. Duties of the Contractor

698. A contractor is obliged to accomplish the work in accordance with the contract. For example, the contractor is liable if it uses a thinner steel frame than the contract specifies for constructing a building even if the frame satisfies the technical safety standards.[522]

699. If this obligation is not fulfilled in accordance with the contract, general rules of contractual liability apply (Articles 414, 415, 541 and 542), and specific rules of contractual liability for a sale contract also apply *mutatis mutandis* (Articles 559, 562 and 566). Thus, the client can resort to the remedies of claiming damages against the contractor, as well as requiring a reduction in the price, cancellation of the contract or requiring a substitute or repairs, although this last remedy is unavailable if the non-conformity of performance is not significant and the repairs involve excessive costs.[523] The client can opt for any of these remedies as long as they are not inconsistent with each other. For example, the client may require the contractor to repair a defect and pay for damages caused by its late work, but the client may not demand damages in lieu of performance (i.e., expectation damages) and repair of the defect at the same time.

700. However, these are subject to specific rules for a contract for work (Articles 636 and 637). First, a contractor shall not be liable for non-conformity arising due to the nature of the materials supplied or instructions given by a client unless the

522. Supreme Court, 10 Oct. 2003, Hanji 1840-18.
523. *See* generally above Part I, Ch. 6.

contractor knew that the materials or instructions were inappropriate but did not disclose this (Article 636). The reason for this exemption is that the client should assume liability if denying the discretion of the contractor that should be allowed in a contract for work.

701. Second, the contractor's liability claim expires after one year of the delivery of the outcome of the work or, if delivery is not necessary, the completion of the work (Article 637). This is laid down because delivery of the outcome of work is not required in some contracts for work, in contrast to sales contracts.

B. Duties of the Client

702. For its part, the client is obliged to pay remuneration upon taking delivery of the outcome of the work if the delivery is necessary or after completion of the contractor's work (Article 633). However, in reality, the standard form of a building contract usually provides that remuneration shall be paid in three separate steps – (1) on starting the job, (2) during the job and (3) on taking delivery of the construction.

703. (a) If a contract for work is cancelled before completion of the contractor's work or (b) if completion of the work becomes impossible due to an impediment not attributable to the contractor, partial remuneration shall be paid to the contractor corresponding to the benefits that the client receives from the separately existing outcome on which the contractor has worked (Article 634). However, if the contractor cannot continue work due to the client's (in)action, the client shall pay the whole amount of remuneration even if the contractor's work has not been completed (Article 536 II).

III. Original Ownership of a Building

704. There has been some discussion about which party – the contractor or the client – originally owns the completed building in a building contract. The Civil Code has no provision on that point, so two views compete with each other.

705. The first view is that the building belongs to the contractor, unless the contractor uses materials for the construction provided by the client, and that the ownership is later transferred from the contractor to the client when the contractor delivers it to the client in exchange for remuneration. The second view is that the building belongs to the client from the beginning.

706. The first view is based on the idea of Article 246, the rule of processing. The second view objects that this is contrary to the reasonable intentions of the parties to allow the client to acquire the original ownership of the building, regardless of the purpose of the building contract. The first view considers that assigning the original ownership of the building to the contractor is the most effective way to protect its claim for remuneration against the client, because the contractor can sell it to someone else if the client does not pay for the building. Although the second view argues that there are alternatives to this, such as a statutory lien for construction work for immovable properties (Article 327), this cannot be an option in practice because the budgeted expenses for the work are in fact difficult to register (as required by Article 338) before construction actually starts. This is why the courts adopt the first view, which is now also extended to the ownership of the unfinished building.

707. In practice, the parties to a building contract sometimes expressly agree that the completed or incomplete building belongs to the client from the beginning. The Supreme Court recognises the effect of such an agreement between the parties, even to a subcontractor, arguing that the legal position of a subcontractor is the same as that of the contractor, at least in relation to the client.

IV. Termination

708. As explained above, the client can cancel a contract for work if the contractor does not fulfill his or her obligation to accomplish the work in accordance with the contract. Moreover, the client can cancel the contract for work at his or her will at any time before the contractor completes his or her work, but the client must pay the contractor for damages arising from the cancellation of the contract (Article 641). Cancellation at will is allowed because it would be pointless to make the contractor finish the work that the client no longer wanted.

709. On the other, a contractor can cancel a contract for work if the client receives an order of commencement of bankruptcy proceedings (Article 642). In such a situation, the Bankruptcy Act gives a bankruptcy trustee the right to cancel a bilateral contract, i.e., a contract for work here (Article 53), but the Civil Code also allows the contractor to cancel it before the completion of work because the contractor needs to avoid the risk of not being paid after completing the work contracted for.

Chapter 6. Leases

710. Leases are the third and final category of loans in Japanese contract law and are currently addressed in Articles 601–621 of the Civil Code. Leases and loans for use[524] are closely related, with the former essentially functioning as a lease without rent. As with loans for consumption[525], leases are governed not only by the contract law provisions found in the Civil Code but also by special laws regulating specific kinds of transactions, e.g. the Act on Land and Building Leases (ALBL) and the Agricultural Land Act. This section will reference commonly invoked provisions of these special laws but focus on the basic Civil Code provisions, and separately address (a) leases in general, (b) commercial leases and (c) agricultural leases.

§1. Leases

711. Leases encompass all loans by a lender of an object to a borrower for rent, with the object itself to be returned at the conclusion of the lease. This category of loans covers everything from rental DVDs, to rental cars, to rented buildings and land.[526]

712. A lessor may enter into a valid lease agreement to lease property to which she does not have ownership rights.[527] If, however, the owner subsequently demands return of the property, the lessee may terminate the lease and demand damages from the lessor.[528]

713. Leases are considered promissory agreements taking effect not at the point of transfer, but at the time of the agreement, when one of the parties 'promises to make' a certain thing available (Article 601).

714. Under the Civil Code, a leasehold of immovable property is perfected by registration (Article 605). If not perfected, the new owner of the property has the right to force the lessee to vacate the property. In other words, the lessee possesses no rights under the lease vis-à-vis the new owner and is limited to a claim against the original owner for breach of contract.

715. The Act on Land and Building Leases (ALBL) changes this. The statute modifies the rights of the lessee in possession where ownership of the leased property has been transferred by providing that even where a lease of land is not registered, if a building on the land is registered, the lessor of the land may assert that registration as a defence against the new owner (Article 10(1) ALBL). Similarly,

524. *See* below Part II, Ch. 10.
525. *Ibid.*
526. In other words, this category also covers both real and personal property. The Civil Code itself refers designated 'things'.
527. Great Court of Cassation, 17 May 1906, Minroku 12-773; Great Court of Cassation, 17 May 1918 Minroku 24-971.
528. Shiomi, *supra* n. 105, 150.

even if the lease of a residence is not registered, the act of occupying the residence provides a defence against a new owner seeking removal (Article 31(1) ALBL).

716. If the ownership of a leased immovable is transferred, the lessee who has perfected its right in the manner explained in paragraphs 714 and 715, the status of the original lessor is automatically transferred to the new owner (transferee) (Article 605-2(1)). Registration of the transfer of ownership is necessary in order for the transferee to assert the transfer vis-à-vis the lessee (Article 605-2(3)). The transferee succeeds the transferor's obligation to reimburse expenses as well as the obligation to return the deposit money (Article 605-2(4)). The transferor and transferee of the immovable may agree that the transferor retains the status as the lessor, but such agreement does not take effect unless the parties also agree that the immovable is leased from the transferee to the transferor (Article 605-2(2)). In that case, the relationship between the transferor/lessor and the lessee is a sublease.

717. A 'mandatory' provision in the Civil Code (*kyouko kitei*) provides that no lease or renewal may exceed fifty years in duration (Article 604(1) & (2)).[529] The Civil Code further limits the duration of leases entered into by those with no authority to dispose of the item (a) six months for the loan of a movable object; (b) three years for the lease of a building; (c) five years for the lease of land; and (d) ten years for the lease of a forest (Article 602(1)).[530] If the term of a lease is beyond these term limits, that portion of the lease beyond these term limits is void without invalidating the entire lease (Articles 604(1) and 602(1)).

718. The Act on Land and Building Leases creates exceptions to the Civil Code's twenty-year maximum term by (a) stating that the Civil Code's limits do not apply to building leases and (b) establishing a default duration of thirty years for land leases, with longer durations permitted when extended by agreement (Articles 3 & 29(2) ALBL). The statute treats land and building leases with a stated term of less than one year as leases without a defined term (Articles 3 & 29(1) ALBL).

719. Where the term of the lease is specified and beyond one year, the lessor must, in order not to renew, provide notice of intent not to renew from six months to one year prior to the expiration of the lease and, if contested, a justifiable basis for not renewing the lease.[531] First, the courts and now also the statute itself permit the lessor to exercise its right not to renew or object to a request to renew only if she possess a 'justifiable reason' (*seito na jiyuu*) for doing so (Articles 6 & 28 ALBL).[532]

529. Prior to the 2017 Reform, this period was 'twenty' years. One reason for the extension to fifty years is that there are business needs for agreeing on a lease with longer period. *Ichimon Itto Minpo (Saikenkannkei) Kaisei [Questions and Answers on the Civil Code (Obligations) Reform]*, 315 (T. Tsutsui and H. Muramtsu eds., Shojihomu 2018).
530. Article 603 further restricts the renewal of short-term leases.
531. Shiomi, *supra* n. 105, 211.
532. Shiomi, *supra* n. 105, 211. Haley, *supra* n. 55.

720. In determining whether a justifiable reason exists, the Act on Land and Building Leases requires consideration of (a) the relative needs of the lessor and lessee for the leased property; (b) the length of the lease, payment of rent and performance of other terms of the lease to date; (c) the condition of the property leased; and (d) any offers by the lessor to the lessee of financial assistance to facilitate vacating the property (Articles 6 & 28 ALBL).

721. This last consideration, financial quid pro quo offered by the lessor to the lessee, is commonly characterised as 'eviction money' (*tachinokiryou*). The courts state that this payment of extra-contractual eviction fees will not justify an objection to renewal of the lease, but it does 'support' a finding that the non-renewal is reasonable.[533] Regardless of the terms of the lease, some courts have required payment of a specified amount of eviction money as a condition to ordering the lessee to vacate the property.[534]

722. The courts determine whether or not justifiable reasons exist at the time the lessor objects.[535] However, absent evidence of bad faith, courts will consider any additional offers of eviction money made by the lessor to the lessee up to the point that the court concludes argument on the subject.[536] This rule presuming renewal does not apply if the contract is either a fixed-term lease of a building (*teiki shakuyaken*) or a 'fixed-term lease' of land (*teiki shakuchiken*) of a certain minimum length (e.g., fifty years in case of standard lease of land) (Articles 22–25 & 38–40 ALBL).

723. Fixed-term leases are not simply leases that explicitly define the length of the contract. They are, under Japanese law, leases for a specific term that explicitly reject any right of renewal by the lessee. They must be in writing, confirmed by notarisation or otherwise, and specifically state that there is no right of renewal (Article 38(1) ALBL). The lessor must provide to the lessee documentation specifically detailing that there is no right of renewal and explain it to the lessor, and the lessor must provide notice of the termination of the contract between six months and a year prior to the end of the term (Article 38(1) ALBL). If the lessor completes these steps the lessee has no right of renewal.[537]

724. The parties may implicitly renew a lease if the lessee continues his or her use and the lessor knows of, but does not object to, this continued use (Article 619). Under the Land and Building Least Act, presumptive rights to renew a lease attach

533. Supreme Court, 1 Mar. 1963, Minshu 17-2-290; Supreme Court, 25 Oct. 1994, Minshu 48-7-1303.
534. Supreme Court, 25 Nov. 1971, Minshu 25-8-1343. *See also* Osaka District Court, Apr. 28, 1982, 476 Hanrei Taimzu 130, translated by J. M. Ramseyer, *reprinted in* C. J. Milhaupt, J. M. Ramseyer and M. D. West, *The Japanese Legal System: Cases, Codes, and Commentary*, 467 (2nd ed., Foundation Press 2012).
535. Supreme Court, 1 Mar. 1963, Minshu 17-2-290.
536. Supreme Court, 25 Oct. 1994, Minshu 48-7-1303.
537. These fixed-term leases which recognize the lessor's 'right not to renew' are recent developments enacted in 1992 and 2000 respectively and intended to revitalize the property market and direct property to more efficient uses. Shiomi, *supra* n. 105, 214. However, strict compliance with the writing requirements are necessary in order for the fixed terms to be enforced. Supreme Court, 16 Jul. 2010, Hanji 2094-58; Supreme Court, 13 Sep. 2012, Minshu 66-9-2363.

if: (a) the lessee demands renewal and the lessor fails to promptly object to the renewal based on justifiable grounds or (b) the lease ends, the lessee continues use of the leased property and the lessor fails to promptly object, again based on justifiable grounds (Articles 5 & 26 ALBL). The lease becomes a lease without term, with termination subject to the notification requirements of one year for land, three months for leased buildings or one day for movables (Articles 619(1) and 617).

725. Practices vary by region but lessors, pursuant to the initial contract, commonly assess a renewal fee (*koshinryo*) at the end of the lease term if the parties agree to renew the lease.[538] The renewal fees can be substantial, the equivalent of one to two months' rent, although amounts are sometimes negotiable.[539] Some courts have invalidated what they considered to be excessively high renewal fees as a violation of the Civil Code's good faith requirements incorporated into Article 10 of the Consumer Contract Act (Act No. 61 of 2000).[540] The Supreme Court has held that an unambiguous renewal clause does not violate good faith requirements and the Consumer Contract Act, absent 'special circumstances suggesting, *inter alia*, that the amount of the renewal fee is too high in light of such factors as the renewal term of the lease contract'.[541]

§2. Lessor Duties

726. Under the Civil Code, the lessor assumes an obligation to make the repairs necessary for use of the item, e.g. fixing a leaking roof, unless the repair became necessary by a cause attributable to the lessee (Article 606(1)). A duty to repair will not arise if the cost of the repair approaches the purchase price of a new replacement.[542] The lessee must give notice to the lessor of the need to repair (Article 615), and she may demand repayment for necessary costs expended as a result of the lessor's failure to make repairs (Article 608). Failure to repair also provides a basis for the lessee to withhold payment of rent in proportion to the interference with use by the lessee caused by the defect.[543] The Civil Code's duty to repair provision is a default provision that the parties may modify in whole or part.[544]

727. The lessor assumes a duty, in certain instances, to facilitate the lessees efforts to accomplish the purposes of the lease. Courts have found, for example, that the lessor has a duty to assist in filing applications for approval of the lease of agricultural land and to enjoin third parties from interfering with the lessee's use of the land.[545]

---

538. Nakata, *supra* n. 61, 467.
539. *Ibid.*
540. Osaka High Court, 27 Aug. 2009, Hanji 2062-40.
541. Supreme Court, 15 Jul. 2011, Minshu 65-5-2269.
542. Great Court of Cassation, 6 Mar. 1940, Shimbun 4551-12.
543. Great Court of Cassation, 26 Sep. 1921, Minroku 27-1627; Great Court of Cassation, 22 May 1916, Minroku 22-1011.
544. Supreme Court, 25 Jun. 1954, Minshu 8-6-1224.
545. Supreme Court, 11 Oct. 1960, Minshu 14-12-2465; Supreme Court, 31 Jan. 1975, Minshu 29-1-53.

728. A lessor has a general duty to ensure the safety of the item leased. Courts have imposed, based on general good faith requirements in the Civil Code, a duty to take reasonable steps to ensure the safety of the lessee's person and property.[546]

§3. Lessee Duties

729. The Code provides a default time for payment of rent: at the end of the month for movables and residential land and buildings; the end of the year for the lease of other land; and after harvest for agricultural leases (Article 614). Absent agreement otherwise, the right to demand payment of rent arises after use of the item leased.

730. Agreements relating to security deposits are contracts accessory to the contract of lease. In theory, it enters into effect only after the security deposit is actually deposited. This means that the lessee is not obligated to pay and payment of which the lessor may not demand; however, if the parties have agreed to the payment of a security deposit, a lessor may terminate the lease if the lessee refuses to pay the agreed security deposit.[547] In practice, security deposits are almost universal. Courts have recognised that they function as collateral and allowed the lessor to apply the security deposit to unpaid rent or other damages caused by the lessee.[548] Courts have also held that the lessee must vacate the property prior to demanding return of the security deposit.[549]

731. Apart from security deposits, many lessors will contractually impose an obligation on the lessee to make a non-refundable lump sum payment equivalent to one to two months' rent as 'key money' prior to occupancy.[550] In some contracts this key money is styled as 'thanks money' (*reikin*), a payment made in 'thanks' to the lessor for making the leased item available. In other contexts, courts have held this money, paid for obtaining a right to lease the property (*kenrikin*), to constitute pre-payment of rent, quid pro quo for the right to obtain profits from the use of the leased property, or quid pro quo for rights within the lease such as the right to sublease the property.[551] Regardless of how the payment is titled, some courts, as discussed above, have found 'excessive' sums of key money and renewal fees charged in residential leases to violate the Consumer Contract Act and invalidated those terms. *See* paragraph 725.

546. Supreme Court, 17 Oct. 1991, Hanji 1404-74 (imposing a duty to maintain a safe premises where a leased building caught fire and resulted in the destruction of the lessee's personal goods).
547. Shiomi, *supra* n. 105, 219.
548. Supreme Court, 2 Feb. 1973, Minshu 27-1-80; Great Court of Cassation, 10 Mar. 1930, Minshu 9-253.
549. Supreme Court, 9 Sep. 1974, Minshu 28-6-1152.
550. Shiomi, *supra* n. 105, 222.
551. *See*, e.g., Supreme Court, 27 Jun. 1928, Minshu 22-6-1427; Tokyo District Court, 26 Apr. 1956, Kaminshu 7-4-1045. Shiomi, *supra* n. 105, 222.

732. Lessors in Japan also commonly demand personal guarantors for leases.[552] The terms of the contract will require the lessee to designate a personal guarantor who agrees to be jointly and severally liable for any unpaid rent or damage caused by the lessee. For regulations of guarantee contracts, *see* Part II, Chapter 8.

733. The lessee assumes a duty to use the leased item in conformance with its reasonably intended use given the nature of the item or in conformance with the terms of use established by the contract (Article 616 applying *mutatis mutandis* Article 594 on loan for use). Special provisions regarding use are common with leased properties and include, e.g., prohibitions against keeping pets, causing 'inconvenience' (*meiwaku*) to other tenants or neighbours, and using the premises in association with members of organised crime.[553]

734. Absent agreement otherwise, the lessee owes a duty to exercise the care of a 'good faith manager' (*zenryou naru kanrisha*) to maintain the leased property (Article 400). This includes notifying the lessor of the need to make repairs or of interference with the lessor's property rights by a third party (Article 615).

§4. Reduction in Rent

735. Default provisions in the Code also provide that, for non-residential land leases such as agricultural leases, if profits from the land are less than the rent as a result of force majeure, lessees may demand a reduction in rent (Article 609).[554] Lessees may similarly seek reduction in rent if a part of the leased item is lost due to reasons other than the causes attributable to the lessee (Article 611).

736. The Act on Land and Building Leases also codifies a right to seek a reduction in rent. If rent for either land or a building becomes 'unreasonable' as a result of changes in taxes, land prices or the rent departs from comparable rents for similar properties in the vicinity, the parties may request a rent increase or decrease. They may do so regardless of the contract terms, and if the parties cannot agree on the increase or decrease, the renter may pay an amount it deems reasonable, pending judgment by the court. If the court finds that amount insufficient, the lessee must pay the difference, with interest (Articles 11 & 32 ALBL).

737. These provisions of the act are mandatary, meaning that even if the parties expressly agree to the amount of rent and scheduled rent increases, the courts, on

552. *See,* e.g., N. Nishimura, 'Zenchu Articles 446-465 Hoshosaimu [Guarantee Obligations]', in *Chushaku Minpo [Commentaries on the Civil Code]*, Vol. 11, 155 (N. Nishimura ed.,Yuhikaku 1965).

553. Shiomi, *supra* n. 105, 160.

554. They may cancel the contract if, as a result of force majeure the rent exceeds profits from the land for more than two (2) years (Art. 610). The MOJ advisory committee has proposed eliminating these provisions given the remedies are now available in the Agricultural Land Act. *See*, MOJ, *supra* n. 104, 161; Art. 20 Agricultural Land Act. However, no change was added.

petition by one of the parties, will re-evaluate the fairness of the rent in light of the intent of the parties and current economic conditions.[555]

738. Claims for rent adjustment are common, as was related litigation following the collapse of Japan's economic bubble in the early 1990s. During the bubble, developers approached landowners with proposals for the landowners to build buildings and the developers to rent them, *in toto*, and then sublease portions of the buildings to individual tenants. Owners often did so based on express rent guarantees in the contract and bank financing for the construction. After the collapse of the bubble and developers' consequent inability to sublease the property, developers demanded reductions in rent.[556] Many courts complied, and a series of Supreme Court judgments on subleases held that the parties' negotiated rent should be reviewed, and revised as necessary, considering the 'totality of the circumstances'.[557]

§5. Subleases

739. The Civil Code prohibits assignment or subleasing the object of the lease without the consent of the lessor (Article 612(1)). If assignment or sublease is carried out without consent, the lessor is entitled to cancel the lease (*See* paragraph 742 below).[558] With consent, the sub-lessee assumes a direct obligation to the lessor; in other words, the lessor may demand payment of rent from either the lessee or sub-lessee (Article 613(1) & (2)).

740. The Civil Code also provides that a lessee's advance payment of rent provides no defence against a claim by the lessor against the sub-lessee, and nothing precludes the lessor from exercising rights as enumerated in the underlying lease (Article 613(1) & (2)). In other words, regardless of the fact that the sub-lessee signed no contract with the lessor–owner, the lessor–owner can pursue payment from either the lessee or sub-lessee and enforce against both rights enumerated in the underlying lease.

741. Cases have held that if a lessee defaults on the original lease, the lessor may demand that the party subletting vacate the property.[559] At that point, the sublease is terminated because its underlying legal basis is lost.[560] The cancellation requires an advance notice to the lessee demanding payment, but such notice need not be provided to the sub-lessee.[561]

555. *See*, e.g., Supreme Court, 29 Feb. 2008.
556. *See* Pardieck, *supra* n. 59, 599.
557. *Ibid.* 613-617.
558. The original drafters incorporated this requirement of consent and afforded the lessor a termination right given the reliance on relationships in traditional Japan. Shiomi, *supra* n. 105, 183.
559. Supreme Court, 21 Dec. 1961, Minshu 15-12-3243; Supreme Court, 25 Feb. 1997, Minshu 51-2-398.
560. Supreme Court, 25 Feb. 1997, Minshu 1-2-398.
561. Supreme Court, 29 Mar. 1962, Minshu 16-3-662.

742. The Civil Code grants the lessor a right to cancel the lease if a lessee subleases without consent (Article 612(2)). The courts have, however, restricted this termination right. Courts have long required not only that the lessee execute a sublease, but also that the third party actually uses the object, before recognising the lessor's right to termination.[562]

743. Courts have also applied the 'abuse of rights' doctrine and interpreted general good faith requirements to restrict termination to those cases where there exists 'acts which constitute a breach of faith' (*haishin teki koui*).[563] The courts and scholarship now generally refer to this as the 'doctrine of broken trust' (*shinrai kankei hakai no houri*).[564] It imposes the burden of proof on the lessee to assert that the circumstances surrounding the sublease without consent do not rise to the level of a breach of faith.[565]

744. The majority of courts evaluate personal factors as well as the economic consequences of the sublease in determining whether there has been a breach of faith.[566] Courts have found no breach of faith where the lessee merely changed corporate form or transferred use of the leased property to a common law spouse.[567]

§6. Cancellation or Termination of the Lease

745. Case law had been clear that if a leased item is destroyed in its entirety or otherwise becomes completely unusable, this automatically terminates the lease[568]. This rule was codified in the 2017 Reform as Article 616-2.

746. Unless otherwise specified, pursuant to the Civil Code, the parties may terminate a lease at any point following notice of one year for leases of land; three months for leases of buildings; and one day for leases of movables and hired venues (Article 617). Even where the right to terminate the lease at any time during a specified term is reserved by one or both parties, the above notice provisions apply (Article 618). Similarly, where a lessee continues in possession following the expiration of a lease, without any objection from the lessor, continuation of the lease on the original terms is presumed and the above notice provisions for termination apply

562. Great Court of Cassation, 16 Apr. 1938, Hanketsu Zenshu 5-9-8.
563. Supreme Court, 25 Sep. 1953, Minshu 7-9-979. *See* also, Haley, *supra* n. 55, 151 and 162; and more generally Nottage, *supra* n. 11.
564. Supreme Court, 21 Apr. 1966, Minshu 20-4-720; Supreme Court, 17 Sep. 1991, Hanji 1402-47. Shiomi, *supra* n. 105, 183.
565. Supreme Court, 27 Jan. 1966, Minshu 20-1-136.
566. Shiomi, *supra* n. 105, 184.
567. Supreme Court, 15 Oct. 1963, Minshu 17-9-1202, Supreme Court, 19 Nov. 1964, Minshu 18-9-1900; Supreme Court, 30 Jun. 1964, Minshu 18-5-991; Supreme Court, 18 Jun. 1965, Minshu 19-4-976.
568. Supreme Court, 3 Dec. 1957, Minshu 11-13-2018; Supreme Court, 21 Dec. 1957, Minshu 15-12-3243.

(Article 619(1)).[569] On termination of the lease, courts have imposed on the borrower an implied obligation to return the leased item in the condition in which it was received, with an exception made for normal wear and tear, including age-related changes.[570] The 2017 Reform codified this rule as Article 621.

747. In case of breach of a contract, the starting point is that if one party (the obligor) breaches the contract, the other party (the obligee) may cancel it if the obligee gives notice specifying a reasonable period of time within which the obligor is to perform, and if the obligor does not perform within that period of time (Article 541).[571] However, for cancellation of lease, case law significantly restricts this general principle, with its application of the 'doctrine of broken trust' (*shinrai kankei hakai no houri*) discussed above in paragraph 743.

748. The doctrine, in the context of a breach of lease contract claim, states that the breach must be so substantial that it destroys the trust that supposedly exists between the lessor and lessee.[572] As a result, minor breaches, such as a one-off delay in payment of rent, or violations of the lease's terms of use, such as a prohibition against keeping pets, may subject the lessee to claims for damages, but they will not provide a basis for the lessor to terminate the contract.

749. By contrast, courts have dispensed with the notice requirement, explained in paragraph 744 above, where the breach is such that it clearly destroys the relationship of trust.[573]

750. Courts have held that where a lessor and lessee agree to terminate the underlying lease, the lessor may not, absent a breach of contract by the lessee, assert the agreement to terminate against any sub-lessees to the property.[574] Courts hold that a voluntary relinquishment of rights should not adversely affect related rights lawfully obtained by a third party. Where a commercial building was leased in its entirety to the lessee with the intent that the lessee sublet space to individual tenants and the lessee declined to renew the lease at the end of its term, courts have held that good faith requirements precluded the building owner–lessor from evicting individual building tenants.[575]

751. The courts have also addressed leasing arrangements where the ownership of land is separate from ownership of buildings sitting on that land. Where a lessor

---

569. *See also* special rules under the Act on Land and Building Leases (ALBL) regarding automatic renewal explained in paras 718–722 above.
570. Supreme Court, 16 Dec. 2005, Hanji 1921-61.
571. Shiomi, *supra* n. 105, 164. *See* Part I, Chapter 6, §4, II.
572. Shiomi, *supra* n. 105, 164.
573. Supreme Court, 25 Apr. 1952, Minshu 6-4-451. *See* also, Taylor 1993, *supra* n. 30.
574. Great Court of Cassation, 7 Mar. 1934, Minshu 13-278; Supreme Court, 24 Mar. 1987, Hanji 1258-61; Supreme Court, 21 Feb. 1963, Minshu 17-1-219. The MOJ Advisory Committee has proposed codifying this principle. *See*, MOJ, *supra* n. 104, 462.
575. Supreme Court, 28 Mar. 2002, Minshu 56-3-662.

of land agrees with the lessee owner to terminate the land lease, courts have held that the lessor of the land may not take action against those renting space within a building located on the land.[576]

§7. COMMERCIAL AND AGRICULTURE LEASES

I. Commercial Lease

752. A commercial lease of land is also governed by the Act on Land and Building Leases, as long as it is made in order for a lessor to own a building on the leased land.

753. Under the Act, a fixed-term lease of land is permitted with its duration of at least more than fifty years, but a commercial fixed-term lease limits its duration to less than fifty but more than ten years. The renewal rules are excluded in a commercial fixed-term lease of land between ten and thirty years term, and may be excluded if the contract specifies so in a commercial fixed-term lease between thirty and fifty years term (Articles 23(1) and (2) ALBL). The commercial lease contract must be notarised (Article 23(3) ALBL).

754. A commercial lease of building is also governed by the same Act.

II. Agricultural Lease

755. The Agricultural Land Act (ALA) (Act No. 229 of 1952) requires the approval of the local Agricultural Commission (*nougyou iinkai*) or Prefectural Governor in order to lease farm land or land used for pasturing animals (Article 3(1) & 3(4) ALA). Leases concluded without this approval are void.[577] The statute also establishes a means for the lessee to request a reduction in rent similar to that found in the Act on Land and Building Leases, discussed above (Articles 21 et seq. ALA).

756. Any worker or entity can make a lease of agricultural land if the agricultural committee approves it (Agricultural Land Act, Article 3(3)). The approval may be given to even a non-agricultural entity if the conditions specified in the Agricultural Land Act are satisfied, e.g. that at least one of their executives is an agricultural worker (Article 3(3) ALA).

757. The lease contract is automatically renewed if a lessor gives notice of intent not to renew to a lessee from six months to one year prior to the expiration of the lease (Article 17 ALA).

---

576. Supreme Court, 21 Feb. 1963, Minshu 17-1-219.
577. Supreme Court, 29 May 1962, Minshu 16-5-1226 (voiding sale of agricultural land without the requisite governmental approval).

758. If the lease contract is made on the larger-scale agricultural land plan decided by a municipal government under the Act on Promotion of Improvement of Agricultural Management Foundation (Act No. 65 of 1980), it does not need the agricultural committee's approval and will end after the stated duration in the plan without being subject to automatic renewal (Article 3(1) Act on Promotion of Improvement of Agricultural Management Foundation).

759. For the lease contract to be terminated, a prefectural governor's approval is necessary except some cases, e.g., where a lessor gives notice of intent not to renew to a lessee cases of the lease contract with more than ten years term (Article 18 ALA).

760. A leasehold of agricultural land is perfected by lessor's possession of the land, or by registration (Article 16 ALA).

Chapter 7. Compromise

§1. General Introduction

761. Settlement or compromise (*wakai*) is a contract under which the parties agree to settle a dispute between them by making reciprocal concessions (Article 695). Any dispute can be settled by the parties as long as the subject matter relates to rights that the parties may dispose of by themselves. Thus, for example, the parties cannot settle a dispute regarding the existence of family relations[578].

762. The vast majority of disputes are settled by this consensual dispute resolution mechanism, rather than by resorting to court proceedings or arbitration (*chusai*) which are adjudicatory in nature. However, even in court proceedings, there is widespread practice where judges recommend settlement to the parties (cf. Article 87, Code of Civil Procedure). If the parties agree to settle the dispute during the court proceeding ('compromise in courts' (*saibanjo-no wakai*)), and if the settlement is entered into court records ('record of settlement' (*wakai chosho*)), that settlement carries the same effect as a 'final and binding judgment' and is thus enforceable (Article 267, Code of Civil Procedure).

763. Conciliation or mediation (*chotei*) is another form of alternative dispute resolution where a neutral third party assists the parties to reach a settlement. The court also administers conciliations (civil conciliations) in which a small committee of conciliators, consisting of judges and private citizens, assists in the settlement. If the parties reach a settlement and enters it in the court record (record of conciliation), the settlement carries the same effect as a final and binding judgment (e.g., Article 16, Civil Conciliation Act, Article 268(1), Domestic Relations Case Procedure Act), and is thus enforceable (Article 267, Code of Civil Procedure). For some types of disputes, such as those involving increase or decrease of rent and family disputes regarding the confirmation or creation of a personal status, civil conciliation must be attempted prior to filing for litigation (e.g., Article 24-2, Civil Conciliation Act; Article 257(1), Domestic Relations Case Procedure Act).

764. Conciliation administered out of courts by certificated dispute resolution organs is given under treatment under the Act on Promotion of Use of Alternative Dispute Resolution (Act No. 151 of 2004). For example, filing for conciliation has the effect of ceasing the prescription periods to run and suspending legal proceedings (Articles 25 and 26). In addition, the requirement that civil conciliation in court must be attempted prior to litigation does not apply, if the dispute resolution procedure in a certificated dispute resolution service was terminated on the grounds that it was impossible to arrange settlement between the parties. In such case, the court in charge of the case may refer the case to conciliation ex officio if the court considers it appropriate to do so (Article 27).

578. Great Court of Cassation, 13 Nov. 1931, Minshu 10-1022.

§2. Finality of the Settlement

765. Once a settlement is reached, it is final and the dispute cannot be reopened, even when it is later discovered that the settlement does not reflect the actual rights of the parties (Article 696). For example, if the subject matter of the dispute is the amount owed by one party to the other, and the parties reach a settlement to that amount, the settlement is final even when it is later discovered that the actual amount was different.

766. However, there is room to avoid the settlement based on mistake (Article 95). It is generally understood that three situations must be distinguished. First is where the mistake relates to the subject matter of the dispute (as described above). Article 696 (finality of settlement) trumps Article 95 (mistake) in that situation. However, in the second situation where the mistake does not relate to the subject matter of dispute, but relates to the 'premise' of the dispute, there is room for Article 95 to apply. For example, where settlement was reached as to the amount of debt, and it was later discovered that the debt did not exist, Article 696 does not preclude Article 95. However, the distinction between the first and second situation can be blurry.

767. The third situation is where the mistake relates neither to the subject matter of the dispute nor to its premise. One example is where settlement was reached that one party will deliver boxes of strawberry jam of a certain brand to the other party as a substitute for paying its debt, and it was later discovered that the quality of the delivered jam was of inferior quality. Article 696 does not preclude the applicability of Article 95.[579]

579. Supreme Court, 14 Jun. 1958, Minshu 12-9-1492 (the strawberry jam case).

Chapter 8. Guarantee Contract

§1. General Introduction

768. A guarantee contract (*hosho keiyaku*) is a contract between an obligee and a guarantor that secures the obligation of the principal obligor by the guarantor's assets. The guarantor is obligated to perform on behalf of the principal obligor if the principal obligor does not perform (Article 446(1)). The principal obligor is not a party to the guarantee contract.

769. In some cases, the guarantor is mandated by the principal obligor to enter into a guarantee contract with the obligee. In other cases, the guarantor enters into a guarantee contract without any such mandate, or even against the will of the principal obligor. These categorisation affect the guarantor's right of reimbursement. The right of reimbursement of a guarantor without mandate is limited in comparison to a guarantor with mandate. *See* Part II, Chapter 8, §4 below.

770. Guarantee contract is a form of personal security where the principal obligation is secured by all of the guarantor's assets, except those prohibited by law to be seized. If the guarantor's assets that secure the principal obligor's obligation are restricted to certain assets, that becomes a situation of a third-party grantor of a real security right (third-party pledge (*butsujo hosho*)). This monograph does not deal with this form of security. Although the English translation used here is 'pledge', which is the same term used for the 'pledge" (*shichi*) explained in below Part II, Chapter 9, they are different in the sense that the latter is a form of possessory security right.

771. In practice, guarantee contracts are used most often to facilitate lending to small- and medium-sized enterprises. Often the owner or operator, such as directors or executive officers, of the enterprise is the guarantor. Guarantee is also often provided by individuals (natural persons) who are family members or friends of the principal obligor. Usually, no fees are charged for providing the guarantee. This is typically an altruistic and gratuitous act based on a sense of moral obligation, and is thoughtlessly entered into without fully recognising the risk of the heavy burden it may have to bear in the case of default by the principal obligor.[580] This has led to increase among courts and lawmakers that protection to such guarantors are necessary. Recent law reform, including the 2017 Reform, has tackled with this issue.

772. Another group of guarantee provided by individuals (natural persons) is fidelity guarantees (*mimoto hosho*). Fidelity guarantors typically secure employer's damages claim, in contract or in tort, against its employees. This is also a risky transaction for fidelity guarantors, who tend to enter into the contract out of sense of kinship or friendship, because fidelity guarantee can be long term, and the amount of damages, if it arises, can be huge. Thus, the Fidelity Guarantee Act

580. Nishimura, *supra* n. 552, 150.

(FGA) (Act No. 42 of 1933) provides protections to fidelity guarantors. For example, the maximum term of fidelity contract is generally limited to five years (Article 2, FGA), and the court is given discretion to limit the amount of the guarantor's liability (Article 5, FGA). Agreements that are more disadvantageous to the fidelity guarantor than the provisions of FGA are void (Article 6, FGA). The courts have also joined the legislature in regulating fidelity guarantees by holding that a fidelity guarantee obligation is not subject to inheritance.[581]

773. On the other, there are also incorporated entities that provide guarantees to facilitate lending to small- and medium-sized enterprises. These are sometimes referred to as 'institutional guarantees'. Most significant in this regard is the guarantee provided by Credit Guarantee Associations (CGA) (*Shin-yo hosho kyokai*). CGAs are non-profit public-interest corporations based on the Credit Guarantee Association Act (Act No. 196 of 1953) and are established in every prefecture and some major cities. They charge the principal obligor fees for the guarantee.

774. The following paragraphs will discuss normal guarantee contracts (Part II, Chapter 8, §2-§4). However, most of the guarantees in practice are joint and severally liable guarantees (*rentai hosho*). We will turn to that in §5 in this chapter below, followed by other special cases of joint guarantees (§6 below), and revolving guarantees (§7 below).

§2. Formation Stage of Guarantee Contracts

I. Writing Requirement

775. The legislative challenge in recent years has been to provide protection to guarantors, particularly individual (natural person) guarantors, who tend to become guarantors without fully understanding the ramifications, or who could not refuse becoming a guarantor out of a sense of moral obligation.[582]

776. The first legislative response came in 2004 when a new provision was added to the Civil Code providing that a guarantee contract is not effective unless it is made in writing, including electromagnetic records (Article 446(2) and (3)).

II. Special Rules on Guarantee by Individuals of Business-Related Obligations

A. Notarised Document Declaring 'Intention to Guarantee'

777. In the 2017 Reform, special rules were added concerning guarantees or revolving guarantees by individuals (natural persons) where the principal obligation

581. Great Court of Cassation, 10 Sep. 1943, Minshu 22-948.
582. Cf. Tsutsui and Muramatsu, *supra* n. 529, 140.

is a loan obligation incurred for the purpose of business. 'Business' can be for profit or non-profit.[583] It was provided that such guarantees are not effective, unless the prospective guarantor has declared its 'intention to guarantee' by a notarised document (*kosei shosho*) created within one month prior to the conclusion of the guarantee contract (Article 465-6(1)). The document must be notarised by a notary public (*kosho-nin*) (Article 465-6(2)). It is expected that the process of going through the steps for notarisation and the verification by the notary public of the prospective guarantor's intention to guarantee will prevent prospective guarantors from thoughtlessly becoming a guarantor.[584]

778. If an individual (natural person) has guaranteed a right of reimbursement arising from a guarantee contract on business-related loans, the special rules explained above do not apply to that guarantee per se. However, since the same protection should be provided to such guarantor, it is provided that the rules explained above apply *mutatis mutandis* to such guarantee (Article 465-8).

779. However, there are important exclusions to the requirement of the notarised document declaring the intention to guarantee. First, if the principal obligor is a corporation, the requirement does not apply when the directors, executive officers or a person equivalent thereto are the ones to become guarantors (Article. 465-9(i)), or when the majority shareholder is the one to become guarantor (Article 465-9(ii)). Second, if the principal obligor is not a corporation, the notarised document requirement does not apply when any person (a) who is jointly doing business with the principal obligor or (b) who is the spouse of the principal obligor actually engaging in the business of the principal obligor (Article 465-9(iii)). The latter is the most controversial as it may significantly curtail the value of the notarised document requirement. Both the House of Representatives and the House of Councillors, when passing the bill of the 2017 Civil Code Reform, adopted a Resolution demanding the government to pay attention to, among others, the possible need to take further necessary steps regarding the exclusion of spouse–guarantors in light of the situation that will emerge following the coming into effect of the 2017 Reform.[585]

B. Principal Obligor's Duty of Disclosure

780. The 2017 Reform also imposed a duty to disclose certain information on the principal obligor, when it mandates an individual (natural person) to enter into a guarantee contract or a revolving guarantee contract where the principal obligation is its obligations, loan or otherwise, incurred for the purpose of business (Article 469-10). Information that must be disclosed are (i) the status of its assets

---

583. Yoshio Shiomi, *Minpo (Saikenkankei) Kaiseihono Gaiyo [An Outline of the Revised Civil Code (Obligations)]*, 141 (Kinzai, 2017).
584. *Ibid.* 140.
585. The Resolutions are available at Tsutsui and Muramatsu, *supra* n. 529, 9.

and its income and expenditure; (ii) the existence of obligations other than the principal obligation, its amount and the status of its performance; and (iii) other collateral that secures the principal obligation. If the principal obligor violates this duty by failing to provide information or by providing false information, and if that causes mistaken belief on the part of the mandated party that leads it to enter into a guarantee contract, and if the obligee knew or could have known of the violation, the guarantor has a right to rescind the guarantee contract with the obligee (Article 456-10(2)).

III. Qualification of the Guarantor

781. There is no restriction on the qualifications of becoming a guarantor.

782. However, if the principal obligor is obligated to furnish a guarantor, the guarantor must be a person of capacity and must have sufficient financial resources to perform the obligation (Article 450(1)). The obligation of the principal obligor to furnish a guarantor may arise under the contract or by law (e.g., Article 650(2) (mandator's obligation to tender reasonable security for obligation incurred by the mandatary for the administration of the mandated business). If the guarantor later comes to lack sufficient resources, the obligee has a right to demand a substitute guarantor (Article 450(2)). However, these rules do not apply if the obligee has designated the guarantor (Article 450(3)). If the principal obligor is unable to furnish a guarantor who meets those requirements, it has the right to furnish other security in leiu (Article 451). If the principal obligor fails to comply with these obligations, it loses the benefit of time and the obligation immediately becomes due (Article 137(iii)).

§3. Obligee and Guarantor: Guarantee Obligation

783. The obligation of the guarantor is to perform the principal obligor's obligation in case of the latter's non-performance (Article 446(1)). Unless otherwise agreed between the obligee and the guarantor, the guarantee obligation secures not only the principal obligation but also the incidentals such as interest, penalty and compensation for damages in connection with the principal obligation (Article 447(1)). The party's intentions in many cases are interpreted to also secure the obligation of restitution in case of cancellation.[586]

I. Accessory Nature (*Fujusei*) of the Guarantee Obligation

784. The purpose of the guarantee obligation is to secure the principal obligation. Therefore, the guarantee obligation is by its nature accessory to the principal obligation.

586. Supreme Court (Grand Bench), 30 Jun. 1965, Minshu 19-4-1143 (guarantee of seller's obligation).

785. Thus, regarding formation or existence of the principal obligation, if the principal obligation is non-existent, void or rescindable, the guarantee obligation is also non-existent or void, except that if the guarantor knew that the contract from which the principal obligation arise is rescindable due to incapacity of the principal obligor, it is presumed that the guarantor has made an independent undertaking which survives rescission of the principal obligor's contract (Article 449).

786. Regarding extinction of the principal obligation, if the principal obligation is fully discharged, the guarantee obligation is also discharged.

787. Regarding the content of the principal obligation, if the burden of the guarantor is more onerous than that of the principal obligor, it is reduced the extent of the principal obligation (Article 448(1)).

788. Likewise, the defences *vis-à-vis* the obligee available to the principal obligor is also available to the guarantor (Article 457(2)). The guarantor is not in a position to exercise the principal obligor's right of set-off, rescission or cancellation, which will result in discharge of the principal obligation, but the guarantor is allowed to refuse performance to the extent the principal obligor's obligation may be discharged based on those rights (Article 457(3)).

789. Further, if the extinctive prescription period of the principal obligor's obligation is renewed or suspended, that effect extends to the guarantee obligation (Article 457(1)).

790. If the principal obligation is transferred, the transferee has the benefit of guarantee obligation. In other words, the guarantee obligation accompanies the principal obligation.[587]

791. However, the reverse of the above is not true: for example, renewal or suspension of the guarantee obligation's extinctive prescription period does not affect the principal obligation.[588]

II. Subsidiarity of the Guarantee Obligation

792. The guarantee obligation is subsidiary to the principal obligation. When the obligee requires the guarantor to perform its obligation, there are two defences available to the guarantor to the effect that requires the obligee to attempt to collect first from the principal obligor, except in the case of jointly and severally liable guarantee (*rentai hosho*) (Article 454). Joint and several liability guarantee is explained in Part II, Chapter 8 §5 below.

587. Nakata, *supra* n. 213, 481.
588. *Ibid.* 498.

793. The first is the 'defence of demand' (*saikokuno koben*), which requires the obligee to demand the principal obligor to perform (Article 452). If the obligee fails to make that demand and is subsequently unable to obtain full performance from the principal obligor, the guarantor is released from its obligation to the extent that the obligee would have received performance from the principal obligee had the demand been immediately made (Article 455). However, this defence is not available if bankruptcy proceedings of the principal obligor has commenced, or if the whereabouts of the principal obligor is unknown.

794. Second, the guarantor has the 'defence of reference (*kensakuno koben*), which requires the obligee to first execute on the assets of the principal obligor (Article 453). In order to avail itself to this defence, the guarantor must prove that the principal obligor has the financial resource to pay its obligation and that the execution would be easy. Similar to the defence of demand, if the obligee fails to execute on the principal obligor's assets notwithstanding the guarantor's proof of financial resource and easiness of the execution, and is subsequently unable to obtain full performance from the principal obligor, the guarantor is released from its obligation to the extent that the obligee would have received performance from the principal obligee had the execution been immediately carried out (Article 455).

III. Obligee's Duty of Disclosure

795. The 2017 Reform added new rules for the protection of guarantors. First, if the guarantee is based on a mandate from the principal obligor, the guarantor has a right to require the obligee to disclose information at any time regarding the existence of non-performance, the remaining amount and the amount already due, with respect to the principal obligation and all the incidentals (Article 458-2). Failure by the obligee to comply with this duty of disclosure will result in the usual remedies available for non-performance including damages and cancellation.[589]

796. Second, if the guarantor is a natural person, the obligee must notify the guarantor of any forfeiture of the benefit of time by the principal obligor. This notification must be given within two months from the time when the obligee became aware of the forfeiture (Article 458-3(1) and (3)). The obligee cannot require the guarantor to pay the interest for delay which has already arisen before the notice is given, except for the interest which would have arisen irrespective of the forfeiture of the benefit of time (Article 458-3(2)).

§4. Guarantor's Right of Reimbursement, Etc.

797. In general, the guarantor has a right of reimbursement (*kyushoken*) against the principal obligor if the principal obligor has benefited by performance or otherwise by the guarantor. However, the extent of the right of reimbursement depends

589. Shiomi, *supra* n. 583, 125.

on whether the guarantee was upon a mandate from the principal obligor or not. The Civil Code contains detailed rules on the right of reimbursement. The following paragraphs can only provide the outline.

I. Right of Reimbursement of Guarantors with Mandate

798. Guarantors with mandate from the principal obligor are given full right of reimbursement. If the guarantor has extinguished the principal obligation by performance on behalf of the principal obligor, or in exchange for its own asset, the guarantor has a right to obtain reimbursement from the principal obligor for the expenditures made, or if the amount of expenditure is larger than the amount of the principal obligation, for the amount the principal obligation was extinguished (Article 459). If the guarantor extinguishes the principal obligation before it is due, the guarantor has a right of reimbursement to the extent the principal obligor benefited at that time (Article 459-2).

799. Under certain conditions, a guarantor with mandate may also claim reimbursement in advance (*jizen kyushoken*), i.e. reimbursement prior to extinguishing the principal obligation (Article 460). Advance reimbursement is available if:

(i) the bankruptcy proceeding of the principal obligor has commenced and the obligee does not participate in the distribution of the bankruptcy estate;
(ii) the obligation is due; provided that, no extension of time granted by the obligee to the principal obligor after the conclusion of the contract of guarantee may be raised as a defence *vis-à-vis* the guarantor; or
(iii) if, without negligence, the guarantor was ordered by court to perform the obligation.

800. Advance reimbursement provides security to the guarantor. However, the provisions on the guarantor's right to advance reimbursement is more restrictive than a mandatary's right to advance payment of the cost of mandated business which would be otherwise be available under Article 649. *See* paragraph 587. Note that the Supreme Court holds that a third-party grantor of security right, even with mandate, is not allowed a right to advance reimbursement against the principal obligor.[590] In reaching that conclusion, the Supreme Court pointed out that unlike mandate of guarantee where the mandate requires the guarantor to owe a guarantee obligation, mandate to provide property as security does not in itself give rise to an obligation of the grantor *vis-à-vis* the obligee. Thus, there is no cost of performance of a guarantee obligation that the third-party grantor can claim against the principal obligor.

801. On the other, the principal obligor will be harmed if the guarantor receives advance reimbursement, but does not extinguish the principal obligation. Thus, until

590. Supreme Court, 18 Dec. 1990, Minshu 44-9-1686.

and unless the obligee has received the full satisfaction of the entire obligation, the principal obligor may, when making advance reimbursement, demand the guarantor to provide security or to obtain the discharge of the principal obligor (Article 461(1)). The principal obligor may also choose to discharge its obligation for advance reimbursement by making a deposit with an official depositary, by providing security or by procuring the discharge of the liabilities of the guarantor (Article 461(1)).

II. Right of Reimbursement of Guarantors Without Mandate

802. In the case of guarantors without mandate, the guarantor has a right to demand the principal obligor to reimburse it for its performance only to the extent that such performance enriched the principal obligor at the time of such performance (Articles 462(1) and 495-2(1)). Thus, reimbursement of expenditures cannot be claimed.

803. However, if the guarantee was against the will of the principal obligor, the amount of reimbursement is further limited to the extent that the principal obligor is actually enriched at the time reimbursement is claimed (Article 462(2) first sentence). In such case, if the principal obligor asserts that it had, prior to the day of the demand for reimbursement, grounds for set-off against the obligee, the guarantor may demand that the obligee perform the obligation which would have been extinguished by operation of such set-off (Article 462(2) second sentence).

III. Guarantor's Duty of Notice

804. In order to avoid double performance by the principal obligor and the guarantor, or to avoid depriving the principal obligor the opportunity to raise any claims it has against the obligee, a guarantor with mandate is imposed of a duty to notify the principal obligor before or after its acts of extinguishing the principal obligation.

805. Guarantor's duty of advance notice. If the guarantor fails to provide advance notice to the principal obligor, the principal obligor may assert *vis-à-vis* the guarantor all defences it had against the obligee (Article 463(1)). Guarantors without mandate do not enjoy the benefit of making advance notice. The scope of reimbursement for such guarantors is already limited to the extent the principal actually benefits from the guarantor's act. *See* II. of this chapter above.

806. Guarantor's duty of ex post notice. If the guarantor fails to provide notice after extinguishing the principal obligation, and if the principal obligor performs its obligation without knowing that the principal obligation was so extinguished, the principal obligor may deem that its own act of performance has extinguished its obligation (Article 463(2)). It follows from this that the guarantor loses its grounds for the right of reimbursement if it fails to give such ex post notice. Instead, such guarantor may claim unjust enrichment against the obligee who received double performance (Article 703). Guarantors without mandate do not enjoy the benefit of ex post notice, if the guarantee was against the will of the principal obligor. They are not allowed to claim reimbursement against the principal obligors who performed in good faith. However, if the principal obligor performed knowing of the absence of the obligation, such performance by the principal obligor amounts to *solutio indebiti* (*hisai bensai*) and restitution may not be claimed against the obligee (Article 705).

IV. Multiple Principal Obligors

807. If there is more than one principal obligor, the obligation to reimburse the guarantor is divided among the principal obligors, if the principal obligation itself is divisible. Unless otherwise agreed, each obligor owes equally proportionate obligations (Article 427). However, if the guarantor guaranteed only part of the multiple principal obligor's obligations, the guarantor has no right of reimbursement against other principal obligors.[591]

808. If the principal obligation is indivisible (e.g., delivery of an automobile) or is a joint and several obligation, the obligation to reimburse is also indivisible or is a joint and several obligation. If the guarantor guaranteed only part of the multiple principal obligor's obligation, the guarantor has the right of reimbursement against other obligors only to the extent of the portion such obligor is to bear (Article 464).

§5. Jointly and Severally Liable Guarantee

809. Jointly and severally liable guarantees (*rentai hosho*) are guarantees under which the guarantor is jointly and severally liable with the principal obligor against the obligee. This is the case when the obligee and guarantor so agree. In addition, if the principal obligation arises from a commercial transaction, or if the guarantee contract is a commercial transaction, the guarantee is a jointly and severally liable guarantee (Article 511(2) Commercial Code).

810. Guarantor's obligation vis-à-vis the obligee. In practice, most of the guarantees are jointly and severally liable guarantees, as they are more favourable to the obligee. First of all, the 'defence of demand' and 'defence of reference' is not available to a jointly and severally liable guarantor (Article 454). *See* §3.II. of this chapter above. In other words, the guarantee obligation of such guarantor is not supplementary to the principal obligation. This allows the obligee to demand the jointly and severally liable guarantor to perform without first demanding the principal obligor to perform, or without first executing on the assets of the principal obligor. Second, if there are more than one jointly and severally liable guarantor,

591. Shiomi, *supra* n. 583, 708.

they do not have the benefit of division which is available to regular guarantors (Article 456). This means that each guarantor is obligated to perform the entire obligation, not only a divided portion.[592]

811. The effect of occurrence of an event affecting one guarantor on the principal obligor. Another difference is that while occurrence of events that affect the guarantee obligation, other than discharge by performance does not affect the principal obligation in regular guarantees, with respect to jointly and severally liable guarantees, discharge of the guarantee obligation by novation, set-off and merger also discharges the principal obligation (Article 458). Prior to the 2017 Reform, request for performance to a jointly and severally liable guarantor also affected the principal obligation (former Article 434 which was deleted in the 2017 Reform). This rule enabled the obligee to renew (*koshin*) (or 'interrupt' (*chudan*) in the terminology of the Civil Code prior to the 2017 Reform) the extinctive prescription period of the principal obligation by demanding performance to a jointly and severally liable guarantor (cf. former Article 153 which corresponds to Article 150 of the Civil Code as revised in 2017). This was considered to be favourable to the obligee,[593] but that is no longer the case under the 2017 Reform. Other events that occurred to the jointly and severally liable obligor that affected the principal obligation, prior to the 2017 Reform, were the release of one of such obligors (former Article 437, which is now deleted) and expiration of the prescription period with respect to one of such obligors (former Article 439, which is deleted). However, there was general consensus that these rules do not apply to jointly and severally liable guarantees, because they presuppose that each guarantors are liable for a portion of the obligation, while that is not the case with respect to jointly and severally liable guarantors.[594]]

812. Right of reimbursement. If such guarantor extinguishes the principal obligation, it has the right of reimbursement according to the regular rules of reimbursement. *See* §4.II. of this chapter above.

§6. Joint Guarantee *(Kyodo Hosho)*

813. Joint guarantees are guarantees under which there is more than one guarantor who guarantees the same principal obligation. Joint guarantees can be entered into by separate guarantee contracts.

814. Guarantor's obligation vis-à-vis the obligee. In principle, the 'defence of demand' and 'defence of reference' are available to joint guarantors. *See* §3.II. of this chapter above.

592. Nakata, *supra* n. 213, 506.
593. Nakata, *supra* n. 213, 451, 506.
594. S. Wagatsuma, *Shintei Saiken Soron [Revised Obligations in General],* 502 (Iwanami Shoten 1964).

815. Likewise, joint guarantors enjoy the benefit of division *vis-à-vis* the obligee: each of them owe equally proportionate guarantee obligations (Article 456). However, this does not apply (i) if the principal obligation is indivisible (e.g., delivery of an automobile); (ii) if the joint obligors agree among themselves that each will perform the entirety of the principal obligation *vis-à-vis* the obligee; or (iii) if the guarantee is a jointly and severally liable guarantee (in which case the defence of demand and defence of reference are not available either).

816. The effect of occurrence of an event affecting one guarantor on other guarantors. The occurrence of an event to one joint guarantor does not affect other joint guarantors, except when the joint guarantors agree among themselves that each will perform the entirety of the principal obligation *vis-à-vis* the obligee, or if they are jointly and severally liable according to Article 511(2) of the Commercial Code (*see* paragraph 809). Even when the joint guarantors are jointly and severally liable guarantors, they are jointly and severally liable with the principal obligor, but not with the other guarantors. Therefore, occurrence of an event to one joint guarantor does not affect other joint guarantors, unless their relation falls under the exception explained above.[595]

817. Right of reimbursement. Joint guarantors who have extinguished the principal obligation have a right of reimbursement against the principal obligor in accordance to the regular rule on right of reimbursement explained in §4.II. of this chapter above. In addition, each joint guarantor also has a right of reimbursement against other joint obligors only if it performed obligations in excess of the portion it should bear (Article 465). The rights of reimbursement against the principal obligor and against other joint obligors are separate and independent rights.

§7. Revolving Guarantee

818. Revolving guarantee (*ne-hosho*) is a continuous guarantee that secures more than one unidentified obligation, present and future. The Japanese term '*ne-hosho*' literally means 'root guarantee'. This can be much riskier than usual guarantees that secure an identified obligation of a fixed amount, and which can be discharged by one-time performance of the principal obligation or guarantee obligation. At the other end of the spectrum is the 'comprehensive revolving guarantee' that do not limit the scope and amount of the secured obligation, and continues for an indefinite period of time. Courts and the legislature have been attentive to the danger of revolving guarantees, and have developed a set of rules that regulate them.

819. One type of revolving guarantee is the fidelity guarantee regulated by the Fidelity Guarantee Act already explained in paragraph 772 above. Revolving guarantees guaranteeing lessee's obligation to pay rent or damages are also seen in practice. However, the most important is the revolving guarantee that secures monetary

595. Supreme Court, 15 Nov. 1968, Minshu 22-12-2649.

obligations that arise from continuous business transactions. It often involves credit to small- and medium-sized enterprises (e.g., securing future receivables incurred in continuous sale, or securing bank's lending in a continuous banking transaction).

I. Case Law Development

820. Courts have developed rules for protection of guarantors in revolving guarantees that apply to revolving guarantees in general. First, if the revolving guarantee does not place a limit to the scope and amount secured, courts will limit them to 'a reasonable extent' in light of the general sense of trade (*torihikitsunen*).[596]

821. Second, if no time period is agreed for a revolving guarantee, courts allow the guarantor, after a reasonable period of time has passed since the contract, to cancel (*kaiyaku*) the revolving guarantee with an advance notice of a reasonable period.[597] Furthermore, if there are reasonable grounds (*sotona riyu*) to cancel the contract, such as breach of trust between the principal obligor and the guarantor, the guarantor may cancel the revolving guarantee immediately.[598]

822. Third, the courts held that the guarantee obligation under a revolving guarantee contract is not subject to inheritance, except for the principal obligation that has already arisen at the time of inheritance.[599]

II. Legislative Response

823. The legislature has also spoken. In addition to the writing requirement applicable to any guarantee contracts (Article 446(2)) which was introduced into the Civil Code in 2004, as explained in §2. I. of this chapter above, the following development which applies to certain revolving guarantees took place.

A. Regulation of Revolving Guarantee by an Individual

824. A revolving guarantee contract involving a guarantor who is a natural person that secures one or more unidentified obligations within a certain specified scope is not effective unless the contract includes a stipulation of the 'maximum amount' to be secured (Article 465-2(2)). The applicability of this rule, when it was first introduced in 2004, was limited to guarantee of loan obligations. That limitation was lifted in the 2017 Reform.

596. Great Court of Cassation, 2 Dec. 1913, Minshu 5-769.
597. Great Court of Cassation, 17 Dec. 1932, Minshu 11-2334.
598. Great Court of Cassation, 27 Feb. 1934, Minshu 13-215; Supreme Court, 18 Dec. 1964, Minshu 18-10-2179.
599. Supreme Court, 9 Nov. 1962, Minshu 16-11-2270.

825. Second, in order to protect the guarantor from an extended time limit which may increase the amount to be secured, rules on manners of determination (or fixation) of the principal were introduced in 2004. They are the rules on 'date of determination' and 'grounds for determination'.

826. The rule on 'date of determination' fixes the principal of the principal obligation at a specified date ('determination date of the principal' (*ganpon kakutei kijitsu*)) (Article 465-3). It provides that, (i) if the agreed date of determination is not within five years from the date of concluding the revolving guarantee, that agreement is ineffective; (ii) if the agreed date of determination is on or after five years from the date of conclusion of the revolving guarantee, or in the absence of agreement on the principal determination date, the date falls on the day on which three years have elapsed from the conclusion of the revolving guarantee. This rule applies only to revolving guarantee by individuals securing loan obligations, even after the 2017 Reform.

827. Thc rulc on 'grounds for determination' provides grounds, the occurrence of which determines the principal. Three of the grounds apply to every revolving guarantee by an individual (Article 465-3(1)). The grounds for determination of the principal is (i) the filing by the obligee for compulsory execution of a monetary obligation or enforcement of a security right securing a monetary obligation on the guarantor's asset; (ii) commencement of bankruptcy proceedings of the guarantor; and (iii) the death of the principal obligor or the guarantor. With respect to (i), the occurrence of such event signals that the obligee considers that the financial condition of the guarantor is deteriorating. In such situation, it was considered inequitable for the obligee to require the guarantor to guarantee any further extension of credit to the principal obligor, and therefore, it is considered that the principal to be secured should be fixed.[600] With respect to (iii), this ground stems from the consideration that revolving guarantees by individuals are based on a mutual trust relationship between a specific principal obligor and a specific guarantor. It was considered that the guarantor should not be required to guarantee obligations incurred by the successors of the principal obligor, and also that the grantor's successor should not be required to be subject to revolving guarantee securing obligations incurred by a principal obligor with whom no mutual trust relationship exists.[601]

828. There are two other grounds for determination of the principal which apply only to revolving guarantee by an individual of loan obligations (Article 465-3(2)). They are (i) the filing by the obligee for compulsory execution of a monetary obligation or enforcement of a security right securing a monetary obligation on the principal obligor's asset and (ii) commencement of bankruptcy proceedings of the principal obligor. With respect to (i), the occurrence of such event signals that the obligee considers that the financial condition of the principal obligor is deteriorating. In such situation, it was considered to be inequitable for the obligee to require

600. *Kaisei Minpono Kaisetsu [Explanation of the Revised Civil Code]*, 47 (T. Yoshida and T. Tsutsui eds., Shojihomu 2004).
601. *Ibid.* 52–53.

the guarantor to guarantee any further extension of credit to the principal obligor, and therefore, the principal should be fixed.[602] This is also a situation that is likely to fall under the case law that allows the guarantor to immediately cancel a revolving guarantee with no time period.[603]

829. The purpose of limiting the applicability of the last two grounds to revolving guarantee of loan obligations is because it was considered that these grounds are inappropriate for other revolving guarantees. For example, in a revolving guarantee of the lessee's obligation, the principal need not be fixed by filing of execution on the assets of the lessee or by the commencement of bankruptcy proceedings of the lessee. This is because the lease is not automatically terminated when these grounds occur.[604]

B. Regulation of Revolving Guarantee by a Corporation

830. If the guarantor in a revolving guarantee is a corporation, the legislative protection under Article 465-2 through 465-4 explained in §7. II. A. of this chapter above, do not apply. Therefore, there may be revolving guarantee contracts with no agreement on the maximum amount to be guaranteed. Under that circumstance, if an individual (natural person) has guaranteed the guarantor's right of reimbursement against the principal obligor, there is no legislative limit to the amount the individual guarantor must guarantee. Therefore, in order to protect such individual guarantor, it is provided that such guarantee is ineffective if the revolving guarantee by a corporation (i) lacks an agreement on the maximum amount or (ii) if there is no agreed 'determination date of the principal' or if the agreed date is not within five years from the date of conclusion of the revolving guarantee (Article 465-5).

602. *Ibid.* 47.
603. *Ibid.* 45.
604. Shiomi, *supra* n. 583, 136–137; Tsutsui and Muramatsu, *supra* n. 529, 138.

Chapter 9. Pledge

§1. General Introduction

831. Pledge (*shichi* or *shichiken*) is a possessory security right that is created by a contract between the pledgor (grantor) and the pledgee (secured creditor) in order to secure a claim. The pledgee may retain possession of the pledged asset (*shichibutsu*) until the secured claim credit is satisfied. It may also have the secured claim paid prior to other (lower-ranking) creditors out of the pledged asset (Article 342 and 347). The retention of the pledged asset has the function of taking hostage of the pledge. The Japanese term for pledge (*shichi*) is the same term used for hostage ('*hitojichi*', meaning '*shichi*' of a person).

832. Any asset, including movables, immovables or intangible rights that are transferable may be pledged (Article 343), unless specifically prohibited by law (e.g., registered automobiles[605]). In reality, pledge of immovables are rarely used. Pledge of movables has been used by pawnbrokers (*shichiya*) as means of providing credit to consumers. Pawnbroker is a moneylending business that extend credits in exchange of a pledge, regulated by the Pawnbroker Business Act (PBA).[606] However, its significance has been diminishing as means of providing unsecured credits to consumers flourished.[607] In addition, the development of non-possessory security right in movables such as 'retention-of-title' sales and 'security by way of transfer' or 'title-transfer security interest' (*joto tanpo*)[608] has lessened the use of pledge for business credits. *Joto tanpo* is a security right where the borrower sells the item to the lender, leases the same back and enters into a purchase agreement effective at the end of the loan term to repurchase the item. Payments on the lease then function as loan payments. On the other, pledge of rights (*kenrijichi*), such as monetary claims (receivables), negotiable instruments or intellectual property rights, is being heavily used for business purposes.[609] For pledge of rights, this monograph will limit its scope to pledge of receivables because there are too many variances for pledge of other rights.

605. Article 20, Automobile Hypothec Act (Act No. 187 of 1951).
606. Law No. 158 of 1950.
607. *See* generally, Pardieck, *supra* n. 26.
608. K. Sono and W. L. Shattuck, 'Personal Property as Collateral in Japan and the United States', 39 *Wash. L. Rev.* 570 (1964); M. E. Hiscock and K. Sono, 'Security Interests and Insolvency in Japan', 44 *Rabel J. Comp. & Int'l Private L.* 757 (1980); Haley, *supra* n. 55, 502; F. G. Bennett, Jr., 'Getting Property Right: "Informal" Mortgages in Japanese Courts', 18 *Pac. Rim L. & Pol'y J.* 463 (2009).
609. For the use of various pledges, *see* H. Dogauchi, *Tanpobukkenho [Law of Security Rights]*, 80 (3rd ed., Yuhikaku 2017).

§2. Creation and Termination

833. A contract to create a pledge takes effect when the pledgor transfers 'actual' possession of the pledged asset to the pledgee (Articles 344 and 345), except in the case of pledge of receivables. The pledgor can be a third party.

834. Unless otherwise agreed, a pledge secures the principal, interest, penalties, expenses of executing the pledge, expense of preserving the pledged asset and the compensation of loss arising from non-performance or latent defects in the pledged asset (Article 346).

835. When the secured credit is satisfied, the pledge is terminated. Upon termination, the pledgee must return the pledged asset it possesses to the pledgor.[610]

§3. Third-Party Effectiveness and Priority

836. The third-party effectiveness of a pledge, in the case of pledge of movables is 'continuous possession' of the pledged asset (Article 352). Priority is determined in the order the possession is made. For immovables it is the registration of the pledge (Article 177). Priority is determined in the order of registration.

837. For receivables, the same rules of third-party effectiveness (perfection) and priority with respect to assignment of receivables apply (Article 364). *See* above Part I, Chapter 4, §2.

§4. Rights and Obligations of the Pledgors, Pledgees and Third-Party Obligors

838. The pledgee may retain the pledged asset until the secured claim is satisfied (Article 347). During the period of retention, the pledgee must preserve the pledged asset with 'the care of a good manager' (*zenryona kanrishano chui*) (Articles 350 and 298(1)). The pledgee has a right of reimbursement of expenses of preservation (Articles 350 and 299). If the pledgee breaches the duty of care, the pledgor may demand that the pledge be extinguished (Articles 350 and 298(3)).

839. In the case of pledge of movables, the pledgee may not use, lease or give as a security the pledged asset without the consent of the obligor. This does not apply, however, for uses necessary for the preservation of the pledged asset (Articles 350 and 298(2)).

840. In the case of pledge of immovables, the pledgee may use and receive the profits from pledged asset (Article 356). Instead, unless otherwise agreed, the

610. *Ibid.* 101.

pledgee cannot demand interest on the secured claim (Articles 358 and 359) and must pay the expenses of management and bear other burdens (e.g., tax) (Articles 357 and 359).

841. With respect to pledge of receivables, the pledgor is obligated to preserve the receivable. For example, the pledgor is not allowed to set off the receivable against its obligations.[611] Further, the pledgor cannot collect from the third-party obligor, unless otherwise agreed between the pledgor and the pledgee.[612] Even if the third-party obligor makes payment to the pledgor or third-party assignee of the receivable, that does not discharge its obligation (analogous application of Article 481). However, the third-party obligor may discharge its obligation by depositing the amount in an official depositary (Article 494), in which case, the pledge will continue on the claim for refund against the official depositary.[613]

§5. Enforcement

I. Out-of-Court Enforcement

842. In case of default, the pledgee may exert pressure on the obligor to perform by retaining (i.e., refusing to return) the pledged asset. On the other, it is prohibited to enter into an agreement, prior to the due date of the secured claim, that will allow the pledgee to acquire the ownership of the pledged asset or to dispose of the pledged asset upon default. Such agreements are void (Article 349 (prohibition of disposition of pledged assets (*ryujichi keiyaku*)). However, this prohibition does not apply to pledge to secure commercial claims (Article 515, Commercial Code) or to licensed pawnbrokers (Article 19, PBA).

843. For pledge of receivables, the pledgee is allowed to collect directly from the third-party obligor provided that third-party effectiveness is achieved as against that obligor (Article 366(1)).

II. Judicial Enforcement

844. The pledgee may also enforce the pledge by judicial auction or, in the case of immovables, execution against profits from secured immovable properties according to the Civil Execution Act.[614] However, judicial auction may not be cost-justified especially regarding movables. Therefore, there is a rule that allows pledgees to demand from the court immediate appropriation of the pledged movable to the satisfaction of claims in accordance with the evaluation of an appraiser if there are reasonable grounds to allow it (Article 354).

611. Supreme Court, 21 Dec. 2006, Minshu 60-10-3964.
612. Dogauchi, *supra* n. 609, 112.
613. *Ibid.* 113.
614. Articles 180–194 Civil Execution Act (Act No. 4 of 1979).

Chapter 10. Loans

845. The current Japanese Civil Code divides loans into three distinct categories: (1) loans for consumption; (2) loans for use; and (3) leases. Loans for consumption and loans for use are addressed here; leases are covered in Chapter 6.

846. As with other transactions, loans are governed not only by the contract law provisions found in the Civil Code but also by special laws, including the Interest Rate Restriction Act and Money Lending Industry Regulation Act. This chapter will refer to commonly invoked provisions of these special laws but focus on the basic Civil Code provisions.

§1. Loans for Consumption

847. Consumption loans are addressed in Civil Code Articles 587–592. As the name suggests, these code provisions are intended to regulate contracts where the item loaned is fungible and to be consumed, and a similar quantity and quality of an item plus interest are to be returned when the loan terminates. The most common example is a loan of money, but this section of the Code has been applied equally to rice and other fungible items.

848. Under the Civil Code, a consumption loan becomes binding at the point at which the borrower receives the item to be loaned from the lender (Article 587). Prior to the point of transfer, a lender is not obligated to lend the item.[615] Courts have relaxed this requirement by recognising binding promises 'to make a consumption loan', including those to extend financing.[616] However, the 2017 Reform added some restrictions to these 'consensual consumption loans'.

849. First, under the 2017 Reform, a writing requirement was imposed for such consensual consumption loans giving rise to the lendor's obligation to lend (Article 587-2(1)). It is explained that the purpose of the writing requirement is to prevent careless conclusion of consumption loans.[617] The writing can be an electromagnetic record (Article 587-2(4)). Second, the Reform provided that the borrower of a consumption loan in writing is entitled to cancel the contract before the lending is consummated (Article 587-2(2)). This in effect means that such consensual consumption loan gives rise to the lender's binding obligation to lend, but the borrower's obligation to borrow is not binding. Additionally, as we *see* in the next paragraph, even after consummation of the lending, the borrower may return the loan at any time (Article 591(2)).

615. Civil law scholars distinguish between 'real contracts' (*yobutsu keiyaku*), taking effect on physical receipt of an item and 'consensual contracts' (*dakusei keiyaku*), which take effect at the point of agreement between two contracting parties. *See* Introduction to the Law of Contracts §3.
616. For example, Supreme Court, 7 Oct. 1965, Minshu 19-7-1723; Supreme Court, 16 Mar. 1973, Kinho 683-25.
617. Tsutsui and Muramatsu, *supra* n. 529. 292.

850. According to the Civil Code, once a loan is consummated, the borrower may return the item at any time (Article 591(2)), and if the term is not defined the lender may demand return or repayment by specifying a reasonable period (Article 591(1)).

851. The item to be lended must conform to the contract. However if there was no agreement for interest, the item need only be of the condition it was at the time it was identified as the item to be lended (Article 590(1)). If the item does not conform to the contract in terms of description and quality, the borrower does not have to return a conforming item. It needs only to return the value of the non-conforming item (Article 590(2)). For example, if the borrower receives second-class rice when the contract was for a consumption loan of first-class rice, the borrower, instead of returning first-class rice, may return the value of second-class rice. If a borrower is unable to return an item of the same kind, quality and quantity, the borrower may return the current value of the item (Article 592).

852. In principle, the lender has no 'duty to explain' the viability of borrower's plan to repay. However, such duty may arise if it was the lendor that was proposing a land development project including its financing.[618]

853. The Civil Code provides, in principle, that the borrower need only return the fungible equivalent of the loaned item at the conclusion of the term of the loan. Absent agreement of the parties, the default rule in non-commercial transaction is that no interest is payable (Article 589). In contrast, the Commercial Code contains a default rule providing for interest payable on a loan made between business entities (Article 513, Commercial Code). In either case, if the interest rate is left undefined, statutory interest rates provided in Article 404 will apply. For an explanation of the statutory interest rate, *see* paragraph 496. Interest, if payable, begins accruing on receipt of the loaned, fungible item (Article 589(2)).[619] This differs from the rule applicable to interest payable as a result of a failure to make timely payment for services or goods in which case, interest begins to accrue on the day following the originally scheduled payment date. *See* paragraph 496.

854. While the parties may agree on interest payable on the loan, Japan heavily regulates commercial lending,[620] and special laws limit the amount of interest that may be charged on consumption loans for money. There are three principal statutes involved. The first, the Interest Rate Restriction Act (IRRA) (Act No. 100 of 1954), applies to any loan (commercial or otherwise) for consumption involving cash. Among other things, this statute caps interest rates at twenty percent per annum for loans up to JPY 100,000; eighteen percent for loans from JPY 100,000 to JPY 1 million; and fifteen percent for loans in excess of JPY 1 million (Article 1, IRRA).[621] The statute provides that an interest rate exceeding these caps are void, thereby

618. Supreme Court, 12 Jun. 2006, Hanji 1941-94.
619. This is codification of Supreme Court, 6 Jun. 1958, Minshu 12-9-1373.
620. *See* generally, Pardieck, *supra* n. 26.
621. The Act imposes additional restrictions on commercial lenders. Arts 5–9 IRRA.

allowing a party to claim a refund of amounts paid in excess of these caps. However, prior to 2006, there was a controversial paragraph 2 to Article 1 of the Act that provided that if the borrower 'voluntarily' paid the amount in exceeding the cap, restitution cannot be claimed (former Article 1(2)). Although the intent of that paragraph had already been trumped by a series of Supreme Court decisions in the 1960s,[622] that paragraph was deleted in 2006 to align with the changes in statutory interpretation of the Money Lending Industry Act by the Supreme Court beginning in 2003. *See* paragraph 856 below.

855. The second, the Acceptance of Investment, Money Deposits and Interest Rates Regulation Act ('Investment Act' or *Shusshiho* in short) (Act No. 195 of June 23, 1954) is a regulatory statute that imposes restrictions on various financial transactions solely as a matter of public law. The legislation, among other things, imposes criminal penalties on any commercial lender lending at rates in excess of twenty percent per annum and for non-commercial lending in excess of 109.5% (Article 5, Investment Act).

856. The third statute is the Money Lending Industry Regulation Act (MLIRA) (Act No. 32 of 1983), which establishes a comprehensive regulatory structure for the commercial lending industry. The Act imposes registration requirements on lending institutions, documentation requirements for loans and limits on collection practices (Articles 3, 16-2, 17, 18 and 21, MLIRA). Prior to 2006, the Act contained a provision that 'deemed effective' voluntary payment of interest exceeding the limitation set by the Interest Rate Restriction Act provided that the lender has complied with certain procedural requirements (former Article 43 MLIRA). This was a push back by the legislature against the Supreme Court decisions that had turned the 'voluntary payment' clause in the Interest Rate Restriction Act into a dead letter.[623] After significant revisions in 2006, however, that provision was deleted in 2006 to expressly incorporate changes in statutory interpretation by the Supreme Court beginning in 2003.[624] The Act now requires compliance officers and imposes a suitability, or 'responsible lending', requirement for lending (Article 12-3 MLIRA). Each lender must evaluate the prospective borrower's ability to repay the loan, refrain from 'unsuitable solicitation', and refer the borrower to credit counselling services in some situations (Articles 13, 13-2, 12-9 MLIRA). The Act also caps interest rates, for public law purposes, at the same levels set out in the Interest Rate Restriction Act (Article 12-8 MLIRA).

622. Supreme Court (Grand Bench), 18 Nov. 1964, Minshu 18-9-1868; Supreme Court (Grand Bench), 13 Nov. 1968, Minshu 22-12-2526; Supreme Court, 25 Nov. 1969, Minshu 23-11-2137. *See* Pardieck, *supra* n. 26, 544.
623. *See* Pardieck, *supra* n. 26, 554.
624. *See* Supreme Court, 18 Jul. 2003, Minshu 57-895. Pardieck, *supra* n. 26, 565.

§2. Loans for Use

857. Loans for use are addressed in Civil Code Articles 593–600, and they deal solely with gratuitous loans of real property or goods. Whether it is a family member loaning the use of a home or a friend loaning the use of a car, the starting premise is that there is a pre-existing relationship between the lender and the borrower and that the very same item loaned will be returned.[625] Non-gratuitous loans for use, loans of real property or goods for rent are treated separately as leases, and dealt with in this text in Chapter 6.

858. Prior to the 2017 Reform, a gratuitous loan for use became effective when the borrower received the item (former Article 593). This is changed in the 2017 Reform which provides that such loan is consensual (Article 593). However, except for cases where the contract is in writing, the lendor has a right to cancel the loan before the borrower receives the item (Article 593-2) and the borrower has a right to cancel the contract at any time (Article 598). This is in line with the regulation of other gratuitous contracts such as gifts (Article 550) and deposits (Article 657-2). *See* Part II, Chapter 2, §2 for deposits.

859. In accepting the item, the borrower assumes a number of obligations: (a) to use the item only as permitted in the contract or as suggested by the nature of the item, and to prohibit use by a third party absent the consent of the lender (Articles 594(1) & (2)); (b) to bear the 'ordinary' costs of use of the borrowed item (Article 595); (c) to return the item upon termination of the contract (Article 593).

860. The lender is treated as a donor and is not liable for any defect in the item, unless the donor has knowledge of the defect and fails to inform the borrower of the same (Article 596, applying Article 551 mutatis mutandis). The lender must bear 'non-ordinary expenses', such as cost to repair damage caused by a typhoon, and 'beneficial expenses', such as the cost of improving land.[626]

861. The contract is terminated by an occurrence certain events, or by cancellation. First, the contract is automatically terminated (a) at the time specified in the contract or, if no time has been specified but the purpose of use has been specified, at the time the purpose of use is satisfied (Article 597(1) & (2)). (b) The death of the borrower also terminates the contract (Article 597(3)).

862. Second, the lender has the right to cancel the contract (a) if the borrower violates the terms of use (Article 594(3)); (b) if the time of return has not been specified but the purpose of use has been specified, after a sufficient time for use has elapsed (Article 598(1)); (c) if both the time for return and the purpose of use has not been specified, at any time (Article 598(2)). On the other, the borrower can cancel the contract at any time (Article 598(3).

---

625. Shiomi, *supra* n. 105, 137.
626. Nakata, *supra* n. 61, 375.

863. Any damages claimed by the lender or reimbursement for expenses claimed by the borrower must be made within one year of return of the borrowed item (Article 600).

Chapter 11. Government Contracts

§1. General Remarks

864. Contracts in which one of the parties is the national or local government (government contracts) are governed by general contract law. The bulk of government contracts are public procurement contracts where the government procures products or services (such as construction services). However, since government contracts impact on national or local finances, and since a high level of transparency and fairness are required, there are special rules that apply for the purpose of proper administration.[627] This monograph will only present a brief outline of the succinct features of (national) government contracts.

865. It is pointed out that several principles govern government contracts.[628] The first principle is that government contracts must be economically reasonable. This leads to the importance of competition in the conclusion of contracts. The second principle is that government contracts must be fair (to the other party). This leads to the need not to abuse government power, and also the need for transparency in the contractual process. These principles lead to the following rules that can be found in the Public Accounting Act (PAA) (Act No. 35 of 1947)[629] and various cabinet orders and ministerial orders, and other sub-rules.

§2. Contract Formation

866. In principle, the government must give priority to selecting its contracting party through 'general competitive bidding (*ippan kyoso nyusatsu*)' (or open tender). Article 29–3(1), PAA provides that in principle, 'before entering into a sale, lease, contract for work or other contract, a Contract Officer or officer responsible for actions authorizing expenditures […] shall put the contract out to tender by issuing a public notice and having persons make offers in respect thereof'.

867. There are two exceptions to this principle. First, if the number of persons who would participate in the tender is small, or if it would be disadvantageous to put it out to tender (e.g., if the construction work requires special technology)[630], such a contract must be put out to 'selective tender' (*shimei kyoso nyusatsu*) where the government preselects the persons who may participate in the tender (Article 29-3(3), PAA).

627. On government contracts, *see* generally M. Usui, *Kokyokeiyakuho Seigi [Details of Public Contract Law]* (Shinzansha 2005).
628. *Ibid*., 8.
629. For local government contracts, the relevant law is the Local Autonomy Act (Act No. 67 of 1947).
630. Usui, *supra* n. 627, 70.

868. Second, if (i) the nature or purpose of the contract does not permit tender (competition), as when the service requires special skill available to a certain person,[631] (ii) a contract cannot be put out to tender due to urgent circumstances, or (iii) it would be disadvantageous to put a contract out to tender (e.g., when the amount of the contract is small)[632], the contract must take the form of a 'discretionary contract (*zui-i keiyaku*)' under which the government selects its contracting party (Article 29-3(4), PAA).

869. It must be noted that, under the World Trade Organization's 1994 and 2012 Agreement on Government Procurement (GPA) to which Japan is a party, the principle of national treatment and non-discrimination applies to foreign nationals (Article 3, GPA). This is implemented by cabinet orders.[633]

870. Except for some exceptions, government contracts must be put into writing (Article 29-8(1), PAA). When a written contract is to be prepared, the contract does not become final and binding until the names and seals of both the government officer and the counterparty have been affixed to the written contract (Article 29-8(8), PAA).

§3. Content and Performance of the Contract

871. Since there is considerable disparity between the government and its private contracting partners, rules have been developed to constrain abuse of government power. For example, the Act on Prevention of Delay in Payment under Government Contracts[634] requires that contents of the contract, including the time of payment, must be specified in writing (Article 4). For public construction contracts, the 'Standard Terms for Public Construction Contracts' (*kokyokoji hyojun ukeoi yakkan*), provides terms to achieve fairness regarding, *inter alia*, modification of construction contracts.

631. *Ibid.*, 201.
632. The amount is designated in Article 99 of the 'Cabinet Order on Budgets, the Settlement of Accounts, and Accounting' (Imperial Order No. 165 of 1947). E.g., when the target price for construction or manufacturing does not exceed JPY 2.5 million; or when purchasing assets at a target price that does not exceed JPY 1.6 million. *See*, Usui, *supra* n. 627, 209.
633. 'Cabinet Order designating special measures regarding procurement procedures of products and specified services by the National Government' (Cabinet Order No. 300 of 1980) and 'Cabinet Order designating special measures regarding procurement procedures of products and specified services by Local Governments' (Cabinet Order No. 372 of 1995).
634. Act No. 256 of 1949.

Chapter 12. Partnership Contract

§1. General Overview

872. Partnership contracts (*kumiai keiyaku*) are contracts under which two or more parties agree to engage in 'joint business' by each party making 'contributions' (*shusshi*) (Article 667(1)). A partnership is created by a partnership contract. Joint ventures for construction or partnerships for law firms are examples of partnerships. The relationship among incorporators of a corporation is also a partnership. The 'joint business' need not be for profit. For example, the 'unit owners association' (*kanri kumiai*)[635] of apartment buildings is a partnership that is not for profit.

873. Unless steps for incorporation are taken according to the provisions of the Civil Code or other law (Article 33),[636] partnerships are not incorporated. This chapter concerns partnerships that are not incorporated.

874. Partnership contracts are consensual and for value. However, whereas the purpose of other contracts is usually for economic exchange, the purpose of partnership is to engage in a joint business, which is not an exchange among the partners. Thus, there are views that consider that partnership contracts are not contracts (bilateral acts of the parties) but 'joint acts' (*godo koi*). The usefulness of such a concept is debated,[637] but the peculiar nature of partnership contracts should not be overlooked. In fact, the 2017 Reform added a provision that provides that the provisions of defence of simultaneous performance (Article 533) and the right to refuse performance in case of impossibility of the other party's obligation (Article 536) do not apply to partnership contracts (Article 667-2(1)). It also provided that partnership contract cannot be cancelled due to non-performance by partners (Article 667-2(2)). Partnership contracts may be terminated only by dissolution, explained in Part II, Chapter 12, §6 below.

§2. Contribution

875. It is necessary that every partner makes contributions. Contributions can be monetary or supply of services (Article 667(2)). When monetary contribution is to

635. Article 3 Act on Building Unit Ownership (Act No. 69 of 1962).
636. Such laws include the following: for profit-making corporations, the Company Act (Act No. 86 of 2005); for non-profit corporations, the Act on General Incorporated Associations and General Incorporated Foundations (Act No. 48 of 2006), supplemented by the Act on Authorization of Public Interest Incorporated Associations and Public Interest Incorporated Foundations (Act No. 49 of 2006), and the Act on Promotion of Specified Non-profit Activities (Act No. 7 of 1998). There are other laws that provide for establishment of specific corporations, such as the Consumer Cooperatives Act (Act No. 200 of 1948), the Agricultural Co-operatives Act (Act No. 132 of 1947), and the Act on Building Unit Ownership, etc. (Act No. 69 of 1962) already cited in *supra* n. 635.
637. Nakata, *supra* n. 61, 557.

be made, a partner who fails to do so must pay interest on the sum and must compensate for any other damages (Article 669). This is an exception to the rule under Article 419, which provides that only interest can be claimed for non-performance of monetary obligations. *See* Part I, Chapter 6, §5.

876. As noted above in paragraph 874, failure by one partner of its obligation to contribute does not give other partners the defence of simultaneous performance, the right to refuse contribution or the right to cancellation (Article 667-2). Contributions must be made.

§3. Management of the Business

877. Management of the business may be delegated to 'operating officers' (*gyomu shikkosha*), who may or may not be partners, but it is not necessary to do so. If no such delegation is made, business determinations are to be made by the majority of the partners, and the determination is to be executed by each partner individually (Article 670(1)).

878. If delegation of management is made to operating officers, those officers will make business determinations and will execute them. If delegation is made to more than one operating officer, business determinations are to be made by the majority of the officers, and are to be executed by each officer (Article 670(2)). Partners can be operating officers (operating partner).

879. Partners who are not operating officers do not have the power of determination or execution, but they have the right to inspect the condition of the business and property of the partnership (Article 673). Moreover, even when there are operating officers, partners may make business determinations if they are made unanimously, which are to be executed by all partners (Article 670(4)).

880. Notwithstanding the above, 'ordinary business' of a partnership may be performed by each partner, but subject to objection by other partners made before the completion of that business (Article 670(5)).

881. Operating officers who are not partners are mandataries and therefore the provisions on the rights and duties of the mandatary apply (Articles 644–450). *See* generally Part II, Chapter 1, §5. When partners make determination and execute the business, the provisions on the duties of mandatary apply *mutatis mutandis* (Article 671).

882. When an operating officer is also a partner (operating partner), that partner cannot resign unless there are justifiable grounds (*seitona riyu*) (Article 672(1)), because otherwise business operation may be disrupted. Likewise, dismissal of operating partners requires justifiable grounds and a unanimous decision of the other partners (Article 672(2)).

§4. REPRESENTATION OF PARTNERSHIP (*KUMIAI DAIRI*)

883. Contracts that a partnership enters into are, unless the partnership is incorporated, contracts in which all of the partners are parties to. However, since it is cumbersome to have all the individual partners manifest their intention to enter into the contract or require each of them to sign the contract, contracts are usually entered into using a representative.

884. Operating officers have the power to represent the partners. If there are more than one operating officer, an officer has that power only if the majority of the officers assent (Article 670-2(2)).

885. If there is one or more operating officer, partners who are not operating partners do not have the power to represent other partners. If there are no operating officers, each partner may have the power to represent other partners, but only if the majority of the partners assent (Article 670-2(1)).

886. Operating officers or partners acting as a representative need not disclose the name of all the partners. It is sufficient to disclose the name of the partnership it is representing (e.g., 'A, representing partnership B').[638]

887. Notwithstanding the above, each partner or operating officer has the power to represent (other) partners for 'ordinary business' (Article 670-2(3)).

§5. PARTNERSHIP PROPERTY

888. The assets of the partnership (partnership property) are isolated from the assets of individual partners (individual property). Thus, *creditors of individual partners* cannot collect from partnership property (Article 677). On the other, in principle, partners owe unlimited liability and therefore *creditors of the partnership* can collect from individual property of the partners (Article 675(2)). However, the partners' liability is limited to each partner's amount of contribution if it is a 'limited liability partnership' (LLP) formed according to the 'Limited Liability Partnership Act' (LLPA)[639] (Article 15, LLPA). LLPs must be formed in writing (Article 4, LLPA) and registered in order to assert limited liability against third parties who do not know or who have justifiable reasons for not knowing that the liability of the partners are limited (Articles 8 and 57, LLPA).

889. Partnership property is 'jointly' owned by all partners (Article 668). The Japanese term used for 'joint ownership' in this provision is '*kyoyu*', which is the same term used for 'co-ownership' (cf. Articles 249). However, it is generally

638. Supreme Court, 31 Jul. 1961, Minshu 15-7-1982.
639. Act No. 40 of 2005.

understood that '*kyoyu*' as it is used in Article 668 is to be distinguished from 'co-ownership'. This widely supported view suggests using the concept of '*goyu*' to refer to the nature of ownership under Article 668,[640] which is translated here as 'joint ownership'.

890. The proportion of share that each partner has in partnership property is determined in proportion to the value of the contribution.[641] Profits and losses that arise from the joint business must also be distributed. Such distribution is determined, unless otherwise agreed, in proportion to the value of each partner's contribution (Article 674(1)). The partners are free to agree on a different proportion in sharing profits and losses. If the proportions of the distributions are specified solely with respect to either profits or losses, it is presumed that the specified proportions are common to both profits and losses (Article 674(2)).

891. 'Joint ownership' (*goyu*) is usually distinguished from 'co-ownership' (*kyoyu*) in the senses that the joint owners are not free to dispose of their shares and that they cannot seek division of the jointly owned property, both of which are possible for co-ownership.[642] However, it is more important to articulate what that right entails.

892. Partners are restricted from disposing of their shares in the partnership property. Even if such disposal is made, such disposal may not be asserted against the partnership or third parties who have dealings with the partnership (Article 676(1)). Furthermore, they may not seek division of partnership property before it is liquidated (Article 676(3)).

893. A *partnership's claim* against third parties (e.g., the joint venture's claim for remuneration for construction work) belongs jointly to the partners. The principle that divisible claims, such as monetary claims, are automatically divided among multiple creditors (Article 427) does not apply to partnership's claims. Partners are not allowed to exercise their share in the claim individually (Article 676(2)).

894. A *partnership's obligation* against third parties (e.g., loan of working capital for the joint business) also belongs jointly to the partners. Here again, the principle that divisible obligations, such as monetary obligations, are automatically divided among multiple obligors (Article 427) does not apply to partnership's obligation. Creditors may exercise their claim against jointly owned partnership property (Article 675(1)). Creditors may also collect from individual property of the partners. In that case, the creditor has the choice of collecting from each partner (i) in the proportion of their shares of losses, or (ii) in equal proportions, except that

640. *See*, e.g., S. Wagatsuma, *Saiken Kakuron Chukan 2 [Specific Obligations]*, 800 (Iwanami Shoten 1962).
641. Nakata, *supra* n. 61, 573.
642. S. Wagatsuma (supplemented by T. Ari-izumi), *Shintei Bukkenho [Newly Revised Property Law]*, 317 (Iwanami Shoten 1983).

(ii) is not allowed if the creditor knew the proportion of share of losses, at the time the claim arose. However, the partners' liability is limited in LLPs. *See* paragraph 888 above.

§6. Change of Partners

I. Admission of New Partners

895. New partners may be admitted by unanimous assent of the existing partners (Article 677-2(1)). New partners must make their contribution (Article 677). They have the same rights and obligations as the existing partners, except that they are not individually liable for obligations of the partnership that arose before admission (Article 677-2(2)).

II. Voluntary Withdrawal

896. The general rule for voluntary withdrawal is as follows. First, if a partnership contract does not specify the duration of the partnership, or specifies that the partnership is to continue for the life of a certain partner, each partner may withdraw at any time by notifying every other partner (Article 678(1)). However, withdrawal does not take effect if it is at a time that is detrimental to the partnership (Article 678(1) proviso). For example, withdrawal may be detrimental if it disrupts the business of the partnership – in which case, withdrawal will not take effect until a successor is found.[643] Second, if a partnership contract specifies the duration of the partnership, partners may not withdraw (Article 678(2)).

897. Nonetheless, even when withdrawal is not permitted in situations explained in the previous paragraph, withdrawal is allowed if there are 'unavoidable grounds' (*yamu o enai jiyu*) (Articles 678(1) proviso and 678(2) proviso). For example, if a partner opposes a business determination made by the operating officers or other partners, there are unavoidable grounds if there is concern that the partner's individual assets will be adversely affected.[644] This is a mandatory rule. The Supreme Court has held that a contract clause that prohibits withdrawal even when there are unavoidable grounds is against public policy (Article 90) and therefore void.[645]

III. Involuntary Withdrawal

898. A partner is also withdrawn in cases of its: (i) death (i.e., no succession), (ii) commencement of insolvency proceedings, (iii) commencement of guardianship or (iv) expulsion (Article 679). Expulsion of a partner may be carried out only

643. Nakata, *supra* n. 61, 581.
644. *Ibid.*
645. Supreme Court, 23 Feb. 1999, Minshu 53-2-193.

if there are justifiable grounds (*seitona jiyu*) and if it is effected by the unanimous agreement of the other partners (Article 680 main clause). For example, there are justifiable grounds if a partner does not perform its obligation to make contributions, or if there is misconduct in executing the joint business.[646] Expulsion may not be asserted against an expelled partner unless a notice to that effect is given to that partner (Article 680 proviso).

899. The partnership itself continues to exist with the remaining partners, even when a partner withdraws. The withdrawing partner may claim a refund of its share according to the partnership property at the time of the withdrawal (Article 681(1)). Refund may be made in money regardless of the kind of contribution the withdrawing partner made (Article 681(2)).

900. A withdrawing partner no longer has rights and obligations as a partner. However, *vis-à-vis* creditors of the partnership, the withdrawing partner is still obligated to perform to the extent it was obligated before the withdrawal (Article 680-2(1) first sentence). In order to protect the withdrawing partner, until and unless the creditor's claim has been fully satisfied, that partner may demand the partnership to provide security or to obtain itself discharge (e.g., by paying the creditor) (Article 680-2(1) second sentence). If the withdrawing partner performs the obligation *vis-à-vis* a creditor, that party has a right of reimbursement against the partnership (Article 680-2(1)).

§7. Dissolution and Liquidation

901. A partnership is dissolved: (i) upon successful completion of the joint business or by impossibility of such successful completion; (ii) by expiration of the stipulated duration of the partnership; (iii) by the occurrence of an event specified in the partnership contract as a cause for dissolution; and (iv) by unanimous assent of the partners (Article 682). In addition, if there are unavoidable grounds for dissolution, the partnership is dissolved at the request of any partner (Article 683). For example, there are unavoidable grounds if the successful completion of the joint business has become extremely difficult, if not impossible, or if withdrawal will not result in a fair resolution of disagreements due to involvement of the majority of the partners in misconduct.[647]

902. Dissolution does not have retroactive effect (Article 684).

903. When a partnership is dissolved, liquidation takes place. Liquidation can be administered jointly by all partners or by one or more liquidator appointed by the majority of the partners (Article 685). The provisions on the management of business and partnership agent, explained in §2 and §3 of this chapter above, apply *mutatis mutandis* to the process of liquidation (Articles 686 and 687).

646. Nakata, *supra* n. 61, 582.
647. *Ibid.*, 584.

904. After concluding current business, collecting debts and performing obligations, the liquidator must distribute the residual assets to the partners in proportion to the value of the contributions of each partner (Article 688).

Chapter 13. Quasi-contracts

§1. *Negotiorum Gestio*

905. *Negotiorum Gestio*, literally meaning 'management of business', is found when a person (hereinafter a 'manager') commences management of the business of another person (hereinafter the 'principal') without being obliged to do so either by contract or by law (Article 697). An example is a person taking care of someone else's dog that strays into a house unaccompanied by its owner.

906. Such an act might invade private autonomy as an interference without the principal's consent, and thus could constitute a tort. However, in some cases it confers a benefit on the principal. This is why the Civil Code justifies the act under certain conditions and provides for its effects.

907. For *Negotiorum Gestio* to exist, first, there must be another person's business that is being managed. In a case where a coheir managed leasing of real property to which all the coheirs succeeded and paid income tax on all rents of that property, as well as all property tax, out of his or her own income, the Supreme Court found management of the business for property tax purposes, but not for income tax. The Court thus allowed that coheir to claim reimbursement of the other coheirs' shares of the property tax paid. In the judgment of the Supreme Court, payment of property tax on behalf of another is reimbursable as management of another person's business, but payment of income tax on behalf of another is not, because the former discharges the other person's tax liability while the latter does not.[648]

908. Second, such management must be done without obligation. If a person is asked to perform such management by another and agrees to it, this is a contract of mandate; it is not *Negotiorum Gestio*.

909. Third, such management must be done with the manager's intention to perform for the principal in a way that is not clearly against the principal's will or benefit. This does not preclude management for one's own benefit as long as it benefits the principal too. An example would be the case where a neighbour repairs the next house's damaged roof in its owner's absence, both to help the owner and also to avoid the possible damage to his or her own roof by loose tiles flying from the next house. However, management cannot be justified if it is clearly against the principal's will or benefit, so the principal may stop *Negotiorum Gestio* by so proving.

910. Upon commencement of *Negotiorum Gestio*, the manager shall notify the principal that management has begun unless the principal already knows it (Article 699). Once a manager starts management, he or she must continue it until the principal or his or her heirs or legal representatives can undertake it unless this clearly

648. Supreme Court, 19 Jan. 2000, Hanji 2070-51.

would be contrary to the principal's intention or interests (Article 700). In managing the business, the manager shall perform in accordance with the nature of the business, using the method that best conforms to the principal's interests, and in accordance with the principal's intention if he or she knows it or at least can infer it (Article 697). This duty of a manager is mitigated where prompt management is necessary in case of an imminent danger to the principal's body, reputation or property, so that the manager would only be liable for damages caused by acting in bad faith or with gross negligence (Article 698). Furthermore, a manager has the same duty as an agent to report to the principal, deliver what he or she has received and compensate the principal for what he or she has consumed during management (Articles 645–647, applied by Article 701). Under Article 415 of the Civil Code, a manager is liable for damages to the principal caused by his or her failure to perform any of those duties mentioned here.

911. On the other, a manager can claim reimbursement from the principal for the beneficial expenses and obligations which he or she has incurred on the principal's behalf. The claim is only allowable to the extent of the actual enrichment of the principal as regards those expenditures made during management against the principal's will (Article 702(1) and (3)). A manager may also require a principal to pay directly to the other party a price for a contract the manager made for the principal (Article 702(2)), although agency is not established between a manager and a principal just because *Negotiorum Gestio* is found between them.

§2. Unjust Enrichment

912. Unjust enrichment is found when a person (hereinafter a 'beneficiary') has benefited at the expense of another person without legal cause. The beneficiary shall be required to return the benefit to the other person who has lost it. The Civil Code provides for the scope of such return according to whether the beneficiary, on receiving that benefit, knew that he or she did not have legal cause to receive it. In general, where the beneficiary did not know, Article 703 limits the scope of the obligation to the extent of the benefit actually remaining on the beneficiary, so that the ignorant beneficiary will not be unexpectedly required to return what he or she has already consumed. On the other, Article 704 requires return of the received benefit together with interest thereon as well as compensation, if any, of damages where the beneficiary did not know.

913. There are exceptions, however, to such general rules. First, Article 708 allows a beneficiary to return nothing to one who provided any benefit for an illegal cause, such as a violation of Article 90. For example, a seller of an illegal drug may refuse to return a price already paid by a buyer, although without Article 708, the seller could not have kept it; this is because a sales contract for an illegal drug is against public policy and thus void under Article 90. Article 708 is based on the clean hands principle, by which a claimant (the buyer here) is not allowed to obtain a remedy (restitution of payment here) because he or she engaged in unethical conduct (an illegal drug deal here). However, this denial of return shall be lifted if the illegal cause existed solely on the part of the beneficiary, and also according to the Supreme Court if the illegality of the cause on the part of the beneficiary is so strong as to make feel as if there is no illegality of the cause on the part of the person who provided the benefit[649]. In those cases, the hands of the claimant can be said to be clean enough to apply general rules for return of the benefit he or she provided.

914. The second exception is provided in Article 121-2(1) and Article 545, which regulate the effect when a contract is rescinded, void and terminated. Under those articles, each party to a contract must restore the other party to the original position regardless of whether the beneficiary knew, when the contract was formed, of a cause for invalidating such a contract from the beginning. These articles are provided specifically to exclude general rules of unjust enrichment, so that the scope of return will not be limited to the extent of current actual enrichment in the case of an ignorant beneficiary (as in Article 703). This is because it is unfair to allow a contract party not to return everything he or she received from the other party while claiming against the other party for restitution of everything he or she has given the other party.

915. The second exception, however, is not always reasonable and therefore is modified. This is the third exception to the general rules, which is found in Article 121-2(2) and (3). Under those provisions, if a party with no or limited capacity to make a contract needs to return what he or she received from the other party, due to the contract being rescinded or void for his or her lack of capacity, the scope of return is limited to the extent of current actual enrichment. This is also true where such a beneficiary, for the same reason, needs to return what he or she received as performance by the other party to a gratuitous contract, such as a gift or a loan without interest. This limitation of the scope is allowed in those two cases even if the beneficiary knows the cause for a contract being rescinded or void for his or her protection. A person with no or limited capacity needs special treatment, and it is unfair to allow a party not to return everything he or she received from the other party while claiming against the other party for full restitution.

916. *See* paragraph 56 for the situation of claiming restitution for a value conferred under a contract against a third person.

§3. Money Paid Without Obligation

917. A person who pays without obligation can demand restitution of the payment from the recipient according to enrichment without cause. Article 705 permits this claim unless a person pays while knowing that such an obligation does not exist. It is fair in light of the estoppel principle to prevent a person with knowledge of the situation from claiming restitution of what he or she paid.

649. Supreme Court, 31 Aug. 1954, Minshu 8-8-1557.

918. It may appear that the same reasoning could apply where a debtor pays before the due date, but Article 706 negates this. Such payment can be deemed a waiver of the debtor's benefit of a time limit regardless of whether the debtor has knowledge of the situation, because it would become advantageous to the debtor anyway. Article 706 only allows a debtor who makes such a payment by mistake to claim the benefit he or she would have gained by waiting until the due date to pay.

919. More careful treatment is provided in Article 707 for a case where a person pays another person's debt while mistakenly believing the debt is his or her own. Although logically the payor can claim for what he or she paid, Article 707 denies this claim if the creditor, justifiably thinking the payment was validly made, has lost or damaged the instrument or waived the security, or lost his or her right to demand payment by prescription. This protects the innocent creditor. Of course, the payor is allowed to demand restitution from the real debtor what he or she paid that debtor's creditor.

Selected Bibliography[650]

General Overviews of Contract Law in Japan

Baelz, M., Dernauer, M., et al. (eds.), *Business Law in Japan: Cases and Comments* (Kluwer 2012).

Chino, M. C., Kashiwagi, N., and Okada, A., 'Contract and Tort', in *Japanese Business Law*, 173–204 (G. P. McAlinn ed., Kluwer Law International 2008).

Dogauchi, H., 'Outline of Contract Law in Japan', *Transparency of Japanese Law Project* (undated), available from: www.tomeika.jur.kyushu-u.ac.jp/transaction/contract.html.

Kato, M., 'Contract Law' in *Business Law in Japan,* 77-173 (L. Nottage ed., Tokyo: CCH Japan, 2008).

Kitagawa, Z., 'Contract', in *Doing Business in Japan* (Z. Kitagawa ed., New York: Matthew Bender, looseleaf, 1997-) (eBook available from: https://www.overdrive.com/creators/296588/professor-zentaro-kitagawa, US only).

Oda, H., *Japanese Law* (Oxford University Press, 2009) 113–63.

Books and Theses

Dernauer, M., *Verbraucherschutz und Vertragsfreiheit im japanischen Recht [Consumer Protection and Freedom of Contract in Japan]* (Mohr Siebeck 2006).

Nottage, L., 'Form, Substance and Neo-Proceduralism in Comparative Contract Law: The Law in Books and the Law in Action in England, New Zealand, Japan and the U.S', (PhD Thesis, Victoria University of Wellington, 2001), available from http://hdl.handle.net/10063/778.

Ramseyer, J. M., *Second-Best Justice: The Virtues of Japanese Law* (University of Chicago Press 2015).

Sawada, T., *Subsequent Conduct and Supervening Events* (University of Tokyo Press, 1968).

---

650. Abridged (excluding most references in German or French) and updated from H. Baum et al, *Japanese Business Law in Western Languages: An Annotated Selective Bibliography* (Hein, 2nd ed. 2013).

Visser 't Hooft, W., *Japanese Contract and Anti-Trust Law: A Sociological and Comparative Study* (Routledge Curzon, 2002).

Articles and Chapters

'Asian Law Symposium', *Washington Law Review* 42(2) (1967).
Bennett, F.,'Civil Law – Contract Law – Doctrine of Frustration – Change of Circumstances', in *Business Law in Japan - Cases and Comments*, 17 (M. Baelz, M. Dernauer, C. Heath and A. Petersen-Padberg eds., Kluwer 2012).
Dernauer, M., 'The 2017 Reform of the Law of Obligations in Japan: Impetus, Rule-making Process, and Outcome' ANJeL Research Publication (April 2018) via https://sites.google.com/prod/view/anjel-network/research (accessed 17 June 2018).
Doi, T., 'Binding Force of a Distributorship Agreement Signed by Export Manager of the Manufacturer but Subject to Approval by its Authorised Officer', in *International Business Transactions: Contract and Dispute Resolution*, 16 (T. Doi, ed., Institute of Comparative Law, Waseda University, 1996).
Doi, T., 'Sale of Goods Transactions, Domestic and International: Contract Law and Conflict of Laws', in *International Business Transactions: Contract and Dispute Resolution*, 218 (T. Doi, ed., Institute of Comparative Law, Waseda University, 1996).
Foote, D. H., 'Evolution in the Concept of Contract', in *United States / Japan Commercial Law and Trade*, 695 (V. Kusuda-Smick ed., Transnational Juris, 1990).
Frank, R., 'Law of Obligations' in *History of Law in Japan Since 1868*, 261 (W. Rohl ed., Brill, 2005).
Fujiwara, M., 'Civil Law – Case to Seek Return of Money Equivalent to Unjust Enrichment – *Actio de in rem verso*', in *Business Law in Japan: Cases and Comments*, 55 (M. Baelz, M. Dernauer, C. Heath and A. Petersen-Padberg eds., Kluwer 2012).
Gray, W., 'The Use and Non-Use of Contract Law in Japan: A Preliminary Study', 17 *Law in Japan*, 119 (1984).
Haley, J. O., 'Relational Contracting: Does Community Count?' in *Japan: Economic Success and Legal System* 167 (H. Baum ed., de Gruyter 1997).
Haley, J.O., 'Rethinking Contract Practice and Law in Japan', 1 *Journal of East Asia and International Law 1,* (2008).
Haley, J. O., 'The Preliminary Contract for Substitute Performance: A Reflection of Japanese Judicial Approach,' 7 *Law in Japan* 133 (1974).
Hasegawa, S., 'Perspectives on the CISG from the Viewpoint of Japanese Civil Law', 26 *Nihon University Comparative Law* 77 (2009).
Hoshino, E., 'The Contemporary Contract', 5 *Law in Japan* 5 (1972).
Ishikawa, H., 'Codification, Decodification, and Recodification of the Japanese Civil Code', 10 *University of Tokyo Journal of Law & Politics* 80 (2013).
Kaiser, A., 'The Construction Contract in Japan from a German Perspective', 36 *Journal of Japanese Law* 217 (2013).

Kamo, A., 'Crystallization, Unification, or Differentiation? The Japanese Civil Code (Law of Obligations) Reform Commission and Basic Reform Policy (Draft Proposals)', 24 *Columbia Journal of Asian Law* 171 (2010).

Kano, N., 'Reform of the Japanese Civil Code: The Interim Draft Proposal of 2013', 36 *Journal of Japanese Law* 261 (2013).

Karaiskos, A., 'Regulation of Unfair Contract Terms in Japan', 28 *Waseda Bulletin of Comparative Law* 44 (2010).

Kashiwagi, N., 'Accession by Japan to the Vienna Sales Convention (CISG)', 25 *Journal of Japanese Law* 214 (2008).

Kato, M., 'One Phase of Japanese Contract Law: Although Western, it is a Little Different', in *International Contract Litigation, Arbitration and Judicial Responsibility in Transnational Disputes*, 21 (R. Sturner and K. Masanori eds., Mohr Siebeck, 2011).

Kawakami, S., 'Japan' in *Pre-Contractual Liability: Reports to the 13th Congress, International Academy of Comparative Law,* 207 (E. Hondius ed., Kluwer 1991).

Kawano, M., 'Comparative Study of Contract Litigation', in *International Contract Litigation, Arbitration and Judicial Responsibility in Transnational Disputes*, 11 (R, Sturner and K. Masanori eds., Mohr Siebeck, 2011).

Kawashima, T., (C. Stevens trans.), 'The Legal Consciousness of Contract in Japan', 7 *Law Japan* 1 (1974).

Kinoshita, T., 'A Comparative Study of Reasonable Expectations and Lost Profits in American and Japanese Law', 7 *Law in Japan* 112 (1974).

Kitagawa, Z., 'Damages in Contracts for the Sale of Goods', 3 *Law in Japan* 43 (1969).

Kitagawa, Z., 'Unfair Contract Terms in Administrative Guidance', *Rechtstheorie* 200 (1985).

Kitagawa, Z., 'Use and Non-Use of Contracts in Japanese Business Relations: A Comparative Analysis', in *Japan: Economic Success and Legal System*, 165 (H. Baum ed., Berlin: Walter de Gruyter, 1997).

Kitagawa, Z., 'Japanese Civil Law and German Law: From the Viewpoint of Comparative Law' in *The Identity of German and Japanese Law in Comparative Perspectives*, 11 (Z. Kitagawa and K. Riesenhuber eds., Walter de Gruyter 2007).

Kozuka, S., 'Judicial Activism of the Supreme Court in Consumer Law: Juridification of Society Through Case Law?' 27 *Journal of Japanese Law* 81 (2009).

Kozuka, S., 'The Impact of Japan's Contract Law Reform on Franchise Agreements', 20 *International Franchising* 24 (May 2016).

Kozuka, S., and Nottage, L., 'The Myth of the Careful Consumer: Law, Culture, Economics and Politics in the Rise and Fall of Unsecured Lending in Japan', in *Consumer Credit, Debt and Bankruptcy: Comparative International Perspectives*, 199 (J. Niemi et al. eds., Hart 2009).

Kozuka, S., and Nottage, L., 'Policy and Politics in Contract Law Reform in Japan' in *The Method and Culture of Comparative Law*, 235 (M. Adams and D. Heirbaut eds., Hart 2014), with a longer version at http://papers.ssrn.com/sol3/papers.cfm?abstract_id=2360343.

Lewi, R., 'Japanese Perspectives on Long Term Contracts', in *Long Term Contracts*, 14 (K. Dharmananda and L. Firios eds., Federation Press 2013).

Markel, A., 'American, English and Japanese Warranty Law Compared: Should the US Reconsider Her Article 95 Declaration to the CISG?', 21 *Pace International Law Review* 204 (2009).

Matsui, S., 'Cloudy Weather, with Occasional Sunshine: Consumer Loans, the Legislature, and the Supreme Court of Japan', 22 *Pacific Rim Law and Policy Journal* 598 (2013).

Matsumoto, T., 'Protection of the Weaker Party in Japanese Contract Law' in *Proceedings of the Symposium: Dutch and Japanese Laws Compared,* 108 (ICCLP et al eds., International Center for Comparative Law and Politics, University of Tokyo, 1993).

Matsumoto, T., 'Privatization of Consumer Law: Current Developments and Features of Consumer Law in Japan at the Turn of the Century', 30 *Hitotsubashi Journal of Law & Politics* 14 (2002).

Matsushima, T., 'Perspectives on the CISG from the Viewpoint of Japanese Commercial Law', 51 *Nihon University Comparative Law* 291 (2009).

Michida, S., (V. Taylor trans), 'Contract Societies: Japan and the United States Compared', 1 *Pacific Rim Law & Policy Journal* 199 (1992).

Miwa, Y. and J. M. Rameyer, 'Rethinking Relationship-Specific Investments: Subcontracting in the Japanese Automobile Industry', 98 *Michigan Law Review* 2667 (2000).

Morimura, S., 'Justifying Contractual Enforcement: Yasaki, Mitsukuni (ed.), East and West: Legal Philosophies in Japan',30 *Archiv für Rechts und Sozialphilosophie: Beiheft* 114 (1987).

Mukai, K., and Toshitani, N., 'The Progress and Problems of Compiling the Civil Code in the Early Meiji Era', 1 *Law Japan* 25 (1967).

Nakata, K., 'Civil Law – Contract Law – Purchase Contract – Extinctive Prescription for Damage Claims Under the Warranty against Defects' in *Business Law in Japan – Cases and Comments*, 53 (M. Baelz, M. Dernauer, C. Heath and A. Petersen-Padberg eds., Kluwer 2012).

Nottage, L., 'Form and Substance in US, English, New Zealand and Japanese Law: A Framework for Better Comparisons of Developments in the Law of Unfair Contracts', 26 *Victoria University of Wellington Law Review* 292 (1996).

Nottage, L., 'Consumer Rights' in *Japanese Consumer Dynamics*, 31 (P. Haghirian ed., Palgrave Macmillan 2010).

Nottage, L. 'Contract Law and Practice in Japan: An Antipodean Perspective' in *Japan: Economic Success and Legal System*, 197 (H. Baum ed., Walter de Gruyter, 1997).

Nottage, L., 'Contract Law, Theory and Practice in Japan: Plus ca Change, Plus c'est la Meme Chose?', in *Asian Laws Through Australian Eyes*, 316 (V. Taylor ed., Law Book Company 1997).

Nottage, L., 'Economic Dislocation in New Zealand and Japan: A Preliminary Empirical Study', 26 *Victoria University Wellington Law Review* 97 (1997).

Nottage, L., 'Planning and Renegotiating Long-Term Contracts in New Zealand and Japan: An Interim Report on an Empirical Research Project', *New Zealand Law Review* (1997): 482.

Nottage, L., 'Tracing Trajectories in Contract Law Theory: Form in Anglo-New Zealand Law, Substance in Japan and the United States', 4 *Yonsei Law* Journal 271 (2013), also available at http://ssrn.com/abstract=2270889.

Nottage, L., 'Comparative Law in and for Japan' in *Oxford Handbook of Comparative Law*, forthcoming (M. Reimann and R. Zimmerman eds,, 2nd ed., Oxford University Press 2019).

Okino, M., 'Recent Development in Consumer Protection in Japan', 4 *University of Tokyo Soft Law. Review* 18 (2012).

Pardieck, A., 'Japan and the Moneylenders: Activist Courts and Substantive Justice', 17 *Pacific Rim Law & Policy Journal* 594 (2008).

Pardieck, A., 'Layers of the Law: A Look at the Role of Law in Japan Today', 22 *Pacific Rim Law & Policy Journal* 666 (2013).

Rahn, G. 'Law, Contract, and Society in Japan: A Personal View', in *Japan: Economic Success and Legal System*, 185 (H. Baum ed., Walter de Gruyter, 1997).

Sakamoto, R., 'Perspectives on the CISG from the Viewpoint of International Business Transaction Laws', 26 *Nihon University Comparative Law* 58 (2009).

Siesta, V. J., 'Out at Home: Challenging the United States-Japanese Player Contract Agreement under Japanese Law', 33 *Brooklyn Journal of International Law* 1098 (2008).

Sono, H., 'Japan's Accession to the CISG: The Asia Factor', 25 *Journal of Japanese Law* 205 (2008).

Sono, H., 'Japan's Accession to and Implementation of the United Nations Convention on Contracts for the International Sale of Goods (CISG)', 53 *Japanese Yearbook of International Law* 437 (2010).

Sono, H., 'The Diversity of Favor Contractus: The Impact of the CISG on Japan's Civil Code and Its Reform', in *Towards Uniformity: The 2nd Annual MAA Schlechtriem CISG Conference,* 179 (I. Schwenzer and L. Spagnolo eds., Eleven International Publishing, 2011).

Sono, H., 'Private Enforcement of Consumer Law: A Sketch of the Japanese Landscape', 63 *Hokkaido Journal of New Global Law & Politics* 63 (2012).

Sono, H., 'Integrating Consumer Law into the Civil Code: A Japanese Attempt at Re-codification', in *Codifying Contract Law: International and Consumer Law Perspectives*, 130 (M. Keyes and T. Wilson eds., Ashgate 2014).

Takahashi, K., '*Walford v. Miles in Japan: Lock-in and Lock-out Agreements in Sumitomo v. UFJ*', *Journal of Business Law* 182 (2009).

Tanikawa, H., 'Risk of Loss in Japanese Sales Transactions', 42 *Washington Law Review* 482 (1967).

Taylor, V., 'Continuing Transactions and Persistent Myths: Contracts in Contemporary Japan', 19 *Melbourne University Law Review* 398 (1993).

Taylor, V., 'Contracts with the Lot: Franchises, Good Faith and Contract Regulation', *New Zealand Law Review* 481 (1997).

Taylor, V., 'Japanese Commercial Transactions and Sanctions Revisited: *Sumitomo v. UFJ*', 8 *Washington University Global Studies Law Review* 426 (2009).

Uchida, T., 'The New Development of Contract Law and General Clauses: A Japanese Perspective', in *Proceedings of the Symposium: Dutch and Japanese Laws*, 119 (ICCLP et al. eds, International Center for Comparative Law and Politics, University of Tokyo 1993).

Uchida, T., and Taylor, V., 'Japan's Era of Contract' in *Law in Japan: A Turning Point*, 454 (D. H. Foote ed., University of Washington Press 2007).
Uchida, T., 'Contract Law Reform in Japan and the UNIDROIT Principles', *Uniform Law Review* 717 (2011).
Visser 't Hooft, W.,'Japanese Law and the Unilateral Termination of Distribution Agreements: The Breakdown of Distribution Keiretsu', in *Yearbook of Law and Legal Practice in East Asia*, 137 (A. De Roo and R. Jagtenberg eds., Kluwer 1996).
Waer, P., 'Frustration of Contracts in Japanese Law: The Doctrine of Changed Circumstances', 20 *Law in Japan* 212 (1987).
Wagatsuma, H. and A. Rosett, 'Cultural Attitudes Towards Contract Law: Japan and the United States Compared', 2 *UCLA Pacific Basin Law Journal* 97 (1983).
Westhoff, J., 'Civil Law – M&A – Binding Nature of Letter of Intent – Obligation to Negotiate in Good Faith – Confidentiality Clause – Injunctive Relief Business Law' in *Business Law in Japan – Cases and Comments,* 29 (M. Baelz, M. Dernauer, C. Heath and A. Petersen-Padberg eds., Kluwer 2012).
Yamamoto, K., 'Civil Law – Contract Law – Nullity of Contracts (Juristic Acts) Due to a Violation of Mandatory Public Law Provisions', in *Business Law in Japan – Cases and Comments*, 5 (M. Baelz, M. Dernauer, C. Heath and A. Petersen-Padberg eds., Kluwer 2012).
Yamamoto, K., 'The Role of Private Law in a Constitutional System',1 *Kyoto Journal of Law & Politics* 59 (2013).
Yoshida, S., and Cassidy, P., 'Top 10 Major Revisions to the Civil Code: From the Viewpoint of the Transportation and Shipbuilding Industries' *Higashimachi LLP* (Newsletter) (2017) http://www.higashimachi.jp/column/images/column205.pdf.
Yoshimasa, T., 'The Reform of the Japanese Contract Law – From the Perspective of Self-Responsibility' *Journal of Japanese Law* forthcoming (2018).
Yoshimasa, T., 'The Reform of the Law on Remedies for Breach of Contract in Japan' in *Reactive Instruments of Social Governance* (A. Bruns & M. Suzuki eds., Mohr Siebeck forthcoming).
Young, M. K., et al., 'Japanese Attitudes Towards Contracts: An Empirical Wrinkle in the Debate', 34 *George Washington Law Review* 852 (2003).

Index

The numbers here refer to paragraph numbers.

Index

www.ingramcontent.com/pod-product-compliance
Ingram Content Group UK Ltd.
Pitfield, Milton Keynes, MK11 3LW, UK
UKHW020137290926
15471UKWH00003B/538